Roman Conquests:
Macedonia and Greece

Roman Conquests: Macedonia and Greece

Philip Matyszak

Pen & Sword
MILITARY

First published in Great Britain in 2009 by
PEN & SWORD MILITARY
an imprint of
Pen & Sword Books Ltd
47 Church Street
Barnsley
South Yorkshire
S70 2AS

ISBN 978 1 84415 968 0

Printed and bound in the UK by
the MPG Books Group

Pen & Sword Books Ltd incorporates the imprints of
Pen & Sword Aviation, Pen & Sword Family History, Pen & Sword Maritime,
Pen & Sword Military, Wharncliffe Local History, Pen & Sword Select,
Pen & Sword Military Classics, Leo Cooper, Remember When,
Seaforth Publishing and Frontline Publishing.

For a complete list of Pen & Sword titles please contact
PEN & SWORD BOOKS LIMITED
47 Church Street, Barnsley, South Yorkshire, S70 2AS, England
E-mail: enquiries@pen-and-sword.co.uk
Website: www.pen-and-sword.co.uk

Contents

Acknowledgements

Putting together a history as complex as the Macedonian Wars needed considerable research. I'd again like to thank Cambridge Faculty of Classics Library for their generous help, and also those including Jo Berry, Ian Hughes and Adrian Goldsworthy who read and commented on parts of the text. Special thanks go to Jackie Whalen and Avi Shah who took precious time on their visits to Thermopylae, Sparta and Athens to personally check and photograph the relevant terrain. Finally I'd like to thank those on the UNRV forum (particularly Nephele, Caldrail, Ursus and Viggen) without whose instructive feedback this would have been a much poorer book.

Maps

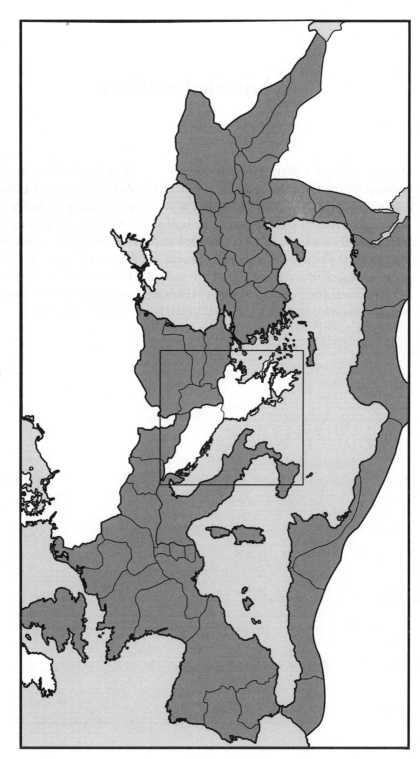

Map of the Roman Empire at its greatest extent with the area covered in this volume highlighted.

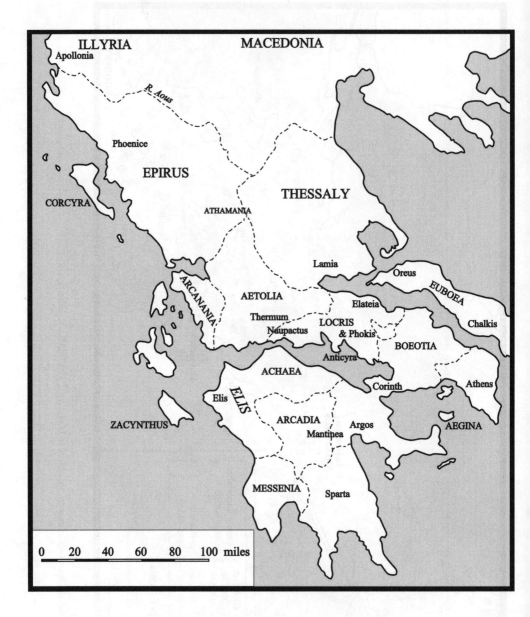

Map of the regions of the Greek mainland.

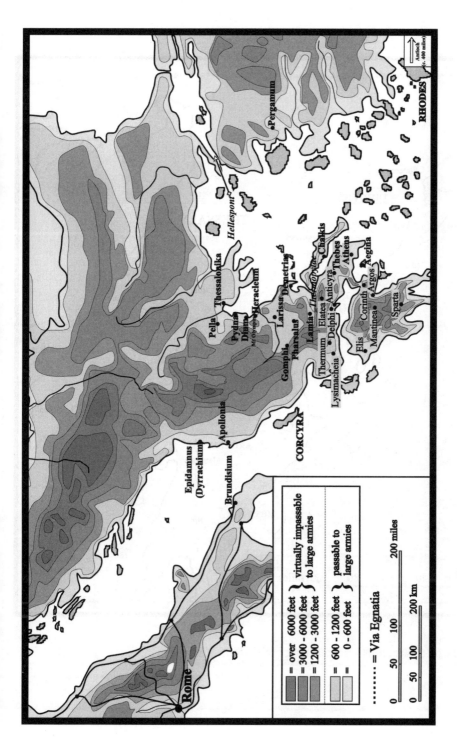

Map showing the topography of southern Italy and the Balkan Peninsula.

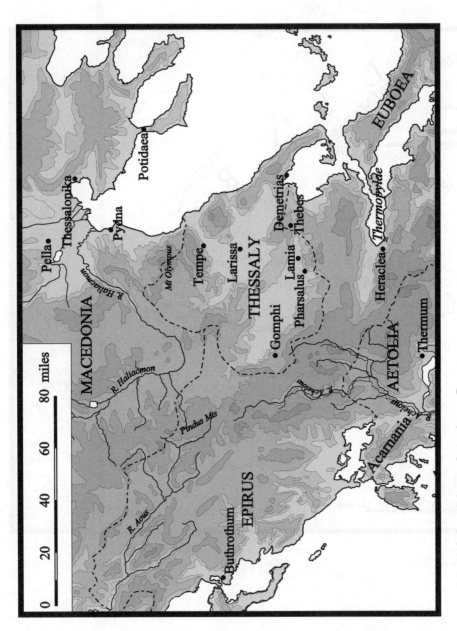

Map of the regions of northern Greece.

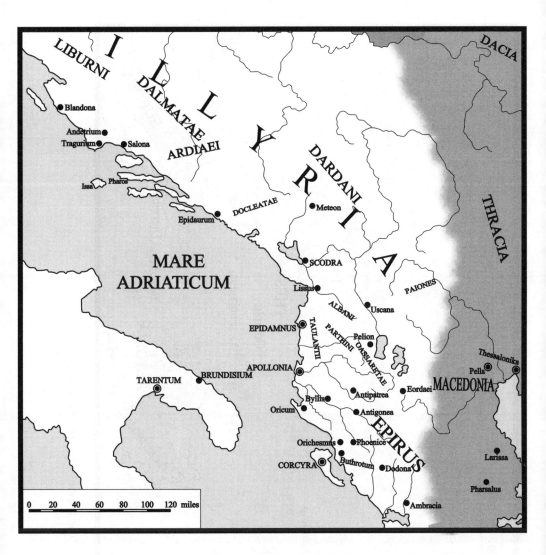

Map of Illyria.

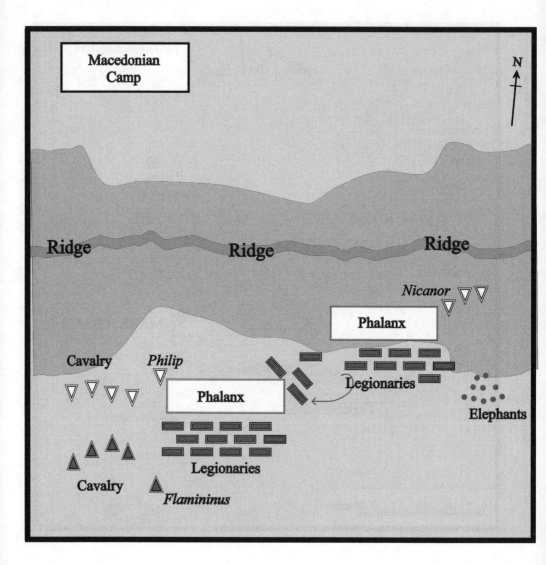

Diagram of the Battle of Cynoscephalae.

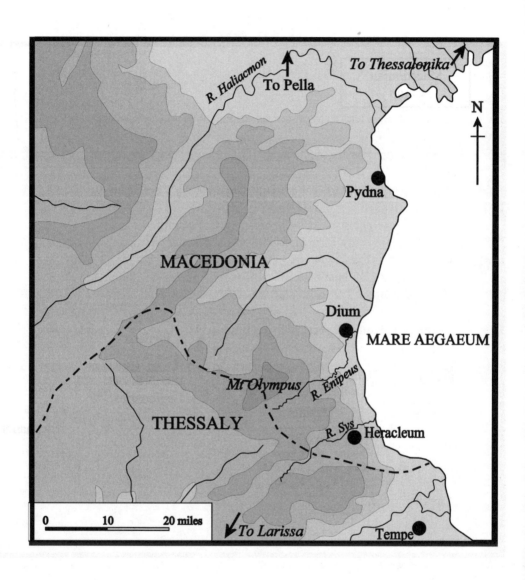

Map of eastern Greece.

List of Illustrations

A legionary from the altar of Domitius Ahenobarbus. (Picture by Adrian Goldsworthy)

A Roman officer from the altar of Domitius Ahenobarbus. (Picture by Adrian Goldsworthy)

A cavalryman from the altar of Domitius Ahenobarbus. (Picture by Adrian Goldsworthy)

The site of ancient Sparta. (Picture by Jackie Whalen)

The remains of the walls of Sparta. Picture by Jackie Whalen

Macedonian cavalryman. (© Johnny Shumate)

A Roman cavalryman in a stand-off with a Greek peltast. (© Johnny Shumate)

A Roman *hastatus* at Pydna finishes off a Macedonian phalangite. (© Johnny Shumate)

Numidian elephant riders on campaign in Greece. (© Johnny Shumate)

A view of the stoa of Attalus. (Picture by Avi Shah)

The mountains of Thessaly as seen from the Nevropolis Plain. (Picture by Jackie Whalen)

View of Thermopylae. (Picture by Jackie Whalen)

The tip of Euboea as seen across the Malian Gulf. (Picture by Jackie Whalen)

Introduction

> For who is so worthless or indolent as not to wish to know by what means ... the Romans have succeeded in subjecting nearly the whole inhabited world to their sole government – a thing unique in history? Or who again is there so passionately devoted to other spectacles or studies as to regard anything as of greater moment than the acquisition of this knowledge?

Thus Polybius starts the story of how Rome grew in his own lifetime from being the dominant power on the Italian peninsula to ruler of an empire that included Spain and his own homeland of Greece.

There have been numerous debates as to the character of the Romans during this period of conquest and expansion. Were the Romans reluctant imperialists, forced into acquiring an empire by a process of 'mission creep'; whereby securing one set of borders involved conquering the adjacent country which led to a fresh set of borders to secure? Or were the Romans, as one writer famously put it, 'the pirates of the land', aggressively bent on conquest and plunder at all costs? Did the Romans take the initiative in starting their wars, or were they reacting to the perceived hostile intentions of others? The answer to all these questions, as will become clear over the following chapters, is 'yes'. Rome was not a monolithic polity. At this time Rome was a democracy, albeit a limited one, and Rome's foreign policy broadly reflected the electorate's swings in opinion. This opinion was, with greater or lesser success, manipulated by the senate, which was itself torn by faction fighting and the personal ambitions of powerful men.

Therefore we should not look for a Roman master plan underlying any aspect of the Roman conquest of Greece and Macedon. It will become clear that at times the Romans had no idea what they were doing from one year to the next, so far were they from having a master plan which they studiously followed during the century of intermittent fighting which it took to bring the Greek peninsula under their sway. It would be fair to describe the Roman conquest of Greece and Macedon as a strictly ad hoc affair, in which all of the attitudes described above prevailed at one time or another.

The footnotes in this book refer those readers interested to the minutiae of the accompanying academic debate (which is partly about these attitudes) and inform where further information can be found. However before one plunges into the debate as to why matters came to pass, it is essential to understand exactly what came to pass. This book is centred on this latter aspect; how Rome came to conquer Greece and Macedon, and exactly what happened in the century that this conquest took. This conquest was of epochal significance as it completed the merging of Greek and Roman culture into the single entity on which modern Europe is founded.

Given the massive importance of the topic, it is surprising that so little has been written about it, and much of what has been written is not for the general reader. In part this is because the story of the Roman conquest of Greece is a complex one, which shuttles between the convoluted internecine spats of relatively minor city-states and the complex strategies of trans-Mediterranean power politics. This means that it is not an easy tale to tell, especially as attempting to simplify it does violence to the reality of what took place.

Fortunately this is a tale with strong characters, including the grim yet brilliant Philip V, who lights many a page with his mordant humour even when his back was firmly pressed against the wall; the flamboyant and egotistical Flamininus, and Polybius himself, who watched fascinated and appalled as his world tumbled into ruin. Then there are the peoples of Greece: the Achaeans, caught between the millstones of Rome and Macedon; the tragi-comic Aetolians, an unlovable people with a fascinating knack for doing exactly the wrong thing at the wrong time. There are the recalcitrant Spartans, and above all, the proud and stubborn Macedonians, a people on the wrong side of history who, for decade after decade, held back apparently unstoppable waves of enemies and for whom even the mighty Roman legions were just one more problem, albeit a major one.

Romans and Macedonians had much in common, and shared a grudging mutual respect even as their similar characters meant that neither was readily prepared to accept defeat for long. In the end the superior soldiery and resources of Rome prevailed, but it was not an easy victory, and the Macedonians went down fighting - repeatedly.

A final player in the saga is the sublimely beautiful but impossibly rugged landscape of Greece itself. The problems of fighting over terrain which was 80 per cent mountains affected strategy and tactics time and again. It is impossible to understand what happened in Greece between 230 BC and 145 BC without understanding the geography of the land itself, and it is to that which we now turn.

Chapter 1

Greece 221 BC: Anatomy of a War Zone

The Invader's Point of View

For a military historian, the most significant period in the history of Greece was the Palaeocene, an era about 60 million years ago. This is when Greek landscape of today was created when the tectonic plate which included what was then the island of Africa came slowly crunching into the Eurasian landmass to create the Mediterranean basin. In the process the platelet containing Crete was pushed downward, its mountain peaks becoming the 2,000 or so Greek isles which are even now being slowly ducked underwater by the millimetre. The same collision buckled the Balkan peninsula into a series of mountain ranges known as Alpine folds.[1] The Alps and Himalayas, created at about the same time, are much higher, but though the average Greek mountain chain peaks out at less than 1.25 miles high, these young mountains are steep and rough. The country itself is basically a collection of such ranges running from northwest to southeast. Though dominating over 80 per cent of the landscape, the mountains are of little interest other than to goatherds and itinerant geologists. The history of Greece has occurred in the remaining 20 per cent of the country, which consists of stony valleys and an occasional coastal plain.

Less than 1 per cent of the mainland is lakes or marshes, and there are no navigable rivers. Like the mountains, the sea dominates life in Greece. The elaborate folds and curves of the terrain mean that Greece has a length of coastline more appropriate for a small continent (more than twice the coastline of Italy), and few parts of Greece are more than 60 miles from the sea.

In antiquity these factors shaped the destiny of the Greek peoples, or Hellenes, as they preferred to call themselves. Most of Greece was considerably harder to attack than defend, as the mountains channel any invader through a limited number of routes, and battles had a tendency to be fought repeatedly at the same choke points.[2] Communication between cities was hard enough for individuals, and doubly so for armies and their supply chains. Greece was as unproductive for empire builders as it was for farmers. There were over 100 city-states in Greece and until the third century most were relatively poor, fervently independent, and passed their time in feuding with neighbours a few days' march away.

This inbuilt parochialism meant that Greeks kept their geopolitics local. For example, the feud between Megalopolis and Messene meant more to those townspeople than wars between the great Hellenistic powers of Seleucia, Macedon and Egypt, and even as the armies of Rome and Macedon rolled across their landscape, the principal concern of Greek cities tended to be how this would affect the local balance of power.

Yet at the same time, the Greeks were internationalists who knew and used the sea better than any other people in antiquity. If their politics were local, their culture was spread across the Mediterranean and beyond. There were Greek colonies in Messalia, looking westward to the Pyrenees, and others on the Black Sea with the Crimean cornfields at their back. The Greeks were traders, interested in other lands and peoples whilst remaining convinced of the superiority of their own. Sea routes connected the land of Hellas with Egypt, Phoenicia, Judea and the far flung colonies of the Greeks themselves.

However, whilst the sea was an useful avenue for trade and exploration, invading armies much preferred to keep their feet on solid ground, even with cases such as Greece, where much of this ground was vertical. As the Persians were reminded when much of their fleet went underwater in a storm at Cape Athos in 492 BC, ancient naval military transport had a tendency to lose dramatically in the contest with wind and wave. In the third century the Romans proved the point yet again during the First Punic War, when their attempts to take the battle to the Carthaginians resulted in entire armies going directly to the bottom of the sea. An estimated 100,000 men died in a single storm off Cape Pachynus in 255 BC, and this disaster, though the largest of its kind, was far from unique. In all of antiquity, no-one successfully invaded Greece by sea.

Macedon

Further up the Balkan peninsula, on the northern border of Greece, was the state of Macedon.[3] There was considerable disagreement among the Hellenes of further south whether Macedonia counted as part of Greece. Some argued (as does the Greek government of today) that the

Macedonians were undoubtedly Greek whilst others were more dubious; there was even an attempt to prevent the Macedonian royal family from participating in the Olympics on the grounds that they were barbarians.[4] Certainly, ancient Macedon was not a typical Greek state in terms of geography, economy or politics. There is also some dispute among academics as to how close the Macedonian tongue was to the language of the rest of Greece, although recent archaeological discoveries of text strongly suggest that the Macedonian language was similar to the dialects of northwestern Greece.

Macedonia is very un-Greek in possessing a wide southern plain and a number of large rivers, while several valleys in the more mountainous north connect the region with the Danube itself. However, in deference to the general landscape of the Balkan peninsula, most of Macedonia's rivers run in a southeasterly direction. The main rivers of the kingdom of Macedon, counting from east to west, were the Nestus, which enters the Aegean sea well to the north and east of the Greek peninsula, the Strymon, which meets the sea by the city of Amphipolis (modern Amfipoli) just east of the distinctive trident of Chalcidice, the Axius which runs to the western side of Chalcidice, and the Haliacmon which defies tradition by running west to east across the fertile plain which is the defining feature of southern Macedonia.

From 512–479 BC Macedon was the most westerly province of the Persian Empire, though as the Macedonians later pointed out to the reproachful Greeks, the geographical accessibility of the kingdom from the east meant that they had little choice in the matter. However reluctant its submission to the Persians, there is no doubt that the Macedonian kingdom benefitted considerably from this arrangement. The Persians annexed the Epirot tribes of the west to create western Macedonia, and when the Persians were driven out after their defeats by the southern Greeks, the Macedonian forces followed them eastward, and took control of the territory west of the River Strymon.

Philip II, father of Alexander the Great, inherited a tidy little kingdom and enlarged it considerably by a drive to the north which incorporated both the Greek cities of the region and the barbarous tribes in their hinterlands. Chunks of Illyria, Thrace and all of Chalcidice followed soon thereafter, creating another cultural difference between Macedonia and the Greeks of the south. The latter were (with minor differences) a culturally and linguistically homogeneous mosaic of independent city-states, while Macedon was a polyglot, multicultural but centralized kingdom: a kingdom which Philip set about equipping with a superb army. Whilst Greek states enjoyed the luxury of squabbling among themselves, Macedonia was the peninsula's involuntary bulwark against the barbarians, and whilst southern Greece was generally safe from incursions, in Macedon barbarian invasions were generally either imminent or occurring. There were Illyrians in the mountains to the west (who came close to conquering all of northwestern Macedonia in 360 BC) Dardanians to the north, and Thracians to the east. In good times these warrior peoples were subdued and some were even incorporated into the army as useful auxiliary soldiers. In bad times the various tribes, singly or in unison, came raiding and pillaging onto the Macedonian plain.

It helped the country's defenders that Macedon was more resource-rich than her neighbours to the south. Cattle were abundant on the Macedonian plain, but a rarity in southern Greece, where even the people of relatively well-farmed Attica preferred to raise pigs, goats and sheep. Only Thessaly, Macedonia's southern neighbour, rivalled the kingdom in the number and quality of its horses, while Macedonia's resources of timber were unmatched by any Greek state and provided the kingdom with useful export revenues. Another source of hard cash was numerous silver and gold mines (especially in the region around Mount Pangaeus once this was conquered and taken from Thrace) and also reserves of iron ore for weapons to keep outsiders at bay.

A flexible, tough and well-equipped army was not the only reason why no-one had successfully invaded Macedon since the Persians. While the barbarian tribes were a menace to those living on Macedon's frontiers, anyone wanting to invade Macedonia from the north or west had first to get through them. This factor, combined with mountainous terrain made it very difficult for any large army to approach except from the south or east. With the fall of the Persian empire, there was no-one with the resources to try to bulldoze through Thrace to the east, which meant that approaches to Macedon had to be by a less-than-optimal route going first through the Greek cities to the south and then over one of a few highly defensible passes into Macedonia proper. Nor was Macedonia inclined to wait to be attacked. The inherent advantages of the country: superior resources, political unity and an army hardened by barbarian assaults, meant that from the fourth century until the coming of the Romans, aggressive armies had tended to march out from Macedon rather than in the opposite direction.

Macedon and Greece in the Century after Alexander the Great

Ever since Philip II crushed Theban resistance at the Battle of Chaeronea in 338 BC, the kings of Macedon had considered the hegemony of southern Greece as a natural right. Few Greeks dared oppose this opinion after Philip's son, Alexander III (the Great), practically wiped Thebes off the map for attempting to rebel against Macedonian overlordship. After Alexander, Greece was effectively dominated by Macedonia's Antigonid dynasty who were descendants of Antigonus Gonatas, grandson of one of Alexander's generals. Gonatus (the name roughly means 'knock-knees') took over Macedonia in 277 BC after the country was almost wrecked by a wave of invading Gauls (Galati) who eventually went on to found the state of Galatia in Asia Minor. After this Antigonus had still to fight off the attentions of Pyrrhus of Epirus (he of the Pyrrhic victories in Italy) before Macedon was anything near to being militarily secure. Through all of this Antigonus Gonatus managed to preserve the Macedonian grip on Greece, albeit by increasingly tyrannical measures. However, such was the devastation and depopulation caused by the invasions of Macedonia's heartland that even at the end of the third century the kingdom's population had not fully recovered.

Consequently, under the rule of Antigonus Gonatas' successor, Demetrius II, Macedonian power in the south slipped somewhat as Greek cities discovered the benefits of confederacy on their own behalf. Though there had been loose federal states throughout Greek history, the first such league of Greek cities to become a power in third century Greece was the Achaean League, an ancient confederacy which was revived in 281 BC. 'In a condition of general weakness, when every city relied only on itself, Greece was swiftly coming apart ... by inclusiveness with their neighbours, some by peaceful agreements, by protecting some and freeing others from tyrants, all were brought into a single community', says the biographer Plutarch in his description of the League's formation.[5]

Under its leader, Aratus, the League initially deferred to the Macedonians. Less obliging were the cities of the Aetolian confederacy, which fell out with Demetrius when he intervened to thwart their attack on the Achaeans. Demetrius' intervention promptly caused Achaeans and Aetolians to forget their differences and ally against him, and for a while it looked as though Greece might be on the verge of regaining its ancient freedom.

This hope was set back by the shrewd military and diplomatic skills of the next ruler of Macedon, Antigonus Doson who came to power in 229 BC. Antigonus Doson was Demetrias II's half brother, and he was originally regent for Demetrias' young son Philip. Antigonus Doson was a skilled commander who won victories against the Dardanian tribesmen and in northern Greece. In a politically adept move, he married Demetrias' widow, the mother of Philip, adopted her son and leveraged his military reputation to have himself proclaimed king. He also acquired a retinue of skilled administrators and advisors to run Macedon, which under his rule became one of the better-managed states of antiquity.

Antigonus' political skill was applied equally deftly in Greece. The confederacy of the peoples of northern Greece, the Thessalian League, had become disorganized. Now it was reconstituted into a pro-Macedonian alliance, binding Thessaly to its northern neighbour. Further south, Antigonus played upon the rivalry between the Achaean League and Sparta, eventually allying himself firmly with the Achaeans. Having decided that, on the whole, Greek leagues made the entire country more manageable, Antigonus organized all his allies into an over-arching Hellenic League. At the head of this he marched his army into the Peloponnese in 222 BC, crushed the Spartans and occupied their city. Whilst technically a free nation, the peoples of Greece were for practical purposes once more under the heel of Macedon. Antigonus placed reinforced Macedonian garrisons in the citadels of Corinth, Chalcis, and the fortress port of Demetrias. These three fortresses were known as 'the fetters of Greece', as any state which controlled them could keep a military grip on the entire southern peninsula. Corinth dominated access to the Peloponnese; the Phocians, Locrians and Boeotians were kept subdued by the garrison at Chalcis; and the Thessalonians could be controlled through the fortress of Demetrias.

However, even with Greece under control, no Macedonian king could rest on his laurels for long since the barbarians in the north could be counted on to upset the general tranquillity. So it proved for Antigonus, who had to hurry north in 221 BC to pre-empt yet another Dardanian attack.[6]

This attack proved unexpectedly lethal, for Antigonus burst a blood vessel whilst in battle, and died on the field. Antigonus' heir, as he had promised, was his half-brother's son whose rule he had supplanted in 229 BC. This boy, now at the tender age of 17 years, took up the reins of the kingdom as Philip V of Macedon.

The Geopolitics of Greece: 220 BC

To the Greeks of the third century, Macedon was a bully, jealous of its hegemony and quick to interfere in the affairs of supposedly-free cities. Yet the Macedonians saw themselves otherwise. Greece was the prize which Macedon guarded from the large and predatory states of the Hellenistic world; and both the Seleucids of Asia and the Ptolemies of Egypt had made plain their interest in taking over Greece should Macedon's power weaken. As the Seleucids were, like the Ptolemies and Macedonians, successors to the empire of Alexander, the rulers of these states felt that they had the right to intervene in Greece should Macedon be preoccupied in the west or along the Danube.

Thus Macedon had surly Greeks to the south, predatory superpowers to the east, and unpredictable barbarian hordes to the north and west. If Macedon was a compact, well-run and highly-organized kingdom, it was because its rulers and peoples agreed it could not be otherwise and still survive. Young Philip V, looking beyond the borders of his kingdom in 220 BC, would have seen the following situation.[7]

Illyria

To the west and north of Macedonia was Illyria. As the historian Appian explains:

> the Greeks call those people Illyrians who occupy the region beyond Macedonia and Thrace from Chaonia and Thesprotia to the River Ister (Danube). This is the length of the country. Its breadth is from Macedonia and the mountains of Thrace to Pannonia and the Adriatic and the foothills of the Alps. Its breadth is five days' journey and its length thirty. [8]

'Illyrian' was something of a generic name for the barbarous peoples of the western Balkans. These peoples were Indo-Europeans of Dorian stock, and their tattooed warriors had, at the dawn of civilization, swept southward and destroyed the Mycenaean kingdoms of Greece.[9] In the third century the Illyrians confined their attacks on civilization to raids by land and sea. In fact so enthusiastic was the piracy of the Luburni (a people from the region of modern north Croatia) that 'liburnian' came to be the generic name for a light pirate vessel. Illyria was a more or less unified kingdom, though the authority of the king did not stop the various tribes from sometimes having their own foreign policy or conducting violent feuds tantamount to small civil wars. Though the Illyrians had been a constant thorn in Macedon's side, the one thing that could be said for this unruly and mountainous kingdom was that it acted as a buffer against the new and aggressive power of Rome, which had arisen to dominate the Italian peninsula.

Rome had already discovered a taste for overseas adventure following its victory over Carthage in the long war of 264 to 241 BC. After their naval successes in that war the Romans were not prepared to tolerate Illyrian predations on their Adriatic coastal trade, and had launched a sustained effort by land and sea to prevent this (see Chapter 2). From the Macedonian strategic viewpoint, Rome and Illyria cancelled each other out at present, but both states had a worrying potential for trouble in the long term.

Epirus

Closely linked to the Illyrians were the Molossians, the leading tribe of the rough country south of Illyria and west of Thessaly known to the Greeks as Epirus. Reluctantly admitted to be Greeks by their fellow nationals, the Epirots claimed descent from a son of Achilles who had settled there after the Trojan War. Thirteen other tribes were also part of Epirus, a region which is particularly afflicted by the Greek landscape, and especially by the Pindus mountain chain, which makes Epirus a land of narrow valleys and tiny plateaux cut across by massive mountain ranges. The humid summers and freezing winters made Macedonian soldiers nostalgic for the mountains of upper Macedonia which the Epirot landscape and climate closely resembled.

Among the Greeks, Epirus was famed principally for its huge and ferocious Molossian hounds, which were the ancient world's premier hunting and guard dogs (and which are possible ancestors of both the St Bernard and Rottweiler breeds). Epirus was also known for the oracle and sanctuary of Zeus at Dodona. The oracle was of great antiquity and even predated that of Apollo at Delphi. Like Illyria, Epirus was more or less a kingdom on those occasions when its various tribes agreed to be so, though the rulers (generally from the Molossian tribe) styled themselves 'protectors' rather than kings. Macedon tended to dominate Epirus, but both states were united in their distaste for the Illyrians, who, whenever given the chance had a tendency to plunder either nation indiscriminately. A marriage alliance between Macedon and Epirus produced the most famous of Epirot exports – the warlike King Pyrrhus. Though he began his rule as a minor and with a co-ruler, Pyrrhus rapidly established himself as the sole power in Epirus and quickly went on to make Epirus the principal power in Greece. Like Alexander, Pyrrhus had a taste for conquest, which he first took out on the Illyrians by annexing their southern territory, probably as far north as the Greek city of Epidamnus. He then secured that flank by allying with King Bardylis of Dardanos, and decisively broke Macedon's power over his kingdom. Pyrrhus was undone by over-reaching his strength in an attempt to conquer southern Italy from the Romans. He attempted to restore his fortunes by attacking Macedon, and even managed to seize the kingship there in 274 BC. Eventually ejected from Macedonia, Pyrrhus turned on the Peloponnese and eventually died whilst attacking Argos.

The career of Pyrrhus represented the high tide of Epirot fortunes. Though he established Ambracia as the Epirot capital and embellished the shrine at Dodona, the most enduring legacy of Pyrrhus was the entrenched enmity of Illyria, Macedon and Greece towards his kingdom. By 232 BC the embattled state was crumbling under constant attacks from its neighbours. The monarchy was dissolved, allowing the tribes greater independence in a loose confederacy.

Thessaly

To the east of the Pindus range, in the shadow of Mount Olympus, highest of Greek mountains and home of the Gods, lay the land of Thessaly, stretching across the south of Macedon to the Aegean Sea. The northwest to southeast slant of the mountain range makes Thessaly a lopsided triangle, wider in the north than in the south, where the mountains extend all the way into the sea to form the Magnisia Peninsula, one arm of the Bay of Pagasai, from where in legend Jason and his Argonauts launched their boat to search for the golden fleece.

By the time it has reached the sea, the mountain chain has broken to allow small fertile basins and leafy valleys alongside the small rivers which flow from the flanks of the mountains across Thessaly's two major plains into the Aegean. These plains are rich in alluvial soil which in antiquity allowed the breeding of such cattle and horses as were able to keep their heads above water through the region's frequent inundations. The temperate climate was excellent for grain, but allowed few areas where olives or vines could be successfully cultivated.

The plains, which were an agricultural blessing, were a military handicap, for the mountains were pierced by a series of passes with the generic name of *tempe* and these passes left Thessaly vulnerable to the armies of north and south. Consequently the region seldom enjoyed an independent political existence apart from a spell of dominance in the sixth century under a king called Aleuas the Red. The main cities of the region were Larissa, Pherae and Pharsalus, and though technically a federation, in reality and in true Greek tradition, these cities were frequently at loggerheads with each other when not fighting the Boeotians to the south and Macedonians to the north.

This internal political weakness meant that uniting the people of Thessaly needed the external and ungentle intervention of Philip II of Macedon. He left the land under four separate rulers called tetrarchs who were in turn firmly under his thumb. With this arrangement in place, the Thessalians, especially as cavalrymen, gave sterling service to Philip's son and successor, Alexander the Great, during his campaigns in Asia Minor. On Alexander's death, Thessaly joined in the general Greek attempt to rebel, and was defeated along with the Greeks in a brisk little conflict called the Lamian War after the Thessalian city which was the principal theatre of action.

Defeat meant that in practical terms Thessaly was effectively partitioned into a 'Thessalian League' in the north which was subject to Macedon, and the south which was under the domination of the nascent and restive Aetolian Confederacy.

Aetolia

This had long been a somewhat barren and backward area in west central Greece. Aetolia filled a rough triangle with its widest side along the Corinthian Gulf, and the tip of the triangle in the north at Mount Tymphrestus. Apart from the Achelous River valley to the west, the entire country was rugged and mountainous, famous in Greek mythology as the scene of the hunt for the fearsome Calydonian boar. The principal occupation of the peoples of Aetolia appeared to their long-suffering neighbours to be brigandage. Large bands of men who knew the terrain were able to move and conceal themselves with relative ease, a fact which led to the undoing of the Athenian general Demosthenes when he tried to invade during the Peloponnesian war of the fifth century, and to the later discomfiture of the Gauls in 280 BC.

Polybius, a supporter of the rival Achaean League, had little good to say about the Aetolians. 'These people are inherently unscrupulous, and insatiably greedy for the property of others.' he complains. 'Because of their lust for plunder, they thought almost any excuse was good enough for attacking people who had done them no wrong.' [10]

By the third century, greatly abetted by Philip II of Macedon who gave them the economically valuable and long-coveted port of Naupactus, the Aetolians surprised the rest of Greece and themselves by becoming a formidable military power. The Aetolian confederacy, formerly little more than a name, became a political reality, and a genuine democracy, with power vested in an assembly which met twice a year, and a military commander elected annually.

Aetolia itself was strengthened against invasion by the fortification of the cities of Calydon, Pleuron, Lysimachia and Arsinoeia, and the Aetolians themselves went adventuring eastward toward the pass of Thermopylae, and gained control of Delphi and Phocis in the 270s BC. In the west the Aetolians were also successfully expansionist and partitioned the area of Acarnania with the Epirots. By now the Macedonian government was bitterly regretting its earlier encouragement of the Aetolians, and the two states were rapidly settling into entrenched positions of mutual hostility. This was partly countered by the diplomacy of Antigonus Doson who brought the Aetolians into his alliance against Sparta, but the Aetolians were, like most Greek states, incapable of remaining in a single alliance for long. By the time of Philip V in 220 BC Aetolia was engaged in a cold war with Macedon and an altogether more fiery series of spats with the Achaean League and Epirus.

The Achaean League

Later historians are well informed of the history and constitution of the Achaean League, as it was described at some length by both Polybius and Plutarch, both of whom viewed it sympathetically. Achaea was a region of the northeastern Peloponnese containing a dozen or so small cities. The Achaeans had the Spartans as neighbours to the south, and historically were forced to subordinate themselves to the legendary military prowess of that city. However, the weakening of Spartan military power allowed the Achaeans to organize themselves into a confederacy which gave its member states a real degree of freedom. Under Aratus of Sicyon the formerly moribund League revived, and began to accept neighbours beyond its original core of twelve cities.

Despite the claims of Polybius, it appears that the Achaeans were, like the Aetolians, prepared to expand by military action as well as through the more gentle arts of diplomacy. Aratus campaigned in Locris, on the other side of the Gulf of Corinth, and gained considerable renown for expelling the Macedonian garrison from the citadel of Corinth, thus (temporarily) relieving Greece of one of its 'fetters', or at least replacing a Macedonian shackle with an Achaean one. The Achaeans also took Mantinea in Arcadia by military force.

Though on separate sides of the Gulf of Corinth, the Achaeans and the Aetolians clashed early and repeatedly, as both had expansionist ambitions in Locris. Furthermore, Aratus' propaganda painted him as a liberator of the Greeks, and the practical upshot of this was that through the 240s and 230s BC the Achaean League took a stance against the nation's premier 'oppressors' – the Macedonians. This hostility was evidenced, for example, by the expulsion of the Macedonians from Corinth, and by combining with the Aetolians against Demetrius. The anti-Macedonian line became untenable once Aratus' skilled skulduggery gained the League control of Megalopolis in 235 BC, since along with Megalopolis came the entrenched hostility of King Cleomenes of Sparta (see below), who considered Megalopolis a Spartan dependency. Cleomenes, who had expansionist ambitions of his own, persuaded the Corinthians to eject the Achaean garrison from their acropolis, and provoked a war in which he defeated the Achaeans in battle. Aratus was in danger of being boxed between enemies in the north and south. Since peace with Cleomenes was unlikely, Aratus used the long-standing friendship between Megalopolis and Macedon to make peace with his northern enemy.

As related above, Antigonus Doson of Macedon jumped at the chance to ally with Achaea, bring Sparta to heel, and get back control of Corinth. Antigonus also used the Achaeans as a counterweight to the Aetolians, with whom he was on bad terms, and thereafter the Macedonians counted the Achaeans as among their most loyal allies in Greece.

Like the Aetolians, the Achaean League was led by a single general (usually Aratus in the early years) though before 255 BC the League had two such commanders as well as a commander of cavalry. Most of the League's business was run by a council at which the different cities of the League were represented, and at least later in its existence, the cities of the League had laws and currency in common. The council was supplemented by a citizen assembly, and both council and citizens met when there was vital and pressing business on hand such as the declaration of war or the ratification of peace.

Sparta

Once the undoubted military leader of Greece, Sparta had been in decline for over a century. The constitution of the city had the unintended effect of concentrating power and land in the hands of an ever-diminishing body of citizens. As these citizens alone had the right to fight as Spartan hoplites, the Spartan army was smaller than many of its rivals. At the Battle of Leuctra in 371 BC the Thebans proved conclusively that the Spartans could be beaten, and from their former ascendancy, the Spartans were reduced to fighting to retain power in their southeastern corner of the Peloponnese. In the 260s BC they joined Athens in attempting to throw Macedon out of the Greek peninsula and were massively and ruinously defeated. It took another generation before the city underwent a brief resurgence under King Cleomenes III, ruler from 235-222 BC. Cleomenes was supported by Ptolemy III of Egypt who saw a chance of breaking the Macedonian hold on Greece. With Egyptian backing, Cleomenes claimed that Sparta had fallen from the constitutional purity established by its founder Lycurgus, and instituted a number of 'reforms' which incidentally increased his own power.

Cleomenes was able to do this as he was a highly successful military leader, who in the early years of his reign restored Spartan military pride by defeating both the Aetolians in Arcadia and the Achaeans at Laodocia. By 228 BC he was operating in central Greece and had briskly annexed Tegea, Mantinea and Orchomenus. He increased the size of the citizen body, and reorganized the army. With these resources the newly-invigorated Spartan state marched on Argos and captured the city, much to the alarm of the Achaeans who had failed in their attempt to do the same. Corinth too came under Spartan influence. This resurgence of Spartan power made Cleomenes highly popular in Sparta and caused considerable anxiety among Sparta's neighbours.

It was this frightening assertiveness which finally drove Aratus to reconcile himself with Antigonus Doson, and allowed the Macedonian-led Hellenic League to drive southwards. Cleomenes did not go down without a fight. In 223 BC his forces captured Megalopolis back from the Achaeans but he spitefully destroyed the city as he knew Sparta had no chance of holding it.

The following year Sparta was brought to bay at the Battle of Sellasia, and though the Spartans fought with their traditional vigour they were no match for the superior Macedonian formations and tactics. Cleomenes fled to Egypt, and Antigonus entered and took control of Sparta. The recent reforms were undone, and a more traditional government established. Though Sparta had a long history ahead, its last flowering was undone at Sellasia, and the city was never more than a shadow of its former self. For most of the next century Sparta was hardly relevant in even the affairs of Greece, let alone in the wider world, though it was Achaean antagonism to Sparta which later led to the final extinction of Greek independence.

Athens

Athens, another of the great city-states of Greece, fared little better than Sparta in the third century. Like the rest of Greece, Athens fell under Macedonian control thanks to Philip II.

The virtual destruction of Thebes after that city's failed rebellion against Macedon kept Athens and the rest of Greece cowed until Alexander's death. When Alexander died in 323 BC, the Athenians joined in the general Greek effort to free themselves from Macedon, a struggle known as the Lamian War (see *Thessaly* above). Athens contributed through her sea power, which had been legendary at the time of the Peloponnesian war. However, as the Spartans were also discovering, the world had moved on, and the Athenian fleet was twice soundly defeated by the Macedonians.

Defeated, Athens had to submit to Macedon's terms. These included the crippling of the Athenian democracy by the disenfranchisement of the poorer citizens and a Macedonian garrison installed in the Piraeus. Later Demetrius, son of the Macedonian king, moved in and became effectively tyrant of Athens. In 287 BC it was felt that the city had behaved well enough for the Macedonian garrisons to be removed, after which Athens gained a precarious degree of autonomy.

Neither Athens nor Greece had given up their dream of full independence, and in Athens an anti-Macedonian faction led by the philosopher Chremonides took power. With help from Sparta, Chremonides attempted to throw off Macedon's grip on the city. Help was also given from Egypt. Indeed, so keen were the Ptolemies to gain a foothold in Greece that they appear from the archaeological evidence to have sponsored the building of some small forts in Attica. The subsequent war is called the Chremonidean War, after Chremonides, its main instigator. Fighting kicked off in 268 BC, and after some minor clashes in the early years Antigonus Gonatus won a major victory outside Corinth in 265 BC and killed the Spartan King Areus I. Athens stood siege until about 262 BC for aid from Egypt. When the Egyptians did get around to sending help, it was probably too late, but it did not matter in any case, as the Macedonians defeated the Egyptian ships at sea well before they reached Athens.

A governor called Demetrios of a family long loyal to Macedon took over the government until 229 BC. During this time Athens was a surly and disaffected ally of Macedon, held down by Macedonian garrisons stationed in forts in Attica and around the city. Nevertheless, Athens stayed out of the frequent clashes between its nominal suzerain and the Aetolians and Achaeans, with all sides apparently happy to accept the city's neutrality.

The construction of garrison forts was about all the building work that was going on, for Athens was at one of the lowest points of its history. A traveller called Herakleides wrote of a trip there: 'The city is not well watered – in fact it is practically dry. Because it is so old, the town layout is poor, the buildings are shabby, and many are uninhabitable. Anyone not familiar with the place would at first be doubtful that this was actually the famous city of the Athenians.' [11]

In 229 BC, again with help from Egypt, Athens rebelled once again. This time, thanks to the preoccupation of Antigonus Doson with Sparta, Athens remained free, though had Doson not perished whilst fighting the barbarians, it is unlikely that this would have remained the case for long.

Chapter 2

The Opening Shots

First Contacts

At the start of the third century, Rome was at best peripheral to Greek affairs. However, whilst few Greeks knew or cared about the existence of Rome, the opposite was not true: Rome certainly knew of Greece which had both directly and indirectly influenced Rome almost since that city's foundation. In fact the Romans believed that they were descended from Trojan refugees who fled their city when it was destroyed by the Greeks after a ten year siege made famous by Homer's *Iliad*.

Whether this is historically accurate is less relevant than the fact that it probably did not make later Roman popular opinion favourable toward the Greeks. Roman perceptions of Greece were not helped by another legendary figure, a Corinthian who settled in the Etruscan city of Tarquinia. His descendants, taking their name from that city, ruled Rome as the Tarquins. So harsh was the rule of the last of these Tarquins that the Romans overthrew him. Deciding henceforth to dispense with kings, the Romans formed a republic.

The leading revolutionary, Lucius Brutus, had, as a young man, travelled to Delphi in Greece to consult the oracle there, and it was to Greece that the nascent republic went again in 450 BC to research the laws which later became the Twelve Tables: the foundation on which was built the massive edifice of Roman Law (and therefore much of later European Law).

During the fourth century, Greece was preoccupied with the growing power of Macedon, and Alexander's subsequent forays against the Persians. Few paid much attention to the west, where the embattled little city-state of Rome fought off Gauls and central Italian hill tribes, and slowly began to expand from central to southern Italy. This eventually brought Rome back into contact with Greece, since the main cities of southern Italy – Naples (which gets its name from the Greek for 'new city', *neopolis*), Tarentum,

Croton and Thurii – were part of the wider Greek diaspora known as *Magna Graecia*.

Thus in the third century, Greece came to Rome in the form of Pyrrhus of Epirus. In the early 280s BC the Romans had fallen out with the Tarentines partly as a result of their support for the Samnites, an Italian mountain people with whom the Romans were having immense difficulty (and who were still not fully subdued 200 years later). With the Romans poised to take Tarentum, the city's citizens appealed to the fellow Greeks of their homeland.

Pyrrhus was ready and willing to help. At this point in his career he had restored the Epirot kingdom, had an initial go at taking over Macedon, and, on being ejected by Lysimachus (the predecessor of Antigonus Gonatus) in 284 BC, was looking for a further adventure. Rome was by now large enough to be considered by the predatory Pyrrhus as a tempting target, especially as the general Greek opinion of Rome (when they thought about the place at all) was that its peoples were at best barbarians with pretences towards civilization.

Pyrrhus saw the chance to take over the rising power of Rome and channel its resources into the conquest of Sicily, and from there to absorb Carthage into an empire encompassing much of the western Mediterranean. It was only when his forces actually came into contact with Rome that Pyrrhus realized that his intelligence, both military and personal, might be at fault:

> At the River Siris, he rode up to to get a view of them [the Romans]; and when he had noted their discipline ... and the general arrangement of their camp, he remarked in some surprise to a close companion: 'These seem remarkably unbarbaric barbarians, but the outcome [of the coming battle] will tell us what their discipline amounts to.'[12]

Pyrrhus defeated the Romans in a succession of battles, but he could make no headway against the famed Roman stubbornness which refused either to admit defeat in the field or to compromise in negotiation. In the end, Pyrrhus left Italy with his planned empire stillborn. But Greece now afforded Rome greater attention and respect, whilst the Roman opinion of their Greek neighbours was hardly improved by this latest clash.

By seeing off Pyrrhus, Rome was free to finish extending her hegemony over the remainder of south Italy. Thereafter, Rome and Greece were once again of peripheral interest to one another as Rome embarked on her first epic war with Carthage, and Greece and Macedon settled into bouts of petty wars and politicking.

Rome and Illyria

Rome's re-engagement with its neighbours over the Adriatic Sea was, perhaps not unexpectedly, with that part of the peninsula nearest to Rome. One of the side effects of the war with Carthage was that Rome had become a naval power, and the state itself was becoming increasingly cosmopolitan. Roman shipping moved up the east coast, and Greeks trading with Rome operated out of harbours in Corcyra (modern Corfu).

Illyria had come under the domination of King Agron of the Ardiaei tribe, a man of evidently powerful character who had welded several other tribes into a single political unit. As the Illyrians were naturally a seafaring people, it followed that the combined Illyrian fleet soon became the dominant force in the Adriatic. The Illyrian army was also powerful, and Agron used it with great effect in 230 BC to stop the Aetolians from press-ganging a city called Medion into their confederacy. Having won a splendid victory, Agron celebrated by becoming so royally inebriated that he passed smoothly from being dead drunk to dead. His demise left his equally-capable wife Teuta to take up the reins of government as regent for his young son, Pinnes.[13]

Under Teuta, Illyria became as strong a state as it would ever become. Acarnania was wrested from Aetolian control after Agron's victory, and the small city of Phoenice in Epirus was captured by the simple expedient of bribing the Gallic troops stationed there. Teuta's men then inflicted a punishing defeat on the indignant Epirots who came marching to the city's relief. Phoenice was eventually ransomed back to the Epirots, who were forced into a humiliating defensive pact with Illyria. Teuta, the highly prejudiced Polybius tells us, was so taken with the richness of the spoils from Epirus that she encouraged her people on ever more extravagant expeditions and raids.

Not unsurprisingly, a lot of this wealth came from the Adriatic, robbed from the boats of merchants trading with Rome. The Greek merchants appealed to the Romans, and the Romans agreed to talk to Teuta about it. Thus in late 230 BC two delegates, Gaius and Lucius Coruncanius, arrived as leaders of an embassy to enquire exactly what was going on. The embassy caught Teuta at a bad time. She was on an island called Issa, besieging a town of the same name which, though Illyrian, was a part of Dardanian territory which refused to accept her authority. From the somewhat-confused reports of Appian and Cassius Dio it appears that the Isseans opportunistically took advantage of the appearance of the newcomers to unilaterally throw themselves on the Romans' mercy.[14] The Roman response is unknown, but the Issean appeal undoubtedly soured the atmosphere at the subsequent meeting with Teuta. The queen listened impatiently to the Romans, and when they were done, informed them that the Illyrian state had no hostile intent toward Rome. However, it was not the business of the Illyrian kingdom to suppress piracy among its citizens, and indeed, piracy in Illyria was a respected native tradition.

At this one of the Roman delegation remarked irritably that if she knew what was good for her, Teuta would break with tradition and start making the suppression of piracy the business of the Illyrian state. The queen took umbrage and the meeting broke up with undiplomatic acrimony.

It was evident that the embassy had achieved all that they were going to. Their mission had been to establish the extent of piracy and the degree of involvement of the Illyrian authorities. They had established the official Illyrian position and warned the queen in the strongest terms that this was not acceptable. However, Teuta was still fuming at the characteristic bluntness with which the Romans had made their point, and, before the Romans had left Illyria, she arranged for the assassination of the delegate who had most offended her.

The First Illyrian War

The killing of an ambassador shocked the Romans, who were further infuriated by the fact that, after initially denying that the embassy had even reached her, Teuta hardly bothered to pretend she had not instigated the murder. Consequently, the year ended with the Romans making a commitment to enrol legions at the start of the next campaigning season (i.e. 229 BC) for the state's first military expedition to the Greek peninsula. It was, as Polybius remarks, an event which deserves close attention as it was a significant harbinger of what was to follow.[15]

Teuta did not wait for the Romans to fall on her, and spent the winter kitting out a substantial fleet. She would have known that there was no help forthcoming from Macedon despite her husband's recent alliance with that kingdom. The Macedonians were deeply engaged in fighting Illyria's northern neighbours, the Dardanians, and had neither the men nor the resources to get involved elsewhere. Consequently, Teuta decided on a pre-emptive strike. The following spring a large part of her new fleet set sail for

Epidamnus, a city on the headland of Dyrrhachium (Durazzo in modern Albania). The Illyrians very nearly succeeded in capturing the place by treachery. They claimed to be landing simply to take on water, but by concealing swords under their tunics they almost managed to take the walls. Once they realized their peril the Epidamnians fought off the invaders, and so denied Teuta control of a port which, because of its strategic position, would for the next century become the main gateway for Roman forces arriving in Greece.

Foiled at Epidamnus, the Illyrians recombined their fleet to take on the Corcyrans whose unsporting complaints to Rome were considered the root cause of the problem. Under siege and badly outnumbered, the Corcyrans appealed to both the Aetolians and Achaeans, who in a rare moment of unity agreed to send support. Thus, after Epidamnus, the first action of the Illyrian war was a minor naval action at some islands off the coast of Corcyra, featuring ships from the Achaean League (which had been partly fitted out by the Aetolians) against other Illyrians and ten heavier vessels of the Illyrians' Acarnanian allies.

The Illyrians adopted the unusual tactic of lashing their lighter ships together into bundles of four hulls apiece, and these, turning broadside to the Achaean triremes, positively invited the Greeks to ram them. However an impact that would have shattered one boat simply caused the rammer to become entangled in wreckage which was still supported by the remaining three, and at this point the Illyrians swarmed over the hull and boarded the attacker before it could back off. The Greeks lost five ships in this way before they turned into the following wind and made for safety, leaving the depressed Corcyrans to make what terms they could with their Illyrian besiegers.

One Demetrius of Pharos was given command of an Illyrian garrison which was installed to hold down the island. The remainder of the Illyrians and the rest of their fleet headed for Epidamnus in another attempt to take the city before the Romans arrived.

And the Romans were on their way. Demonstrating a poor sense of timing, Queen Teuta had provoked the Romans during a year when they had no pressing business elsewhere. Therefore, instead of a relatively minor expeditionary force, the Illyrians had the undivided attention of both Roman consuls and their armies. Consul Gnaeus Fulvius Centumalus came accompanied by 200 ships with the task of clearing the sea lanes for his colleague, Lucius Postumius Albinus, who was en route from Brundisium with naval transports carrying 20,000 infantry and 2,000 cavalry. Word of the siege of Corcyra made that island the initial destination of Gnaeus Fulvius and his fleet. Though Corcyra had fallen before the Romans arrived, Demetrius of Pharos did a lightning comparison between the size of his garrison and that of the Roman force bearing down on him and promptly switched his allegiance to Rome.

After the Corcyrans had enthusiastically placed the Illyrian garrison and their own safety in Roman hands, the fleet proceeded north to Apollonia, nearby on the Greek mainland, there to link up with Albinus and his army. Demetrius of Pharos was brought along, both as a hostage and as a guide to the terrain and peoples of Illyria. The combined force then proceeded yet further north to lift the siege of Epidamnus. This they did just with word of their intention, as the Illyrians hastily decamped at the news that the Romans were on their way.

The Romans moved steadily northward, plundering coastal cites as they went and eventually reached Issa where they lifted the Illyrian siege and took up the Issean offer of surrender which had been made to their original delegation.

Illyrian unity, always fragile, was utterly incapable of withstanding the strain of the Roman invasion. Though they administered a sharp setback to the Romans at a place called Nutria, the Illyrians could see the war was unwinnable, and tribe after tribe sent embassies to the Romans to make a separate peace. As a bonus to the Romans, twenty galleys loaded with pirate plunder were captured while the Illyrians were attempting to move their ill-gotten gains to a more secure location. This bounty allowed Fulvius to later celebrate a naval triumph and nicely defrayed the costs of the war. As Demetrius had proven himself a reliable collaborator the Romans placed much of their newly-conquered territory under his control, and spared his native island of Pharos from the attentions of the plundering legions.

Teuta was politically isolated and most of her military force had melted away. She had little choice but to ask for whatever terms the Romans were prepared to offer. After due deliberation the Romans decided that Teuta should give up control of some further areas of Illyria and pay an indemnity large enough to cover those costs of the war still being borne by the Roman treasury. Above all, Teuta was charged with suppressing Illyrian piracy and to severely restrict her own state's naval activity. What naval activity remained was to happen north of the mouth of the Lissus River where it could not threaten the Greek coast.

The Interwar Period

The Romans returned home, Fulvius to his triumph and Postumius to be later re-elected to the consulship. (Which he never took up; whilst still consul-elect he was killed in action against the Gauls, who plated his skull with gold and made it a drinking vessel.) Delegates were sent to both the Aetolian and Achaean Leagues to explain what had driven the Romans to military action so near to their home territory. The Romans retained a nominal presence in Greece, since Corcyra, Apollonia and Epidamnus remained under their protection. It is significant that while it was necessary to justify the war and settlement to neighbouring Greek states, the Macedonians were apparently not consulted, even though Macedon was the hegemonic power in Greece. Demetrius II of Macedon had died at this time, and the country was still weakened by barbarian invasions and seen as a declining force. Antigonus Doson, Demetrius' successor, was an unknown quantity, and the Romans probably judged (correctly) that he would have enough trouble with southern Greece (especially the resurgent Sparta of Cleomenes) to be anything other than grateful that the Illyrians had been slapped down.

Rome's intentions with regard to Illyria seem fairly clear. Rome was not interested in the conquest of Illyria, let alone the rest of the Greek peninsula. They had enough on their hands with the Gallic Boii in the Alps and the absorption of central and southern Italy with its troublesome Samnites. Their main interest in the Illyrians was an earnest hope that they would go away and stop bothering Roman shipping. The recent war was intended to achieve this modest ambition by leaving a chain of independent city-states dependant on Rome along the south-western Illyrian coast, and by keeping the Balkans further north divided, disorganized and no threat to anyone.

What the Romans did not factor into their calculations was the personality of Demetrius of Pharos. It is hard to fully understand what drove this mercurial and ambitious individual. None of the ancient sources have a good word for him, and modern scholars are divided as to his character and motivation.[16] However, it seems reasonable to assume that Demetrius showed his true colours at Corcyra when he was unscrupulous, self-interested and brave enough to take risks if the potential reward was sufficiently tempting.

Certainly Demetrius wasted little time consolidating the position the Romans had left him. He wrested the guardianship of Illyria's young king from Teuta, and brought recalcitrant tribes under his sway. There can be no doubt that the steady reunification of Illyria under Demetrius was exactly what the Romans did not want to see, but there was little ostensible reason for complaint, in that the Illyrians were under no obligation to organize their internal affairs to suit Rome.

Demetrius also reaffirmed the alliance of his people with Macedon. His Illyrians fought alongside Antigonus Doson when he subdued Cleomenes of Sparta, and Demetrius hardly wavered in his alliance with Macedon thereafter. This early venture into foreign affairs was followed up with increasing boldness in succeeding years. It is probable that Demetrius felt that, despite their warnings, the Romans would not concern themselves with Illyria so long as Demetrius did not interfere with trade in the Adriatic.

This view would have been further reinforced when a relative of Queen Teuta, called Sacerdilaidas, led his ships on a massive plundering raid south of the River Lissa in direct contravention of the treaty of 228 BC. It is quite probable that Demetrius read the passive Roman reaction as meaning that Illyrians could get violent with southern Greece as long as such ships as crossed south of the River Lissus did so in a private capacity rather than as warships of Illyria.

Accordingly he took at least fifty boats on a plundering expedition to the Cyclades. The chronology of these events is somewhat confused, but it appears that Demetrius was correct in his judgement that whilst his conduct might irritate the Romans, his adherence to the strict letter of the treaty of 228 BC would allow the views of non-interventionists in the Roman senate to prevail.

Polybius believes that Demetrius was encouraged in his aggression abroad by Rome's difficulties with the Gauls, and because he foresaw further difficulties for Rome with Carthage. Demetrius may have felt that Rome's preoccupations left him a free hand to further strengthen his position in Acarnania and against the Aetolians. However, Polybius appears to overlook the fact that the Romans had been successful against the Gauls in Istria (at the top of the Adriatic Sea) and that the threat of Hannibal in Spain was hardly obvious in the 220s BC. Roman tolerance had its limits.

The Second Illyrian War

What provoked the war which broke out between Rome and Illyria in 219 BC was that Demetrius, overcome with galloping ambition, either himself or (more probably) through proxies, seems eventually to have attacked and sacked Illyrian cities which looked to Rome for protection.

This was a very real cause for war. Indeed, it was exactly the same cause that Rome would evoke the following year when Hannibal sacked Saguntum in Spain, a city under Roman protection. A clue as to which 'city' Demetrius attacked comes from Appian who remarks that Demetrius 'detached the Atintani from [their allegiance to] Rome'.[17] (Atintania was a district south of the River Lissus, somewhere between that river and Phoenice in northern Epirus, and definitely within the area of the Roman protectorate.)

In short, the gambler in Demetrius had compelled him to push his luck further and further, until it finally ran out. In 219 BC Demetrius' ally, Antigonus Dosun, was dead, and Antigonus' young heir, Philip V, was still an untried youngster on the Macedonian throne. Demetrius had probably not helped his case by helping the Aetolians (Macedon's enemies) in their attack on the border town of Pylos. But Philip had troubles of his own in 220 BC and little time to spare either to help or hinder Demetrius.

In 219 BC the Romans had finished their business with the Istrians and had a large experienced army to hand. They may already have received word of Hannibal's aggressive behaviour in Spain, and wanted to secure their eastern front before engaging in the west. Whatever the Roman reasoning, Demetrius received information about its concrete outcome that summer: a Roman force under the consul Lucius Amelius Paulus was on the way.

There is little information about the Roman forces, and none at all about the naval contingent, but it is a reasonable assumption that Paulus had a standard consular army of 20,000 men and 2,000 cavalry. There seems little to credit claims that our main surviving source, Polybius, was following the jingoistic pro-Roman line taken by Rome's first historian Fabius Pictor (whose works are now lost) and that in fact Demetrius was the innocent victim of unprovoked Roman expansionism. Even those who do take this view have to conclude that Rome's intention with the expedition of 219 BC was simply to make sure that their 'placeholder' (the string of cities and peoples under their protection on Greece's eastern coast) was not eroded away by Illyrian encroachments. As with Teuta, Rome sent its legions not to conquer but to chastise, and in the course of chastisement to extract sufficient booty to cover the cost of administering it.

Demetrius decided that he had to weather the storm, and proceeded to batten down the hatches by having his political opponents arrested and executed. He then proceeded to strongly garrison two cities: Dimale (location now uncertain) and his native Pharos.

When Paulus arrived in Illyria he found the enemy fully prepared. Illyrian morale was high, for it was generally believed that their strongpoints were impregnable. They intended that the war would consist of one or two drawn-out sieges during which the Illyrian irregulars would harass the Romans from their mountain redoubts and enrich themselves by raiding Roman supply lines.

Consequently the Illyrians were flabbergasted and appalled when Paulus and his highly-experienced legionaries proceeded in a workmanlike manner to Dimale, briskly set up siege works and took the place within a week. Paulus then packed up his siege engines and set off for Pharos, meeting along the way a stream of Illyrian envoys sent by their demoralized masters to distance themselves from Demetrius and to make terms with the Romans whilst they could still get credit for doing so.

Many Illyrians evidently felt that the island fortress of Pharos was not going to last much longer than Dimale, but Paulus was less sanguine. As his immediate assault of Dimale showed, he was determined not to get drawn into the debilitating siege warfare that Demetrius had planned for him. However, Pharos had thousands of loyal, highly motivated defenders, and was even more strongly fortified than Dimale had been. Since Paulus wanted to crack the Pharian nut with the same dispatch that he had used at Dimale he decided to immediately deploy his best weapon against Demetrius, namely the character of the man himself.

Therefore the opening attack on Pharos consisted of a mere twenty ships. These arrived in broad daylight and disembarked a scratch squad of troops. These took over the harbour and calmly began readying it for the main invasion force. The inference was that the Illyrians were considered too demoralized to sally out of their walls and deal even with this small Roman force. Demetrius, on the other hand, saw a way of obstructing the main Roman landing, and promptly set out to push the Roman beachhead back into the sea. Against expectations, the Romans did not re-embark in the face of superior enemy numbers, but fought back stubbornly, and Demetrius was forced to throw more and more men into the fray until his entire garrison of some 6,000 men was engaged.

At this point it became apparent that the Roman advance party was not in fact preparing the harbour for the main Roman army. The main Roman army had already landed the previous evening on the other side of the island and had spent the night making its way across to the fortress. The Roman troops in the harbour had been sent to draw the Illyrians out of their defences, and whilst these had been in action, the main Roman army was smugly forming up on a hill between the Pharians and their city.

The Pharians gamely changed tack, and drew up their lines to storm the Romans on the hill. While impressed by the Illyrian resolve, it is unlikely that the Romans were deeply perturbed by an outnumbered force of irregulars trying to attack uphill against legionaries in formation. The legions waited until the Illyrians were committed to their advance, and then fell upon them while the troops from the harbour attacked the Illyrian rear. It was a brief, one-sided battle.

Illyrian warriors were soon either dead or scattered all over the island. The majority wisely refrained from taking shelter in the town, since the Romans now proceeded thence and razed it to the ground, having first looted their campaign expenses from the premises. This outcome was not a total surprise to Demetrius. He, for all his impetuous nature, knew his opponents well enough to have prepared a Plan B. This consisted of a carefully-mapped escape route, some fast ships tucked away in a secluded cove, and sufficient supplies to carry Rome's scapegrace ex-protégé to shelter in the court of Philip of Macedon.

With Demetrius gone, and the vaunted Illyrian strongpoints collapsed like two houses of cards, the rest of Illyria showed little fight. The war turned into a triumphal procession during which Paulus subdued the rest of Illyria, organized the place 'as he saw fit' and returned home for a well-merited triumph, having been away for just over two months.[18]

Meanwhile, back in Macedon

In 219 BC Philip V had been king of Macedon for a matter of months, but he would have known from the outset that, even without the Romans complicating his life, that his was no easy job. Though ranked as one of the great Hellenistic powers, for more than a century Macedon had been 'punching above its weight' as modern military parlance puts it. A relatively small and partly mountainous country, with limited resources of manpower, Macedon had an abundance of barbarian enemies to occupy its armies; as if holding down the fractious statelets of the Greek peninsula was not effort enough. As pointed out earlier, Macedon compensated for its weakness in manpower and military overstretch by having both a superbly organized army and an efficient administration.

Since the king of Macedon was the linchpin of that administration, it was natural that Macedon's enemies would test the mettle of that linchpin, who was, after all, a 17-year-old boy. As Polybius remarks:

> The Aetolians had for long been dissatisfied with peace and with a way of life limited to their own resources, as they had been accustomed to live on the wealth of their neighbours ... Nevertheless

whilst Antigonus was alive, they kept their peace through fear of Macedonia, but when the king died leaving as his successor Philip, who was almost a child, they thought this new king could be safely ignored.[19]

More or less the same thought had occurred to the Dardanians, the warlike people to the north of Illyria against whom Antigonus Doson had probably been campaigning at the time of his death. Assuming a state of confusion whilst Philip picked up the reins of power, the Dardanians lost no time in launching a quick raid on Macedonia. Philip had been expecting this and had prepared his response with the speed and flair that was to become his trademark.

The Dardanians were driven back in confusion to their mountains, but before Philip could follow up this early success word reached him of trouble to the south. The Aetolians had started a war with the small city-state of Messenia. Since the Hellenic League created by Antigonus Doson to deal with Cleomenes of Sparta had never been dissolved, the Messanians called for aid from their former allies, above all the Achaeans and Macedon.

Aratus, leader of the Achaeans at this time, responded promptly to the Messanian plea without waiting for Philip, whom he knew to be busy with the Dardanians. However, the Achaeans were out-manouvered and soundly beaten by the Aetolians, which is why it became essential for Philip to hurry to Corinth to take matters in hand. The contingencies of the international situation meant that rather than seeking an immediate military solution, the king was initially inclined towards negotiations.

Trouble was brewing to the east where a war had broken out between Rhodes and Byzantium, enthusiastically encouraged by the Ptolemaic Egyptians. Also with Egyptian encouragement, Athens had revolted from Macedon, and Sparta was becoming restless once more. The outlook to the west was ominous. Relations between Rome and Carthage were deteriorating rapidly as a result of Hannibal's unchecked expansion in Spain, and the two Illyrian leaders, Demetrius and Sacerdilaidas were becoming increasingly assertive. Sacerdilaidas had vigorously joined in the Aetolian aggression, and not to be outdone, Demetrius had embarked on the expansionist policy on the borders of the Roman protectorate which was to bring the legions down on his head. In short, Philip was emphatically not looking for trouble if he could talk his way out of it instead.

Leaving Demetrius to be dealt with by the Romans, Philip bribed Sacerdilaidas to his side and thus secured his western frontier. However, the

Aetolians had already shown how little they feared Macedon's intervention. Aetolia's privateers had captured a ship of the Macedonian royal navy, and taking it to Aetolia, sold the ship and enslaved its captain and crew. Now convinced that Philip had come south to fight, the Aetolians pre-empted negotiations by resuming hostilities. The war which followed is known as the Social War, since it involved the allies of Macedon. It was basically another spat between the Greek confederations. However this spat was more important than most because it established the military and political situation which prevailed at the time of the coming of Rome.

In response to Aetolian attacks Philip arrived in Epirus via Thessaly. He ignored an Aetolian attempt to distract him by a very substantial raid into Macedonia and took the city of Ambracus. Then, with a combined army of Macedonians, Epirots and Achaeans he pushed deep into the Aetolian heartland. However, his hopes of finishing the war that year were dashed by news that the Dardanians were preparing a larger and more organized assault on his kingdom. Philip was desperately needed in the north once more. It was while en route to deal with the latest crisis that Philip added to his entourage, Demetrius of Pharos fresh from his drubbing by the Romans. It was unlikely that Philip would look kindly on Roman intervention in Illyria, which he perceived as part of his bailiwick, and his kindly reception of Demetrius was probably a reflection of his pique.

Hearing of Philip's immanent return, the Dardanians abandoned their plans for invasion. It was now late in the campaigning season, and everyone assumed that hostilities were now concluded for the year. Consequently it came as a shock to the Aetolians and their allies when Philip suddenly reappeared in Corinth with a picked force of some 6,000 men and advanced through the winter snows into Arcadia in the eastern Peloponnese.

A highly profitable and successful campaign followed in which Philip's conduct and generalship aroused near-universal admiration in Greece. The end of the year 219 BC saw Philip back at the city of Argos with the Aetolians packed out of the Peloponnese and the peninsula largely subdued apart from Sparta, soon to be under the rule of King Nabis, a ruler in the tradition of the late Cleomenes. At about this time, word reached Philip that Rome was on the brink of war with Carthage, as Hannibal had attacked Rome's ally in Spain (the city of Saguntum) and Carthage had failed to respond appropriately to this outrage by one of its generals. This news, with its momentous implications for the future of Greece and Macedon, was considered of little note at the time.

Summer 218 BC saw Hannibal and his elephants set out for the Alps, and a Roman army head off in the opposite direction to Spain. In the east, the Hellenistic kingdoms of the Ptolemies and the Seleucids began a serious war over possession of an area called Coele-Syria. Between the two, the states of Greece resumed where they had left off the previous winter. Philip had obtained supplies of corn from the Achaeans to compensate for the effects of the Aetolian raid on Macedonia the previous year. Perhaps feeling the Aetolians owed him yet more corn, he suddenly switched his attack from land to sea and, with ships partly supplied by Sacerdilaidas, pillaged the island of Cephallenia, a valuable ally which supplied Aetolia with both corn and ships.

On hearing that the Aetolians had attacked Thessaly, Philip made another lightning change of direction. Taking advantage of the absence of Aetilia's army he attacked the country once more with a force which included Macedonian regulars, Illyrian tribesmen, Thracian irregulars and Cretan bowmen. These made their way through the narrow mountain passes before the remaining Aetolians had time to mount an effective defence, and took and sacked Thermus, the principal city of the Aetolian confederacy.

The Macedonian army then razed much of the town, in contravention of the laws of war as the Greeks perceived them, and so earned Philip the undying enmity of the Aetolians. On hearing of the attack on Aetolia, the Spartans declared against Macedon, and were stunned to find that within days the Macedonian king had departed Aetolia and was plundering their lands.

Philip might have done more, but his commanders were suffering from divided loyalties. There were those who endorsed the operations in Greece, and those who were aware that Thessaly and Macedonia were lightly defended in consequence. Chief among those with the latter view was Philip's counsellor, Apelles. Polybius (who, as an Achaean, was all in favour of Philip beating up the Aetolians) claims that Apelles had expected his seniority to impress the young king to the point where Apelles might have been the de facto ruler of Macedon. When Philip showed himself both highly competent and very much his own man, Apelles became bitter and treacherous. The Macedonian kings traditionally allowed their followers considerable freedom of speech and action, but when they overstepped the mark (as Apelles proceeded to do by interfering with the efficiency of the army) these same kings could also be remarkably abrupt. Apelles and the generals who supported him were promptly executed and their followers purged from the royal court.

By way of appeasing the remainder of Apelles' faction in the army, Philip switched operations the following year to Boeotia, intending to secure this area and so prevent Aetolian raids on Macedon and Thessaly. It was after another substantial victory in this new theatre of operations that news reached Philip that Hannibal had thrashed the Romans at the Battle of Lake Trasimene in Italy.

This was of particular interest to Philip as Sacerdilaidas now felt that his efforts for the Macedonian cause had been insufficiently rewarded and he had turned openly hostile. With Hannibal keeping the Romans out of the game, the Illyrians had returned whole-heartedly to state-sponsored piracy and regional trade was suffering. Urged on by Demetrius of Pharos, Philip began to contemplate patching up a peace with the Aetolians, and subduing the Illyrians once and for all. Then using Illyria as a springboard, Philip might establish a Macedonian presence in war-weakened Italy. Perhaps after all, the master plan of Pyrrhus could be realized.

This was, as Polybius remarks, the moment when the separate threads of Greek and Roman history became intertwined, and events in the west directly affected Greece. It was a moment not only of great opportunity, but of great danger. In the peace conference with the Aetolians which was part one of Philip's ambitious new plan, Polybius has one speaker remark:

> Whether the Carthaginians beat the Romans or the Romans beat the Carthaginians, it is highly unlikely that the winners will be content to rule Italy and Sicily. They are sure to come here. ...if you wait for these clouds gathering in the west to cover Greece, I very much fear these truces and wars and games at which we now play are going to be rudely interrupted.[20]

After their mauling at Macedonian hands over the previous few years the Aetolians were keen to retire and lick their wounds under the mantle of Greek unity. This left Philip free to move his plan to part two and attack Illyria, where he made considerable progress before the winter closed in.

During the winter was all sides in the converging regional conflict mustered their forces for a hectic campaigning season to come. The Romans had elected as consul Aemilius Paulus, the conqueror of Illyria in 219 BC, and were gathering the largest army they had ever put into the field in an effort to push Hannibal from Italy. Philip was busily building a fleet (mostly fast light ships of the Illyrian type) for operations in the Adriatic, and the Achaeans and Aetolians were quietly preparing for another bout of mutual hostilities. Sacerdilaidas was industriously building ships to counter Philip's fleet, and had sent to the Romans for aid. The Romans had problems of their own at this point, but dispatched a small fleet of some dozen ships from Lilybaeum in Sicily with instructions to familiarize themselves with the situation in the Balkans and Adriatic coast.

Philip's fleet, pushing northward, encountered these ships, the first military encounter between Macedonians and Romans. The Macedonians did not engage the newcomers, for Philip had not yet decided on war with Rome. Philip thought he had encountered the full Roman fleet, and was uncertain whether this presaged another major Roman incursion into the region. So perturbed was he by this extension of Roman power that he pulled back his forces which had reached as far as Apollonia and awaited developments.

Though he had not lost any men, this retreat was a blow to Philip's prestige. The setback soured the young king who had heretofore enjoyed little but outright success. He would have further cursed when he realized that he had retreated from Illyria, not before the full Roman fleet, but merely a strong reconnaissance force. None of this would have disposed him favourably to Rome. Later in the year, news reached Macedonia that even as Philip was pulling back from Illyria, in expectation of the arrival of a Roman army, Hannibal was busily wiping out that same army at Cannae, killing, among tens of thousand of others, the consul Aemilius Paulus.

This development appears to have tipped the balance. However, Philip did not immediately declare war on Rome. It is possible that Philip may even have considered that he had left it too late to do so, and that Rome must now surely sue for peace. However, as 215 BC began, and the Romans fought grimly on, Philip could offer assistance to Carthage without appearing simply to climb on to the bandwagon of Hannibal's success. Led by an Athenian, Xenophanes, ambassadors were sent to make an agreement for an offensive alliance against the Romans.

Chapter 3

The First Macedonian War

The Treaty

Before the gods who battle on our side and before the Sun, Moon, and Earth, the Rivers, Lakes, and Waters; before all the gods sovereign in Macedonia and the rest of Greece and all the gods of battle who preside over this oath, Hannibal the general declares, and with him all the Carthaginian senators present, and all Carthaginians in his forces, that for our mutual benefit we should make oaths binding ourselves to be friends, family, and brothers, on the following terms.

(1) That King Philip and the Macedonians and those Greeks who are allied to him shall protect the Carthaginians as a sovereign people, and Hannibal their general, and those with him, and all under the rule of Carthaginian law; and likewise the people of Utica and all cities and peoples subject to Carthage, and the soldiers and allied cities and tribes of Italy, Gaul, and Liguria, and with whomsoever in this country we may later ally ourselves with.

(2) The Carthaginians serving with us shall guard and protect King Philip and the Macedonians and those Greeks allied to him, and so too shall the people of Utica and all cities and peoples subject to Carthage, and their allies and soldiers and all allied peoples and tribes in Italy, Gaul, and Liguria, and any others who may later become our allies in Italy and the region.

(3) We will neither form plots nor set ambushes against against each other but in earnest good fellowship, without deceit or secret reservations, we will be enemies of those making war on the Carthaginians, unless these are kings, cities, or nations with which we have [previously] sworn alliance.

(4) And we, too, will be the enemies of those making war against King Philip, unless these are kings, cities, and peoples with which we

have [prior] treaties of alliance.

(5) You [the Macedonians] will be our allies in the war with the Romans until the gods give us both victory, and will provide such help as we have need or as we agree should be supplied.

(6) Once the gods have given us the victory over the Romans and their allies, if the Romans ask for terms the subsequent peace shall include yourselves and will contain the following conditions: that the Romans will never declare war upon you; that they shall give up Corcyra, Apollonia, Epidamnus, Pharos, Dimale, Parthini, or Atintania, and that they shall return to Demetrius of Pharos all his friends who are in their power.

(7) If the Romans make war on either of us, we will help each other in that war as either side requires.

(8) We will do likewise if any others make war on either of us, excepting always kings, cities, and peoples who are sworn allies.

(9) No clauses are to be withdrawn from or added to this treaty without our mutual agreement.[21]

Such are the terms of the treaty which Philip's ambassadors brought back from their meeting with Hannibal. There are several points of interest to this agreement. Firstly, it is evident that for all Hannibal's alleged hatred of Rome, the treaty appears to anticipate a Roman state that not only survives a Carthaginian victory, but which might later be capable of threatening Macedonia. Secondly, Hannibal agreed to help Philip in his later wars, which suggests that Hannibal saw a future in which Carthage engaged with the Hellenistic powers to the east, much as was actually later to be the case with Rome. Finally, though Philip agreed to help the Carthaginians, the treaty is curiously coy about an outright Macedonian declaration of war against Rome. Indeed, there are suggestions that the Macedonians wanted the treaty to be kept quiet, at least until Philip V had ratified it, but this was not to be. Either by chance or more possibly through shrewd work by Roman intelligence agents, the Macedonian ambassadors were seized as they left Italy. (They were travelling in five ships, and because Hannibal was in Campania at the time, this little fleet had to sail around the whole of southern Italy, which greatly increased their chances of being intercepted.) The treaty fell into Roman hands, along with those Carthaginians accompanying it in order to witness Philip swearing to abide by its terms.

Though unfortunate for Philip, this was something of a windfall for posterity, as the treaty was sent to Rome where it would undoubtedly have been entered into the Roman record office on the Capitoline hill. It is entirely possible that the text above was rendered by Polybius as an exact copy of the original. However, even though his unfriendly intentions were now public, it is unlikely that there were any emendations to the treaty which an embarrassed Philip was forced to resubmit through a fresh set of ambassadors. It did not help that the Romans had seen the first treaty before Philip did, and were already taking pre-emptive measures against hostilities to which Philip had not agreed, but was now committed to undertake on the basis that the Romans evidently considered he was going to.

The captured treaty has formed the basis of a lively historical debate as to what exactly Philip imagined he was getting into when he allied himself with Hannibal. There are those who pass the 'treaty' off as entirely a Roman invention designed to excuse later Roman aggression in the region, and others who see it as a defensive measure by which Philip foresaw the threat Rome offered his kingdom and attempted to nip it in the bud at a strategic moment.

However, both these arguments are centred about Philip's attitude toward Rome in a way that the treaty itself is not. The suggestion is rather that Macedon and Carthage saw their alliance with regard to the war with Rome as a template for their conduct towards each other in their future wars. In short, this agreement shows that Macedon recognized that the western Mediterranean had come of age, and that the size and sophistication of the military forces deployed in the current war meant that Carthage was a military power equivalent to the Hellenistic kingdoms to the east. In allying with Hannibal, Philip was attempting both to secure Macedon's western flank, and to harness the power of Carthage as an ally in future conflicts with Egypt or the Seleucids. As far as Rome itself was concerned, all Philip wanted from the current war was that Rome should give up its protectorates on the Greek mainland and get off his back whilst he sorted out Illyria.

According to our sources, Demetrius of Pharos wanted more, and urged Philip to establish a presence on the Italian mainland. However, the treaty makes it plain that Philip understood that Hannibal's success in Italy meant that the old Pyrrhic master plan was no longer feasible. Better then that Italy become a set of rival city-states under Carthaginian tutelage, in much the same way as Greece was independent under Macedonian hegemony. Rome had a future as one of these city-states, perhaps even as foremost among them, but Philip had no problem with that.

Given these limited aims, Philip might not have expected the bitter indignation which his agreement with Hannibal aroused in Rome. That one of the major powers of the Hellenistic world should have turned on Rome during its darkest hour was seen as an act of opportunistic betrayal. There was no history of antagonism between Rome and Macedon, and the Romans did not consider that they had done anything to merit Macedonian hostility other than that after Cannae they seemed too weak to defend against it. It is highly indicative of the relative strength of feeling on each side that though they were locked in a desperate struggle against Hannibal in southern Italy, it was the Romans rather than Philip who took the initiative.

Rome's Response

Not that the cautious Romans rushed headlong into conflict. There was always the chance that the whole thing was yet another of Hannibal's diabolical plots, conceived without Philip's knowledge and designed to get both the Greek cities of Italy on Hannibal's side (to the extent they were not already there), and to sow antagonism between Rome and Macedon. In any case, given their straitened circumstances, the Romans did not have a large army to commit to this new front. However, the Romans did have a navy available, since after their heavy losses at sea during the First Punic War, the Carthaginians had decided not to challenge Rome at sea this time around. Accordingly, the senate proposed to send a military force somewhere between a large reconnaissance and a small army to this new theatre under the watchful eye of a considerable naval force. (To which, apparently with no sense of irony, the Romans added the five ships which they had captured with the Macedonian ambassadors aboard.)

> It was ordered that the agents be kept in irons, and those with them should be sold into slavery. Another twenty ships were to be fitted out and sent to join the twenty-five already under the command of P. Valerius Flaccus [at Tarentum]. ... Valerius took on board the soldiers from Varro's army and which were there under the command of L. Apustius. This combined fleet of fifty-five warships was to guard the coast of Italy, but also to find out exactly how hostile Macedon intended to be.[22]

If Philip was indeed planning to start ravaging the Italian coast, as per Rome's gloomiest prognostications, Valerius' small force was to land in Greece and attempt to keep Philip busy there instead. The Romans owed some money to King Heiro of Syracuse, but decided that the repayment, already en route, should be diverted to pay for this new enterprise. Heiro appears to have taken this well, and added own his own account supplies of corn for the undertaking. Livy appears to believe that these prompt actions, combined with Philip's need to reratify the treaty with Hannibal, pre-empted and frustrated Macedon's aggressive intentions. More probably, Philip spent most of 215 BC doing exactly what he intended to do all along, which was to gather his forces for another crack at Illyria, though this time the Roman protectorate to the south of Illyria was in his sights as well.

First, and always, there were the never-ending squabbles of Greece to be kept in hand. In this case Philip was asked to interfere in a case of *stasis* in the city of Messene in the Peloponnese. *Stasis* was a particularly disagreeable form of civil war between aristocrats and democrats which had a tendency to rip apart cities where it was allowed to continue unchecked. Either Philip came to Messene too late to stop strife breaking out or he actively encouraged the democratic faction, as some 200 of the opposing party were killed before the conflict was resolved. When Aratus of the Achaean League came hurrying up, he found Philip in control of the situation. To Aratus Philip bluntly put the question: should he take advantage of his situation and keep control of the city? Aratus disagreed with horror, and though Philip followed this advice, thereafter relationships between the two men became irrevocably strained. The weakening of ties between Macedon and Achaea were not due to this incident alone: Philip's credibility had suffered from his first retreat from the Romans, and as Philip matured he was less prone to taking advice from the older Aratus. Demetrius of Pharos increasingly became Philip's preferred counsellor, and Demetrius was never a force for peace and moderation.

It is to this time that both Plutarch and Polybius date the change in Philip from the golden boy of Greece to a gloomy and erratic despot, but the truth is that this change in perception was less to do with a change in Philip's character than a cooling of Macedon's relations with her southern neighbours. It may also be that his encounter with Rome made clear to Philip that wider issues on the international stage were beginning to threaten his kingdom, and he became consequently more irritable and impatient with the continual wrangling and petty wars of Greece.

Certainly Philip was not counting on a Carthaginian victory and the treaty he had made with Hannibal to remove the alien bridgehead which was the Roman protectorate south of Illyria. He intended to do this for himself, and he accordingly started the campaigning season of 214 BC with an attempt on Apollonia with a fleet of 120 light warships. It is uncertain whether this first approach was a serious attack or a diversion, for Philip suddenly switched his troops to the nearby town of Oricum, which he took at the first assault. After this, the siege of Apollonia began in earnest.

The detour to Oricum gave the Romans of Valerius' force time to mobilize, and they set sail immediately to confront Philip. Fifty-five ships were not enough to carry the legionaries, so the remainder travelled aboard merchant vessels. Landing at Oricum, they found Philip already gone, and with the army with which they had intended to engage him the Romans had little trouble taking the town back from its Macedonian garrison. Apollonia lay near the mouth of a river (called the Vjose today, and the Aous in antiquity) and to here Valerius dispatched a force of 2,000 men under a veteran commander called Q. Naevius Crista. Crista landed secretly and sent the ships back to the main force so that the Macedonians would not know they were there. Then, taking a roundabout route calculated to avoid the enemy, he succeeded in bringing his force into Apollonia without the Macedonians being aware that the Romans had arrived.

Admittedly the siege of Apollonia was in its early stages, but it is unlikely that Philip was unaware that some sort of reinforcements had reached the city. However it is uncertain at this point that his spies had yet reported that Oricum had been retaken, or even that the Romans were in the region. Quite possibly Philip took the new arrivals for Illyrian irregulars, as the Illyrian tribes were beginning to muster in the face of the Macedonian advance. The relaxed attitude of the besieging Macedonians certainly suggests that no-one yet knew that their enemies had been joined by veteran soldiers hardened in combat against Hannibal: a foe who seldom permitted mistakes.

Indeed, the only excuse the Macedonians could offer for what happened next is that they believed that they were contending with a terrified and outnumbered city militia and a rag-tag Illyrian force. Had they known that the Romans were present, they would have kept a sharper guard about their camp the following night. The experienced Crista had noted the casual Macedonian approach to their siege and determined to take the fight to the enemy. His men approached the Macedonian camp in complete silence under cover of darkness, and if Livy is to be believed managed to infiltrate over 1,000 men into the camp before someone on the gate guard worked out that the newcomers were not supposed to be there.[23]

Not unexpectedly, when the Macedonians woke up to discover that the Romans had not only arrived but were actually among their tents with swords in hand, total chaos ensued. Few on the Macedonian side were dressed for battle, or indeed dressed at all, and no-one had much idea of exactly where or how many the enemy were. A few perceptive souls realized that the most secure point of retreat was the Macedonian fleet still anchored upriver, and they were rapidly followed thence by the rest of the army. Philip had little chance to retrieve the situation, and was forced to join in the general retreat 'dressed in a manner hardly decent for a common soldier, let alone a king' reports Livy with relish.

Fortunately for the Macedonians, Crista had no cavalry, and Macedonians in their underwear were considerably swifter of foot than Romans in armour. Though much of Philip's force made it safely to the ships (including the king himself) their camp and several thousand men fell into Roman hands. The next day, Philip had to watch grimly as the Apollonians took possession of the catapults and other siege artillery intended for use against their city. These were mounted on the walls of their intended target, making continuation of the siege pointless. In fact it was the Macedonians themselves who were in danger of becoming besieged in their ships, for Valerius now moved his fleet to block the river mouth.

Though fewer in number, the Roman ships were generally heavier, and the confines of the river meant that the superior manoeuvrability of the lighter ships counted for little. There was nothing Philip could do but sail away up the river as far as possible. Then he beached and burned his ships and took his force home to Macedon over the mountains. The first round had gone, emphatically, to the Romans. However, in Philip Rome had found an enemy with a stubborn tenacity equal to her own, and Philip was far from giving up.

His first act on returning to Greece was to attempt to repossess himself of Messene which he had given up on the advice of Aratus. The Messenians, technically allies of Macedon, made it very plain that they preferred their relationship to be at arm's length and emphatically rejected the Macedonian garrison. Macedonian insistence on taking military control led to an open breach, and eventually a siege of the city which saw Demetrius of Pharos killed in action. Having failed to take Messene itself, Philip vindictively ravaged Messenian territory, an act which sent his stock among the Greek cities plummeting yet further, and succeeded only in driving Messene firmly into the arms of the Aetolian confederation. It also led to a final rupture with Aratus, who was dying, possibly of tuberculosis, and possibly, as he appears to have believed, of slow poison administered by Philip's agents. Philip did maintain friendly relations with another of Aratus' family, Aratus' daughter-in-law Polycrateia, who eventually accompanied Philip back to Macedonia as his lover.

The year 213 BC saw Philip back in Illyria, and with Valerius too weak to do more than keep possession of Apollonia, Philip briskly took possession of the rest of the Roman protectorate there. With skill and energy he seized Dimale and the other towns of the region, and defeated Rome's allies, the tribes of the Parthini and Atinantes. With this area secured, he turned his attention fully on Sacerdilaidas and the Illyrians, and in a swift brutal campaign he drove toward the main Illyrian town of Lissus, and there flattened its supposedly-impregnable citadel.

Not only the soldiery, but also the diplomats were busy that year. Livy describes the first contact through what appears to be an attempt to ransom a captured ambassador, 'Damippus, a Lacedaemonian, who had been sent from Syracuse on a mission to King Philip and was captured by some Roman ships'.[24] The Spartans were at this time allied with the Aetolians, and the Romans took this opportunity to sound out the Aetolians about an alliance. The Aetolians were particularly peeved with the Macedonians at this point, since Philip had either permitted or even encouraged Acarnania to escape from Aetolian control.

With Sacerdilaidas and the Illyrians fervently petitioning Valerius for help against Philip, and Philip looking vulnerable after his setback before Apollonia, the Romans saw the possibility of assembling a handy anti-Macedonian confederation. Across the Aegean Sea, on the other side of Greece in Anatolia, the restless and energetic Attalus of Pergamum was looking to expand his kingdom. He had long been on cordial terms with the Aetolians, and had dreams of expanding his control over much of the Aegean, and possibly also Euboea, though he was well aware that the Macedonians would take a dim view of such a programme. Attalus, from a Roman perspective, was certainly worth considering as an ally, especially as this would extend Rome's international reach into Asia Minor for the first time. The Spartans and Thracians were also to be invited to join the enterprise, which, if everyone came aboard, would mean that Macedon would be completely encircled by enemies. (Which, from a cynical Macedonian viewpoint, would simply formalize the de facto state of affairs.)

Some time before 211 BC (the exact date is uncertain) Romans and Aetolians put their agreement in writing. Rome and Aetolia were to jointly make war on Macedon, with the Aetolians helping Rome regain her protectorate, and the Romans helping with the Aetolian conquest of Acarnania. Expenses were to be divided according to the labours of those involved, but Rome was to get any financial benefit accruing from the war, and the Aetolians any territory. This aspect of the agreement was to satisfy firstly those Romans who were opposed to the extension of the war to

Greece, but who accepted that Rome desperately needed cash, and secondly to pacify those Greeks who suspected the Romans of territorial ambitions.

Valerius was to expand his naval activities beyond the protection of Apollonia, and every effort was to be made to encourage the other potential members of the anti-Macedonian alliance to declare themselves as soon as possible. By default, those Greek states which remained allied to Macedon were to be considered enemies of Rome, and given the inaccessibility of Macedonia, it was on those states that the opening blows of this new war would fall. Firstly, to stir the Aetolians by example, Valerius seized the generally inoffensive island and city of Zacynthus south of Corcyra, the southernmost and third largest of the Ionian islands (though he was unable take the acropolis). The Acarnanians also suffered collateral damage as the Romans seized their towns of Oeniadae and Nasus.

Philip Versus the Aetolians

Philip was at Pella in Macedon when news reached him of Rome's alliance with Aetolia. His reaction was to have a rapid bout of what for a Macedonian king might be termed military housekeeping. Instead of attacking Aetolia directly, Philip first decided to weaken or intimidate those tribes on his country's borders which might be thinking of trying something. He had already seized the town of Bylazora, which, due to its strategic position became a bulwark against Dardanian raids in the region of Paionia. Now he launched lightning raids against Apollonia and Oricum, handing a brisk defeat to the Apollonian army which confidently sallied out to meet him. This manoeuvre both intimidated the Illyrians (whose borders Philip ravaged whilst he was about it) and ensured that Valerius thenceforth stayed back to defend this area. From there Philip moved north against the Dardanians, and by taking the border town of Sintia, made it harder for that tribe to gain access to the Macedonian plain. Then he pushed northeast, and delivered a warning raid on the Thracians for the benefit of any tribes planning to join the anti-Macedonian coalition. (As it appears that Attalus had done from the outset, though his early contribution was limited.)

Macedon was not fighting alone. The Achaeans, inveterate enemies of the Aetolians, stayed loyal to their alliance with Macedon, as did Thessaly, much of which was by now almost a Macedonian province. Epirus too gave Macedon support, though this was mostly limited to keeping the Illyrians off Philip's back. Boeotia and Phocis were also allies, the former because Philip had earlier flattened much of the place, and installed his own colonists. Philip's most vulnerable allies were the Acarnanians, who were trapped between the Aetolians and the Romans. With Philip currently too busy to come to their relief, they discovered with fury and despair that the Aetolians were planning a major expedition against them. The Acarnanian response was to make preparations for the entire nation to die fighting. They sent their women and children to safety in Epirus, and almost every male in the country then mustered under arms and marched to the Aetolian border having first sworn a grim oath to take as many of the enemy as possible to the grave with them.

In the face of such ferocious determination, the Aetolians hesitated, and with this hesitation the momentum of the war was lost. Before the Aetolians girded themselves up once more, word reached them that Philip was on his way, having given the tribe of the Thracian Maedi a thrashing sufficient to cause the Thracians to lose their taste for warfare for the time being. The Aetolians gave up their plans for invasion, and, satisfied that Acarnania was safe for now, Philip concluded operations for the season in order to give his footsore army a well-deserved break.

Valerius had by now shifted his base of operations to Corcyra, and in 210 BC he launched from there a combined operation against the city of Anticyra in Phocis, for which the Aetolians supplied the land troops to supplement the Roman ships.[25] With help from the artillery carried by the Roman fleet the town was conquered in a matter of days and the inhabitants enslaved. In accordance with their agreement with the Romans, the Aetolians took the town (they do not appear to have been able to hold it for long) and the Romans took the booty. This was Valerius' last contribution to the war. He was informed in dispatches that he had been elected consul in his absence, and was required in Rome. He was to be replaced by Sulpicius Galba, a man who had already served his consulship and was now a proconsul.[26]

Limited as the success in Anticyra had been, it was apparently enough to encourage Sparta and Messenia to join the war on the Roman side, despite a spirited speech from an Acarnanian ambassador who praised the Macedonians who 'for the greater part of their lives never cease from fighting with the barbarians for the sake of the security of Greece'. The ambassador warned that 'Greece is threatened by foreigners intent on enslavement, men you imagine you are bringing in against Philip, but are actually bringing against yourselves and the whole of Greece'.

Galba's first action of the war was to take the island of Aegina near Athens. As ever, he handed the island over to the Aetolians after first helping himself to the booty. The Aetolians, as landlubberly a people as could be found in Greece, were somewhat nonplussed as to what they should do with their new possession, until Attalus offered to take it off their hands. The Pergamene king thus acquired a handy naval base in the Saronic Gulf for the bargain price of 30 talents and no expenditure of effort whatsoever. This purchase marked Attalus' first positive contribution to the alliance.

But not everything was going the coalition's way. Philip had responded to Attalus' involvement in the war by opening communications with his relative by marriage, Prusias of Bithynia. Prusias was Attalus' neighbour and bitter rival, and he readily promised ships to counter Attalus at sea. Nor were the Romans making many friends. Galba did his fighting by the harsher Roman rules of war, and had caused considerable disquiet by initially not allowing the captured Aeginetan peoples to ransom themselves. Also, with his other borders now beaten into submission, Philip was free to turn his attention south.

The Aetolians attempted to hold Philip out of central Greece at the fortress town of Echinus, possibly because they hoped that the Romans would be able to resupply them by sea. For reasons which are now uncertain, but possibly because of a failure of communication between Galba and Attalus, this did not happen. Indeed, Polybius informs us that though Galba made an appearance, it was Philip who had command of the sea. Polybius' description of the siege is worth giving in detail, as it gives a good account of contemporary techniques. (Philip recently had learned the value of meticulous preparations in storming cities after he failed to take Larissa near Bylazora. Everything had gone perfectly until the Macedonians placed their scaling ladders against the city walls, and found that they were too short.)

> He decided to launch his attack on the city against its two towers. In front of each tower he constructed a sheltering parapet for sappers and a battering ram, and between the towers a parapet parallel to the wall connecting each parapet and ram with the other. The completed design actually looked not dissimilar to the [city] wall, for the protective structure of the parapets ... looked like battlements with [siege] towers at each side.
>
> At the base of the siege towers men levelled the earth to allow the smooth passage of the rollers on which the ram was pushed. On the second story there were water-jars and other devices for extinguishing fires, and also catapults. On the third level, eye-to-eye with the towers of the enemy, a number of men stood ready to attack anyone who sallied out to damage the ram.

Two trenches were dug from the earthworks between the towers towards the wall of the city and three sets of ballistas were put in place. The first set hurled stones weighing a talent, and the other two stones half as heavy. Still more covered passages from the camp had been made for the sappers, so that those coming and going between earthworks and camp were protected against missile fire from the city.[27]

After his elaborate preparations, Philip rolled his towers forward and took the town in short order. He then followed this up with a number of successes further south. The arrival of Macedon seems to have stirred the Achaeans into action, so that, even with the Spartans now on the Aetolian side, things were less hopeful for Philip's enemies than they had seemed at the start of the war. Despite the increased threat from Philip, the Romans were now actually pulling soldiers out of the Greek peninsula, having apparently determined to fight the war (as the historian J.V.P Balsdon memorably puts it) 'to the last Aetolian'.

Philip continued to move swiftly south. He had received Achaean appeals for help, since the Aetolians, reinforced by other members of their coalition, were gathering on Achaea's borders. Hearing of the Macedonian advance, this force decided to block Philip before he could unite with the Achaeans. Consequently a mixed force of Romans (supplied by Galba from his rowers) and Pergamene auxiliaries backed by a larger force of Aetolians met Philip at the old battleground of Lamia. The site of Antigonus' victory was a good omen for Philip, who soundly trounced his foes in one of the few battles in a war which mostly consisted of quick raids, sieges, march and countermarch. The battle appears to have been two separate actions, won each time by Philip, in which the anti-Macedonian coalition lost at least a thousand men each time.

After this beating, the Aetolians thereafter refused to face the Macedonians in the field for the rest of the war. They were told by a triumphant Macedonian ambassador that the Romans were using them to take the brunt of the action, in the same way that expendable light troops are committed to battle whilst the phalanx stand off, ready to take the credit for a victory, or withdraw unharmed from a defeat.[28] The Aetolians did not really need telling, since they were already sending reproachful messages to Rome saying roughly the same thing.

The Doves Gather

By 209 BC the war between the Romans and Hannibal was beginning to take on a Mediterranean-wide dimension. Not only were the Romans and Carthaginians directly at loggerheads in Spain, Italy and Africa, but Philip's treaty with Hannibal had resulted in Pergamum and Bithynia getting involved in the war as well. Furthermore, the powers of Ptolemaic Egypt and the Seleucid Empire were quick to see that Macedon's alliance with Carthage had them in mind as much as it did Rome. Given that Seleucid and Egyptian were constantly battling in Palestine and Phoenicia, the fact that Macedon had an interest in pan-regional alliances was of immediate interest to both parties. However, if Philip were to ally himself with either the Seleucids or Egyptians, he had first to be disentangled from his war against Rome.

Furthermore, the Ptolemaic kingdom had other incentives to broker peace. The Ptolemies had long relied on mercenaries from Greece and Macedon for its own military manpower, both to control the native Egyptian population and for adventures abroad. The current troubles in Greece were hitting Egypt's reserves of military manpower, since professional soldiers currently did not have to travel as far as Egypt to find employment. Finally the Ptolemies had interests in the Greek world in both Cyprus and Crete, and had become de facto patrons of Athens after that city had broken free of Macedon. They were eager to extend their influence further, and were in a good position to broker peace, as they were on good terms with the Romans, whom they had supplied with corn during those years when the war made harvests unavailable in Sicily and southern Italy. It is in fact possible that rumours of a Ptolemaic link-up with Rome were partly behind Philip making his alliance with Hannibal: certainly until 212 BC Philip considered the Hellenistic Empires a greater threat than Rome.

The island states of Rhodes and Chios were also seeking an end to the war. They were perturbed by Pergamum's ambitions in the Aegean Sea, and had decided that ending the war in Greece would deprive Attalus of his pretext for expansion. And after the defeat at Lamia, the most recent and important converts to the peace party were the Aetolians themselves. To the ambassadors who approached Philip after Lamia, they added their own representative, the wily Amynander of Athamania, who was instructed to ask for an armistice.

Philip was definitely interested. Macedon had always had so many military commitments that making them fewer was a worthwhile objective in itself, and Carthage had proven unrewarding as an ally. Instead of bringing

Carthaginian help eastward, and allowing him to expand westward, Philip had found that Hannibal was tied down in southern Italy and it was hostile Rome which had come east. Even the Carthaginian navy would not, or could not, challenge Roman domination of the Adriatic, and instead of gaining in his control of the seas, Philip found himself challenged in the Aegean by the fleet of Attalus. And now ambassadors came from Egypt and Seleucia, each making suggestions as to how Macedon and themselves could profit from an alliance against the other. In short, if peace could be arranged on decent terms, Philip was ready to co-operate.

An armistice of thirty days was agreed, and Philip proceeded to Aegium in Achaea where peace was to be discussed at a meeting of the League. But two developments occurred before the talks were properly under way. Firstly, Attalus turned up with a fleet. He had been expected to make an attempt at Euboea, but, probably on hearing that Philip had anticipated this, he proceeded instead to his new naval base at Aegina. Secondly, Galba had written to Rome warning the senate that peace was in danger of breaking out across Greece. Galba had then moved his fleet from Naupactus to nearer Corinth so as to show the southern Greeks that Rome had still a presence in the area. Encouraged by these developments, the Aetolians made demands that they knew Philip would never accept, and once the Aetolians had started pushing for concessions, others started wanting concessions of their own. Faced with demands that he cede territory to the Messenians, the Aetolians, the Romans and the Illyrians, Philip walked out of the proceedings, saying that he had come to find a basis for peace, whilst his enemies were looking for a pretext for war.

Philip took himself off to preside over the Nemean games at Argos, the city from which legend claimed his line had originated. At the games he became popular with the people by mingling with them freely and on an equal basis, whilst he upset the nobility (already disturbed by his failure to negotiate with the Aetolians) by conducting a series of indiscreetly managed affairs with high-born and married ladies.

The War Resumes

Galba had been sufficiently alarmed by the pacifistic tendencies of his allies to become more proactive in prosecuting the war. Landing troops between Sikyon and Corinth, the Romans started to devastate the countryside. They were unprepared for the speed with which Philip gathered up a force (apparently consisting entirely of cavalry), which fell on the scattered Romans as they returned, laden with plunder, to their ships. Those Romans who escaped did so by abandoning their spoils, and their fleet returned to Naupactus licking its wounds. Philip meanwhile returned to the games, apparently determined to party even harder after his minor victory: the first of any description he had managed over the Romans. During his pursuit of the Romans, Philip had collided with a tree whilst on horseback. Neither rider nor steed were hurt, but one of Philip's helmet fittings broke off, and unknown to the king this souvenir was carried northward, along with a rumour that he was dead.

The games over, Philip went back into action. According to a fragmentary text from Appian, the senate had reinforced Galba with several thousand legionaries. These came as a shock to the Macedonians when, together with the Achaeans, they closed with a mixed force of Aetolians and Eleans near the city of Elis. (Elis had defected from the Achaean League and invited in an Aetolian garrison, and Philip was there to forcibly reintegrate city and League.) Seeing Roman standards amongst the enemy, Philip attempted to withdraw, but the enemy moved forward confidently and engaged his lines. Philip decided that the legionaries were the source of this unwonted exuberance in his foes and decided to take out the threat with his cavalry. Macedonian companion cavalry were formidable shock troops, but after a decade spent fighting Hannibal, Rome's highly experienced legionaries were unshockable. Philip's horse was literally stopped dead by a well-placed *pilum*, and a ferocious fight developed about the king, who was now on foot with his enemies pressing to seize him, and his own men resisting desperately.

After taking substantial casualties, the Macedonians managed to persuade Philip back on horseback, and to leave the action. Despite being unhorsed and unused to fighting on foot, their king had been fighting like a berserker. Though the army took a mauling, the Macedonians providentially retreated to the very strongpoint that the Eleans had decided to use to stash their goods for safety from the Macedonians. Consequently Philip was able to distribute booty amongst his men as though he had won the victory.

During these proceedings messengers arrived with news of massive barbarian incursions to the north. Apparently a garrison commander on the border of Macedon had been bribed to give up his fortress, and this had led to a successful raid, which in turn led the Dardanians, secure in the belief that Philip had perished in Greece, to come flooding onto the Macedonian plain. Philip was forced to put the war in the south on hold and hurry north to persuade the Illyrians and Dardanians that reports of his death were greatly exaggerated. Fortunately the campaigning season was coming to an end, and few developments were to be expected in his absence.

In fact southern Greece remained quiet until the start of the campaigning season of 208 BC, which Galba started by transferring his fleet to Aegina. This signalled that Rome, like Pergamum, would now be operating in the Aegean, and that the emphasis of the war would shift from south-central Greece to the eastern seaboard. Hopes were high in the Roman camp that 208 BC would be a decisive year. Philip had his hands full with barbarian tribes which were either invading or planning to invade, as soon as someone else took the initiative and drew Philip's armies away. The Aetolians had fortified Thermopylae to stop Philip coming to relieve his allies in the south, and Euboea was again in danger.

Philip was more than equal to any of his enemies singly, but if he moved against one, the others would attack. An analogy would be of a wild boar cornered by hunting dogs. If but one dog attacked, the others could fall on the boar and kill it. But that first dog would be comprehensively ripped to pieces. Philip promised his increasingly frantic allies that he would help each of them as far as possible, but deliberately did nothing other than to make sure his army could move rapidly to the first flashpoint as soon as it developed. Having his army set for maximum mobility, he took a chance to raid the town of Heraclea. Attalus was meant to be meeting the Aetolians there, and Philip intended to crash the party. He pushed his army through a series of forced marches, but arrived a few days too late. Nevertheless, as well as the army helping itself to Heraclea's stock of winter wheat, the raid served warning on Macedon's enemies that Philip's army could strike far and fast. A series of watchfires had been set on regional peaks, with a central lookout point on Mount Tisaeos, a signalling system designed to let Philip know as soon as his enemies were on the move.

The fires were soon ablaze, signalling that Attalus and Galba were attacking Euboea. The pair gained their bridgehead by bribing the garrison commander of the town of Oreus, but the allies' main objective, the fortress city of Chalcis, held out reassured by the knowledge that Philip was already storming southward. There was no Spartan-style resistance by the Aetolians at Thermopylae. The garrison there was brushed aside, and Philip descended on Attalus in Locris, where he was sheltering from bad weather and contrary tides which had driven him from Chalcis. The Pergamene king had to make a chaotic retreat, and then found a bad year getting worse with news that Prusias of Bithynia had invaded his kingdom in Asia Minor. This effectively took Pergamum out of the war, and with Attalus hurrying home, a disgruntled Galba had to pull back to Aegina to prepare a new strategy. In fact, though Philip did not know it at the time, the defection of Attalus caused the Romans to virtually abandon Greece to its own devices. They were fully committed in Italy and Spain, and apart from ordering Galba to keep an eye on the Adriatic and Illyrian coastline, they withdrew both troops and interest from the region.

With Pergamum and Rome off his 'to do' list, Philip headed south, to the relief of the Achaeans. Once again, the king had little to do here. The Spartans and Aetolians had been gathering ominously on Achaea's borders once more, but took the arrival of the Macedonian army as a signal to rethink their plans for the summer. To complete Philip's season, even a minor Carthaginian fleet made a welcome, if brief appearance. This had considerable propaganda value, and though it was evident that the Carthaginians had no intention of fighting in Greek waters, their presence was enough to subdue southern Greece once more. The year that had started so ominously for Philip ended with his returning north with a relatively easy mind (effortlessly retaking Oreus in Euboea en route) with only the Dardanians remaining on his agenda.

The Peace of Phoenice

Philip's year kept getting better. Achaea, largely rudderless since the death of Aratus, suddenly found itself under an able and energetic leader called Philopoemen who equipped and trained the Acheans with Macedonian weapons and tactics. So effectively did he do this that when the Achaeans were next threatened by the Spartans, instead of calling for Macedonian help, they set out to deal with the invaders themselves. The two sides met at Mantinea, where the astonished Spartans found themselves soundly defeated. The Spartan commander, Machinidas, made the major error of trying to lead a tightly-paced phalanx over a ditch. He paid for it with his life when the delighted Achaeans fell on his disorganized troops. The Battle of Mantinea had two firsts: it was the first time that the Achaeans had beaten the Spartans (who lost 4,000 killed and several thousand more as prisoners), and the first time heavy artillery (intended for use against the walls of Mantinea) was used in battle against a phalanx. This was also, though no-one knew it at the time, the last major battle which Greek was to fight against Greek before Rome's quarrel with Macedon monopolized the military situation.

The Aetolians were suddenly very lonely. Rome turned a deaf ear to their pleas for help, Attalus and Sparta were effectively out of the war, and negotiations to find further allies among the island states of the Aegean proved fruitless. Having dealt with the Dardanians for the moment, Philip was clearing the last Aetolian strongholds from Thessaly as a preliminary for a vengeful descent on Aetolia proper.

During the abortive peace negotiations of 209 BC Philip had met Amynander of Athamania, and now he used this personal contact to secure the passage of his army through Amynander's territory to Aetolia. Amynander's price for betraying his former Aetolian allies was the island of Zacynthus, which Valerius had occupied early in the war. With the Romans no longer contesting the seas at this point, Philip had simply to occupy the island and hand it over. He then proceeded to get his money's worth from the deal by comprehensively ravaging Aetolia, including a return visit to Thermum to demolish anything that had been constructed since his previous sacking of the place in 218 BC.

The invasion of Aetolia effectively ended the war, as all that remained was for the Aetolians to acknowledge that they had been defeated. This, for most of 207 BC, the Aetolians stubbornly refused to do, apparently hoping that the Romans would eventually return to their alliance. After fighting Hannibal for over a decade, Rome had its own problems. The state was committing all its available reserves to the conquest of Spain, and new recruits were so scarce that volunteer slaves were allowed into the army. Roman allies in Italy were bitterly protesting against Rome's demands on their money and manpower. At the same time the Gauls in the alpine provinces were both restless and aggressive. Economically, most of Italy south of Etruria was a mess: 'The small farmers had been carried off into the armies and there were hardly any slaves available to work the fields, the cattle had been driven off by looters, and the farmhouses had been stripped or burned' reports Livy.[29] The war in Greece had always been something of a sideshow, and one which Rome could ill afford. Beating up the Aetolians was distracting Philip nicely, and with Greece Roman short-term thinking dominated to the point where no-one seemed to have considered what Philip would do when he had finished with Aetolia. 'Little attention was paid to Greece' admits Livy.

In fact, having taken the Aetolians as allies, the Romans seem to have been shocked and hurt when those allies went on to make a separate peace with Philip, although it was their neglect of the Aetolian cause which made that peace almost inevitable. Indeed, it was hardly a peace as much as a surrender, though Philip had the sense to make the terms relatively mild so as to reduce the provocation for a further war.

Nevertheless, the Aetolians lost many of the gains they had made in

Phocis during the preceding decades, as well as the cities of Pharsalus, Echinus, and Larissa. Philip made conciliatory noises about the latter three cities, suggesting that they were not so much Macedonian conquests as hostages for the federation's good behaviour, to be returned at some point in the future. Nevertheless, peace came at a price that left Aetolia much diminished.

With Aetolia subdued, Philip enjoyed the luxury of being able to take the initiative. There was an obvious target for his newly unemployed army, and that was back where the war had begun in the Roman protectorate centred on Apollonia. Intelligence of Philip's intentions was finally enough to stir the Romans to action and in the spring of 205 BC a force of 10,000 men and 1,000 cavalry was sent across the Adriatic under the command of P. Sempronius Tuditanus. Arriving in Illyria, Sempronius (without success) besieged the fortress town of Dimale, a part of the protectorate now in Macedonian hands, and sent his lieutenant Laetorius to rouse the Aetolians back into action. The wisdom of Philip's policy in making his peace with Aetolia on relatively gentle terms now became apparent. The Aetolians were at that time neither so aggrieved with Philip that they thirsted for revenge at all costs, nor so trusting of the Romans that they believed in their continued support. History does not relate precisely what the Aetolians told Laetorius when he came asking for help, but it was certainly a firm, and probably a colourfully expressed 'No'.

With Aetolia peaceful, Philip was able to continue with his original plan and march on Apollonia. Bereft of allies, Sempronius had neither the manpower nor the will to meet Philip in the field, so he stayed behind his walls, and hoped that the Illyrian tribes he had stirred up against Macedon would eventually make the king go away. When this strategy patently failed, Sempronius gave a more sympathetic hearing to ambassadors from Epirus, who, with two large and potentially hostile armies preparing to use their country as a battleground, were understandably eager advocates for peace.

Philip, as always, was prepared to talk. He still had unfinished business with the Dardanians, and also may have already turned his attention to an alliance with either the Ptolemies or Seleucids. Already the Seleucids were looking promising, not least because Egypt had island possessions in the southeastern Mediterranean which could be profitably transferred to Macedon, and Seleucid help would be useful, both for this and for punishing Attalus for his recent presumptuous opportunism.

Rome's objectives were currently limited to holding the area around Apollonia, and getting Dimale back. If these objectives could be achieved by a treaty which allowed 10,000 desperately-needed men to be deployed elsewhere, then the senate was all in favour. The Aetolians had demonstrated they were determinedly pacifistic for the present, and with Sparta licking its wounds, this left no-one on the Roman side with a motive for fighting. When, in the autumn of 205 BC, the Romans met Philip at an inland town of Epirus called Phoenice, most of Greece confidently expected a peace treaty to result.

Chapter 4

From Uneasy Peace to Renewed War

A New World Order?

The meeting which made the Peace of Phoenice followed a personal meeting between Philip and Sempronius. Livy makes the highly significant and sometimes overlooked comment that 'King Attalus, Pleuratus, Nabis tyrant of the Lacedaemonians, the Eleans, the Messenians, and Athenians were included in the treaty by the Romans'. These are the parties involved in the alliance against Philip (apart from the Aetolians who were already at peace with Macedon). It is quite possible that these parties acquiesced in letting the Romans sort out the terms of the treaty. This would be quite reasonable, as parties to the peace such as the little *polis* of Elis would be quite happy to have a heavyweight like Rome negotiating on their behalf, and others such as Attalus had little to negotiate apart from ceasing hostilities, which was the de facto state of affairs anyway. The Spartans and Achaeans had unfinished business between themselves, but this was not directly related to the peace between Rome and Macedon. If Rome did become the representative for smaller Greek states, this set a precedent for the future, when other parties in Greece were to allow Rome to negotiate for them when the stakes were much higher.

As it was, the Peace of Phoenice was little more than agreement to accept the status quo and stop fighting. The Romans wanted their protectorate back, including the town of Dimale, and the hegemony over tribes such as the Parthini which they had enjoyed before the war. The tribe of the Atintani seemed eager to remain under Macedon, and this request was added to the overall terms of the treaty forwarded to Rome for ratification by the Senate. It is unfortunate that we do not know in detail the other terms, particularly what arrangements were made with regard to Athens, as this would help to establish exactly what caused the peace to break down later. We can be certain that the Romans required at least an implicit repudiation of the treaty with Hannibal, insofar as the very making of peace did not already constitute such a repudiation.

It has been suggested that this was not so much a treaty as a truce by which the Romans intended to deal with their wars in series rather than in parallel. By this view Phoenice was never meant to be a permanent settlement nor one which either side had any intention of keeping. The cynical assumption is that the treaty provided a breathing space, after which war was to be resumed when convenient to either party.

This view does something of an injustice to both Rome and Macedon. Firstly, that peace was so easily made shows that, in material terms, Rome and Macedon actually had very little to fight about. When the terms of the peace were announced in Rome they were enthusiastically endorsed by both Senate and people. So satisfied were the Romans with the work of Sempronius that they elected him consul. In short, the basic goodwill required for a peace did exist. It would be a major misreading of events to assume that Rome had marked Greece and Macedon as 'forthcoming business' on some secret master plan for world domination, or even that the Senate already intended to make war on Macedon as soon as the current struggle with Carthage was concluded.

It is unlikely that either Rome or Macedon realized that whatever their intentions, history had set them on a collision course. Rome and Macedon had much in common, including a militaristic society, a policy of opportunistic expansionism and a fear of encirclement in what both perceived as a world of foes. Events were to show that what Macedon and Rome most wanted of the other state was for it to go away. If geography were as amenable to human affairs as politics, both parties would have cheerfully inserted a thousand miles of open sea between their two states and ignored each other thereafter. However almost the contrary situation was true. The expansion of her borders had made Rome practically neighbours with Philip. And Philip's international ambitions meant that Rome would henceforth always be paranoid that Philip might make another anti-Roman alliance, for example with the Seleucids, just as he had allied himself with Hannibal. A century before, Pyrrhus had invaded Italy, showing that a Hellenistic invasion of Italy was certainly practicable.

Rome would not wait passively for such an alliance and invasion to happen. Since Rome's aristocracy depended on victory in war for political success, their response to any potential alliance against Rome would be to strike first and hard for the good of Rome and the furtherance of their careers. The proverb 'he who does not strike first will be first struck' was well known in the ancient world, and was almost doctrinal among some members of the Roman Senate. Since Philip had quit his war with Rome at Phoenice precisely because he wanted to get more closely involved with the affairs of the other Hellenistic powers, given all the goodwill in the world between Macedon and Rome, no sanguine observer of international politics would bet on a lasting peace. But Rome had not goodwill but intense suspicion for Macedon, combined with a smouldering resentment for Philip's support for Hannibal, so a renewed war was almost inevitable.[30]

This was not immediately obvious. Just as the Romans had been pleased to come out of the Macedonian war with their protectorate south of Illyria intact and their legions free to concentrate on the downfall of Carthage, Philip could also congratulate himself on having had essentially a good war. After an initial setback, he had demonstrated his abilities as a commander in no uncertain manner, and had made considerable gains in Illyria and around Larissa in central northern Greece. That perpetual thorn in Macedon's side, Aetolia, had been beaten into abject submission, and Philip and his allies had enlarged their dominions at Aetolia's expense. Aetolia was embittered with Rome and estranged from the rest of Greece. Achaea was securely pro-Macedonian and grateful for Macedonian help, whilst Sparta, now under the dictatorial rule of King Nabis, was essentially a spent force. Thessaly was secure, and Acarnania passionately pro-Macedonian. The kingdom had a promising new ally in King Prusias, whilst on the other hand Attalus of Pergamum was both a new enemy and an excuse for military action in Anatolia.

Anatolia (basically modern Turkey) included Cappadocia, Pergamum and Bithynia, and their nominal suzerain Antiochus III of Seleucia. Antiochus had paid little attention to Greek and Macedonian affairs (and completely ignored the war between Rome and Hannibal) as he had business of his own with far-flung eastern parts of an empire that reached to the foothills of the Himalayas. Whilst Philip had been consolidating his position in Greece, Antiochus had been doing the same in Bactria, in the region just west of modern Afghanistan. He and Philip had finished their respective wars at about the same time, and both turned their attention southwards to Egypt and to the Aegean. Philip's interest in the Aegean was partly stimulated by Attalus' naval ambitions in an area which had been traditionally dominated by Macedon, though that country's problems in previous decades meant that its dominance had slipped somewhat.

Now this dominance was to be restored, even if partly at the expense of Rhodes, a friendly power which had done much to keep the eastern Mediterranean free of pirates (not through altruism, but to encourage the trade which was that island state's lifeblood). Working on the principle that one has to speculate to accumulate, Philip prepared a scratch fleet which he sent to plunder the eastern-Mediterranean territories of his enemies, even if the process sometimes involved making these enemies as a result of looting them. The result of this state-sponsored piracy was a handy haul of booty that Philip used to pay for a more substantial fleet. The king did not sit quietly at home whilst his admiral was away, but proceeded to energetically and bloodily chastise the Thracians and Dardanians for their raids whilst he had been otherwise engaged fighting in the south.

In Greek politics, Philip took a highly pro-democratic line, generally siding with the democrats against the aristocrats whom he felt had been insufficiently enthusiastic with their support for his campaigns. He was generally popular in Greece, not least because some of the captives taken by Galba had been sold as slaves, and Philip had redeemed their freedom at his own expense. Nevertheless, taking the side of the people against the elites of various cities did not prevent Philip himself from becoming steadily more despotic. He often failed to differentiate between allies and subjects, and his arrogant conduct caused strains in his long-standing alliance with the Achaeans, who had developed a higher opinion of themselves after Philopoemen had led them to victory over the Spartans. With Aetolia riven by internal strife, Philip saw no need to return those Aetolian cities which he was holding hostage. It did not appear to disturb the Macedonian king that he was alienating his friends and building up resentments which would later find their outlet in alliances with Rome. This again suggests that Philip regarded interaction with Rome finished for the foreseeable future. After all the Romans had hardly bothered about Greece whilst they were fighting a war there, so why should they be more interested after they and Macedon had made a mutually-satisfactory peace?

Though Hannibal had been recalled from Italy to Africa, Rome and Carthage were still tearing at each other with unabated ferocity. Major battles had been fought around Utica, and feverish politicking swirled about the African kings Syphax and Massinissa as both combatants sought to win or undermine the loyalty of these potential allies. At least until a resolution had been reached in that war, Philip could cheerfully ignore the prospect of Roman interference, and he intended to make the most of the opportunity.

Egypt was troubled by an internal revolt, and Antiochus had begun moving troops towards the Middle East under the ingenuous pretext of having them on hand to 'help' if need be. Philip had also offered to send Macedonian troops to Egypt in the same cause, but the Egyptians had wisely declined to invite either fox into the hen-house. Philip also contemplated becoming a Ptolemy by marriage, as he received a proposal that the young Ptolemy Epiphanes, heir apparent of Egypt, should wed one of his daughters as part of the increasing diplomatic contact between the two states. Yet even as he made diplomatic overtures to Egypt, Philip was plotting furiously with Antiochus.

Thus 203 BC ended with momentous events taking shape. Rome's struggle with Carthage was reaching its climax, and Philip seemed poised to make substantial gains both in the Aegean with his new fleet and in Thrace with his veteran army. He had concluded a full but secret agreement with Antiochus, by which the two kings appear to have agreed to divide Egypt's overseas possessions between them.

The Years of Decision: 202/201 BC

His back protected by his agreement with Philip, Antiochus revealed his intentions with regard to Egypt by launching a massive attack upon Gaza in the closing months of 203 BC. Though the chronology is uncertain, the trigger for this was almost certainly the death of Ptolemy Philopater and the succession of his underage son to the throne. Philip responded by intensifying his own operations. His soldiers paid little attention to Egyptian cities and dependants; they attacked neutrals with great enthusiasm but paid at least lip-service to the integrity of the Pharaoh's territories. (Which suggests that, by nominally remaining at peace with Egypt, Philip was leaving open lines for a later rapprochement.) So fierce was the assault on the free cities of the Aegean that it brought Rhodes and a coalition of island states into open enmity with Macedon. These attempted an early naval assault on Philip's fleet, but were defeated.

Philip's active intervention in Anatolia deeply irritated Antiochus, especially since Philip worked closely with Prusias, to whom Antiochus was hostile. If, as Livy reports, Philip had sent a substantial sum of money and 4,000 men to assist the Carthaginians, this suggests that Macedon was making enemies on all fronts with careless abandon. In part Philip's insouciance was justified. He was well aware that friendship in the Greek world counted for far less than political expediency, and he seems to have believed that no matter how he cultivated allies they would in any case abandon him once matters became difficult. (In this he was partly wrong. Some Greeks, despite his indifference and ill-treatment, were to remain fiercely loyal to his cause.) Philip's aid to Carthage, if this was indeed rendered, would have been inspired by a desire to keep the pot boiling in

Africa for as long as possible. It is quite possible that the Macedonians who allegedly went to fight in Africa were volunteers, at least posing as mercenaries so as not to violate the agreement with Rome. Whether they were there at all, and if they fought with Hannibal against the Romans have been fiercely debated ever since.[31]

The Macedonian incursion into the Aegean brought together the formerly antagonistic Attalus and the Rhodians. Philip took personal charge of a fleet which met his combined enemies in a naval battle off the island of Chios. The fighting was hard, and though Macedonian valour eventually prevailed over Rhodian seamanship, victory, such as it was, came at a cost which crippled the Macedonian navy. Philip had effectively lost his new fleet, but could console himself that he had once more put the annoying Attalus to flight, and captured his flagship as well. Perhaps to give his navy time to effect repairs, Philip made a lightning excursion against Pergamum, perhaps hoping to capture Attalus' capital. However, the canny Pergamene king had foreseen the eventuality, and his capital was well prepared to withstand a siege. Attalus had also taken the precaution of bringing in what crops he could and destroying the rest, so Philip had an army which was unchallenged in the field, but being slowly defeated by hunger. (This was a lesson he was to remember, and attempt to apply to his own enemies in later years.)

Not content to remain quietly behind his walls, Attalus sought to rouse enemies of Macedon nearer home. There was some prospect of this. The Athenians were furious that Philip's control of the Hellespont gave him a chokehold on their supplies of wheat and timber from the shores of the Black Sea, and Philip's new ascendancy in the Aegean deeply worried the nominally-free states of Greece. The Aetolians had already been to Rome, protesting about Philip's retention of their cities. To which the Romans roughly replied: 'You made your peace with him – live with the consequences'.[32] This rebuff is interesting because had Rome been contemplating war with Macedon at this early stage, it would not have been so brutally dismissive of a useful potential ally. It was probably from this embassy that the Romans heard an (exaggerated) account of Philip's assistance to Hannibal. They were deeply indignant at this violation of the treaty, which Philip naturally denied. However, when Macedonian soldiers turned up among the prisoners whom Scipio captured in Rome's decisive victory over Hannibal at Zama, Roman suspicion of Philip deepened.

Attalus' embassy to the Aetolians was always a forlorn hope, given his somewhat weak performance in the earlier war, but the Pergamene king received a more sympathetic hearing in Rome, where the ground had been partly prepared by the earlier Aetolian embassy. It is very probable that this embassy brought with them news that exploded in Rome like diplomatic dynamite: the revelation of the secret treaty which showed that Philip and Antiochus were working in tandem. The rifts already present in that alliance would have gone unmentioned (Antiochus could certainly have made more effort to feed Philip's starving soldiers). Instead the Romans were told how Antiochus, the conqueror of the Far East, was now working with Philip to dismember Egypt. Again it is highly unlikely that the pair actually contemplated conquering Egypt proper, but the Pergamenes would have painted this as a probable scenario, and pointed out that with Egyptian wealth and corn, only Rome would stand in the way of Macedon and Seleucia's dominance of the known world.[33]

Rome hardly needed encouragement from Pergamene diplomats to be hostile to Macedon. Both immediate political reasons and barely-understood socio-economic imperatives were driving the state in the same direction.

Carthage was now defeated, tied down by a treaty and the obligation to pay reparations which guaranteed that Rome's former rival would never possess more than a shadow of her previous power for decades to come. However, whatever compensation Carthage could pay could barely offset the massive damage done to the Italian economy, where the southern half of the country had been a war zone for a decade and a half. Money was also beginning to trickle in from the silver mines of Spain which were now in Roman hands, and the city had already begun the laborious process of repaying its war debts.

But neither Carthage nor Spain could replace Italy's major loss in the Hannibalic War: manpower. Rome had defeated Carthage partly by throwing its vastly-greater reserves of population at the problem. The strategy had succeeded, but the cost had been terrible: it is estimated that Rome itself lost one adult male in three to the war. In a world where disease and infant mortality meant that every woman had to bear at least seven children just to keep the population stable, such losses were hard to replace. Yet within two generations these losses were to be made up by one of the most massive population transfers in antiquity. It is highly unlikely that Rome contemplated war with Macedon in terms of the most massive slave raid in history, yet this was the terrible consequence for Greece, and an underlying cause of the war.

Rome was barely aware of this imperative, but it was reinforced by another social dynamic which everyone knew well. At this time, the Roman political elite were essentially a warrior aristocracy. The political leaders of the state (the consuls) were expected to be generals, and to spend at least a part of the year in command of an army. In fact the word 'province' comes from the Latin *provincia*, a term which defined a consul's area of military operations (the word actually translates to something like 'for conquering'.) No Roman politician could hope to succeed with the electorate unless he had a substantial military background, so most young Roman aristocratic males joined the army in their mid-to-late teens as military tribunes, and had over half a decade of military service behind them before they took even the first steps up the senatorial ladder.

The end of the war with Hannibal left an up-and-coming generation of would-be politicians severely disadvantaged at the polls in relation to their slightly older rivals who could point to success against the most terrifying enemy in Roman history. This new generation needed a good war as desperately as Italy needed manpower to work its fields, and those wanting war had at their disposal the Roman army, by this time undoubtedly supreme among the fighting forces in the known world.

To motive and means was added an excuse. Philip had revealed himself as an expansionist with insatiable imperial ambitions, a new Alexander, or at best a second Pyrrhus. Seen from Rome the Pergamene vision of a Seleucid-Macedonian alliance tearing apart Egypt and then turning its combined force on Rome was at least plausible, if not probable.

In fact, as Philip himself would have gladly explained if given the opportunity, there was not the slightest chance of this happening. Neither Macedon nor Seleucia had the resources to take and hold Ptolemaic Egypt, and even if they did, joint rule was as unfeasible as each trusting the other to rule for their joint benefit. In reality Philip was in the alliance to pick up some Aegean islands, and Antiochus wanted to make gains in southern Palestine and Gaza.

If Attalus' head could end up on a pole and his kingdom end up in Macedon's possession this would be both a satisfactory revenge and more than Macedon would have expected to gain from its Seleucid alliance, but, as it turned out, this had proved beyond Philip's power. He had only managed to extricate his hungry soldiers from Anatolia with considerable difficulty, returning to Macedon in the spring of 200 BC. The man who had failed to take Pergamum would have laughed with sardonic scorn if told he was currently terrifying Rome with rumours he intended to take the Capitoline.

Sadly, the true might of Macedonia (or lack of it) was irrelevant, as was the firmness and intent of Philip's Seleucid alliance. By now Rome wanted, and on a certain level needed, a war and Philip's conduct had provided a defensible pretext. Sulpicius Galba, the general who had commanded operations in Roman operations in Greece during the First Macedonian War was elected to the consulship in 200 BC, an ominous sign of Roman intentions. Three highly-aristocratic Roman envoys were sent, allegedly to mediate between Ptolemy and Antiochus, but also to warn Philip against interfering with Rome's Greek allies and to submit to Attalus' demands for arbitration. The envoys gave themselves a wandering itinerary en route to Philip so as to canvass support for war among the Greeks along the way.

Given that Rome was looking for a fight, as now seems to have been the case, a further pretext could always be found in the continual squabbles of the Greek states. The most obvious excuse was to be found in Athens, and it was here that the envoys eventually turned up.

Two Acarnanian youths had been accused of violating the sanctity of the Eleusian Mysteries, a fertility rite upon which the Athenians set great store. The young men were executed, and Acarnanian protests roughly ignored. The Acarnanians protested more vigorously, this time with an army supported by Macedonian ships and auxiliaries, and the farmlands of Attica were devastated by way of additional emphasis. This military pressure was taken off Athens by the return of Attalus and some Rhodian ships which were ecstatically welcomed in Athens. The Acarnanians, having made their point anyway, withdrew and Philip's supporting troops went with them. Carried away by the arrival of two sets of powerful protectors (Romans and Pergamenes) and the departure of two sets of enemies (Macedonians and Acarnanians), the Athenians promptly declared war on Philip.

This embarrassed the Roman envoys, who had not yet delivered their ultimatum to Philip, and had no authority to ally Rome with Athens, let alone Rhodes and the other members of Attalus' coalition. Even worse, early in 200 BC the Senate had put the proposal to the Roman people that they should go to war with Macedon, and had been soundly rejected. The Roman people knew well that war was the route to political advancement, but it was the aristocrats who actually benefitted, and the war-weary populace had no intention of seeing their menfolk die to advance someone's political career.

The Roman envoys did what they could. When Macedon responded to the Athenian declaration of war with a small army that began devastating whatever the Acarnanians had missed, the envoys went to Nicanor, the Macedonian general, and delivered their ultimatum to him. Nicanor promised to deliver the message to his royal master, and left with his army to do so. Soon afterwards, the Macedonians returned and resumed plundering Attica. Meanwhile Philip, having heard the Roman demand, had responded by moving east and campaigning in Thrace. It appeared that he had no intention of obeying the envoys, especially as, for the first time and directly against the Roman ultimatum, he began to attack Egyptian possessions in the region. With Roman stolidity, the envoys decided to make absolutely sure by sending one of their number to speak to the king personally.

This final ambassador was not sent in a last desperate attempt to make peace, but through Roman religious scruples. Between the two embassies, the Senate (pointing to Philip's aggression against their friend and ally Attalus) had at last persuaded the Roman people to declare war. The motion passed not least because the Senate ruled that any veteran soldiers taking part in the fighting would do so only if they were volunteers. (Since many veterans had returned home to find the family smallholding devastated, the cattle stolen, the labour force run off and the farmhouse flattened, volunteer recruits needing a livelihood proved not hard to come by.)

Nevertheless, the vote for war was conditional on Philip refusing the Roman ultimatum, so it had to be offered for rejection one more time. The Roman ambassador, Marcus Aemilius Lepidus, of Rome's great Aemilian line found Philip engaged in wrapping up the assault of a town called Abydus. He had breached the walls, and the people of the town threatened collective suicide if Philip pressed the attack any further. With his usual grim humour, Philip allowed 'three days respite so that anyone who wanted to slit their throat or wrists could do so' and turned to deal with Rome's young ambassador.[34] Given that his purpose was to provoke the king into war, Aemilius was not diplomatic in presenting the Roman demands. Polybius reports:

> The king was considerably taken aback, but said that he pardoned him [Aemilius] for speaking so arrogantly. He gave three reasons, first because he was young and inexperienced in these matters, secondly because of his looks – and in fact he was the handsomest man of his time – but above all because he was a Roman. 'I ask mainly of the Romans that they neither break their treaty nor make war on me; but if they do so anyway, we will defend ourselves and pray to the gods to help us' the Macedonian king responded.[35]

Philip correctly pointed out that his actions were all legal within the terms of the Peace of Phoenice, and that Rome, in breaking the peace, would be the aggressor. Implicitly conceding the point, Aemilius could only respond by invoking the further demand, not included in the treaty, that Philip cease his assaults on 'Greek autonomy'. Eventually Aemilius was able to persuade the king that there was no point in being reasonable, as Rome was determined to declare war in any case, so Philip may as well reject the ultimatum and get it over with.

Thereafter, briefly recalling the ostensible reason for their embassy, the ambassadors made a quick trip to Egypt to inform Ptolemy that their 'mediation' with Antiochus had been unsuccessful. It is probable that hostilities between Antiochus and Ptolemy were now more to Rome than a vehicle by which to deliver the Roman ultimatum to Philip. If Egypt and the Seleucids remained at odds, the chances of either intervening in Greece and Macedon were considerably reduced.

Thus, in the autumn of 200 BC Rome and Macedon were again at war. In fact, so certain had the Romans been of the outcome of 'negotiations' that even as Aemilius was conferring with Philip, the first Roman transports were crossing the Adriatic bearing the legions to Illyria.

Rome Versus Macedon: Forces and Resources

The warrior poet Archilochus wrote several centuries earlier that 'the fox has many tricks, whilst the hedgehog has only one. But the hedgehog's trick is a very good one.' In the same way, the Roman army was a one-trick army, based on the fact that in a head-on clash, the legionaries could go straight through whatever was in front of them. Even Hannibal was aware of that, and had used the fact to his advantage in his famous envelopment of the Roman army at Cannae. There was much speculation as to how the Roman army would fare against the phalanx, a unit specifically designed to hold pinned any force that attacked frontally so that the cavalry could come round and deal with its sides and back. In the clash of legion against phalanx, the irresistible force was about to meet the immovable object. Victory would go not only to the side which first resolved this paradox to its advantage, but also to the side with the greater resources and the better politicians.

Rome

Both Livy and Polybius have taken the time to describe the Roman army; Livy how it existed before the war with Hannibal, and Polybius the army of his own time. We do not have an exact description of the army between these two dates (the force that went to war against Philip V) but it would not have been much different from the army which conquered Hannibal, and it certainly featured many of the same men.

The core of the Roman army was, and for centuries to come would be, the Roman legion. A Roman legionary was a heavy infantryman, armed with two throwing spears and a stabbing sword. It is possible that for the first time these swords were the Spanish swords which the Romans had seen Hannibal's Iberian mercenaries use to terrible effect.

It is probable that like later Roman swords, these early weapons had a varied carbon content, with a low carbon core, and high carbon density on the surface and edge. The 20-or-so inches of blade (Roman swords at this time were slightly longer than their imperial equivalents) had a slight waist just off the handle and from there tapered to a point at an angle which became particularly pronounced in the last few inches. It was balanced by a wooden pommel, and tended to have a handle of bone or rough ivory. The grip on these swords was particularly important, as unlike many stabbing swords, the *gladius hispaniensis* had no blood runnels to allow air into a wound. Consequently, to avoid flesh clamping about the blade, the soldier had to give it a vicious twist as he withdrew it, creating a wound which shocked Macedonians accustomed to the less ferocious Greek sword which was ubiquitous across the eastern Mediterranean. The Roman sword was worn high on the right-hand side with its own belt, whilst the left hand carried the shield.

This shield, the Roman *scutum*, was rounder and somewhat larger than later versions were to become. Polybius describes it in detail:

> The surface is convex, and 2 feet 6 inches wide and 4 feet long. It is made from two layers of wood secured with bull's hide glue, and then layered first with canvas and then with calfskin. The upper and lower edges are secured with iron bands – the lower in order to protect the shield when that edge rests on the ground, the upper, as it will receive sword strokes. In the centre is an iron boss used to deflect stones, pikes and heavy missiles.[36]

For their armour some of the poorest soldiers still may have borne the old 'heart protector'. This was basically a square brass plate worn across the chest like a heavily defensive training bra which protected little more than the upper thorax. However, anyone who could afford it (and anyone with a decent property qualification could do so), sported *lorica hamata*, a suit of chain mail padded at the shoulders and coming down about to the knees.

The left leg had a single greave (a sort of rigid, footless metal sock) which both prevented the shield from chafing the leg as the legionary put his best foot forward, and protected the leg to some extent from low–flying missiles.

The two *pila* were both spears designed to be thrown as a preliminary to a more personal engagement. The lighter spear was probably launched at about 30 yards, and the heavier *pilum* just before contact. Both weapons had a long metal tang of soft iron, so that the spear would probably bend once it had impaled itself in a shield, but the heavier *pilum* was quite capable of going through the man behind it if he let his guard down, possibly because the lighter *pilum* had made his shield impractically cumbersome. Whether embedded in shield or flesh, the spear's viciously barbed head made it hard to remove. (Most surgeons either used a special extraction tool or simply pushed it through to the other side and then snipped it off.)

At least the front ranks of the Romans attached long blue–black plumes to their bronze helmets which made them look taller and more formidable than they already were. Romans were particularly terrifying enemies, since another aspect of Roman soldiers was that they fought their wars by a somewhat different and more savage code than their Greek opponents. To the Greeks war was a way of life by which *polis* contended against *polis* and the ultimate objective was political advantage rather than the death of the opposing soldiery. Every Greek knew that the fortunes of war might leave him abandoned on a stricken field at the mercy of his enemies, and there were rules for surrendering, ransoming prisoners and at worst, the organized collection of the dead. The average Roman infantryman, hardened by the savage war against Hannibal, cared little for these conventions. He was there to kill his enemy and to do whatever it took to achieve that objective. It was a military culture clash that was to leave both Greeks and Macedonians horrified by their grimly-merciless opponents.

At this time the legionaries fought in maniples - literally 'handfuls' of about sixty men. Each maniple was of either *hastati, principes* or *triarii*. The front-line maniples were the *hastati*, literally 'spearmen' (from *hasta* – spear*)*. These were young men, many seeing combat for the first time, and consequently filled with young men's belief in their own immortality. The maniples of older, wiser *principes* made up the second line. These men knew that victory was their best chance of coming through a battle intact, and were prepared to fight ferociously to achieve it. The back line were veteran warriors armed with long spears. These spears were defensive weapons which allowed the *triarii* to form a bristling phalanx behind which the scattered *hastati* and *principes* could reorganize themselves after a setback.

For centuries after these soldiers had ceased to be a part of the regular army, the expression 'it's come to the *triarii*' remained a metaphor for a desperate situation.

Whilst the Roman citizens of her army were almost exclusively legionaries, the Romans were aware of the need for specialist skills they did not themselves possess, and supplemented their army with auxiliaries. 'Auxiliaries' at this time meant only 'non-legionaries' and could be anything from Italian allied soldiers not much differently armed and equipped from the Romans, all the way to exotic troops such as Cretan archers, Balearic slingers or Gallic mercenary cavalry. It is uncertain how much the Romans initially brought over to Greece in the way of auxiliary forces, as they probably relied on their own light troops *(velites)* and those of the Greek allies they intended to pick up en route.

The *velites* were those Roman citizens rich enough to be recruited into the army, but too poor to afford a full legionary panoply. Often these were young men of families that could only afford a single set of legionary equipment, and had better-equipped fathers already under arms. The velites were skirmishers, lightly armed with shield and throwing spear. Polybius says of them only that they often wore distinctive items such as scraps of wolfskin, so the later practice of invariably depicting these troops clad in complete wolfskins which covered the helmet is probably incorrect.

As with future generations of Roman soldiery, the command and control figure on the ground was the centurion, who despite his name was responsible for some eighty legionaries, and the legion itself came with a complement of some five military tribunes. These 'officers' were generally young aristocrats doing their military service before going into the senate, or on occasion hardened commanders who had risen from command of auxiliary troops. However, the legionary legate who was to command later legions did not exist at this time and the soldiery came under the direct command of the general in command of the army.

However, the legions did have a *praefectus castrorum* (master of the camp) who took precedence even over the *primus pilus*, the leading centurion of the legion, and it was the *praefectus castrorum r*ather than the general who dealt with the day-to-day running of the unit.

The actual forces that Rome was able to field for the war with Macedon were somewhat constrained by two factors: the political necessity of restricting the recruitment of veterans to volunteers; and the surliness of the Italian allies who wanted time to recover from the drain of money and manpower which had resulted from the Hannibalic War. Also, Rome's own budget was somewhat limited, both because the nation did not have much funding available and because the objectives of the Senate in fighting the war were somewhat limited.

The Romans were clear that the objective of this war was to clip Philip's wings and to restrain both his appetite and his capacity for foreign adventure. The conquest of neither Greece nor Macedon was envisaged. In fact far from Greeks being conquered by Rome, the Roman strategy was from the beginning to make sure that as many Greeks as possible should be bribed, persuaded or coerced into taking the field alongside the Romans. Given that Macedon had trouble with the Greeks when they were fighting Macedon on their own, it was believed that only a relatively small Roman force of about two legions would be enough to tip the balance, and force Philip to submit to terms more to Rome's liking than those resulting from the Peace of Phoenice.

Macedon

Philip's problem was that though Macedon's small but highly-competent army was capable of dealing with any threat to his kingdom, these threats seldom came singly.[37] Yet geography had put Macedon in a box from which there was little room to expand, and consequently the kingdom's reserves of manpower were never equal to the demands upon them. On the other hand, geography was also Macedon's ally, in that the same mountains which limited Macedonia's agricultural capacity and population made it very difficult to get at such farms and people as Macedonia did have. The state had never been invaded by a western power, and as the Romans had already discovered, a direct approach through northern Illyria was impracticable, both politically and physically.

All Philip had to do was hold the Romans in the passes, and they would be unable to get at him. The flaw in this strategy was slowly to become apparent, in that the army that Philip intended to hold the mountain passes with was far from ideal for the purpose. The Macedonian phalanx had been created by Philip's namesake and predecessor, Philip II, for a particular task: to defeat the Greek phalanx. From time immemorial, Greek wars had been fought by mutual consent. Either an army stayed behind its walls and refused to fight, or it would come out, select one of the few bits of Greek terrain flat enough for the purpose, and offer battle.

This convention had produced a remarkable oddity: a mountainous country with warriors who fought best and mainly on level ground. Because bounding about rough terrain was not involved, the traditional Greek warrior could wear heavy armour and carry a large shield. The Macedonian contribution was to find a way of concentrating even more spears against those shields than had formerly been possible. The average hoplite phalanx had individuals armed with spears some 6 to 8 feet in length. The average Macedonian phalangite used the *sarissa*, a spear some two to three times longer. This weapon, dating back to the 330s BC, was made of cornel wood, and since 18-foot straight lengths of wood were hard to come by, this *sarissa* generally came in two parts joined in the middle, with a narrow leaf-shaped blade at one end, and a sharpened butt-spike at the other. (This latter was very useful for those occasions when the phalanx had literally marched over the opposition, and finishing off any enemy wounded underfoot simply involved slamming the butt-spike down.)

The shield was a round type called an *aspis*. It was a thin sheet of metal (usually bronze) overlaying a wood base about 2 feet across. The distinctive feature of this shield was that it was designed to be carried on a shoulder strap on those occasions when the bearer was wielding a *sarissa*, a job which required both hands. However, given that the *sarissa* was unsuitable for many of the army's tasks (for example storming the walls of a city) it is highly probable that the *aspis* was a dual-use shield capable of normal usage when the phalangites were fighting with sword and javelin.

The formation of the phalanx allowed at least the first three ranks to bring their *sarissae* into play, and the phalanx was generally even deeper than this, allowing the front ranks to be replaced as they became depleted, or to allow those at the back to literally push those in the front ranks through a thinner enemy line. This formation meant that it was important only for the front ranks to wear armour, and it is possible that the back rankers wore only light linen armour, helmet and greaves.

The rigidity of the phalanx meant that it could only go into battle pointing straight forward, and, as the inexperienced Spartans had discovered whilst trying out this new formation at Mantinea, irregularities in the terrain could cause chaos. Therefore the phalanx was supported by lighter troops called peltasts after the *pelte*, a light, usually crescent-shaped shield which these soldiers carried. Peltasts were not mere skirmishers, as they had both better armour and weapons. In fact some modern researchers have argued that these peltasts were one role played by Macedonian soldiers, at least some of whom could switch from peltast to phalangite as the military situation required. It was the task of peltasts to keep skirmishers and cavalry off the flanks and rear of the phalanx, and to act as a 'hinge' about which the Macedonian cavalry could manoeuvre.

As well as native levies, there were also mercenary peltasts from Greek cities who could be called upon to supplement the army that most needed them. As such peltasts brought their own weapons and armour with them, there was probably considerable divergence of type. But generally a peltast could be assumed to have lighter armour than a hoplite, a good stock of javelins, and probably a thrusting spear for close combat work. Most would also have carried a sword, but unlike the Romans, most Hellenistic armies did not use this as their primary weapon.

The Macedonians comfortably outclassed the Romans in the quality of their cavalry, something which would have given them greater comfort if they were not aware that the Romans expected their cavalry to be inferior and had modified their military operations to work around this disadvantage. In part this was done by co-opting the cavalry of whatever allies they had working with them, and in part by centralizing their supply structure so that the army needed to spread out less to forage, a point at which it became particularly vulnerable to sudden cavalry attacks. As a result of this detail, much of the strategy of the Second Macedonian War was built about the intertwined relationship of Greek geography and Roman lines of supply. Polybius remarks that the Roman cavalry had suffered from a number of handicaps in the past: a lack of armour, poor-quality shields that rotted in the rain, and javelins so light and bendy that they were useless in close combat and impossible to throw properly. On discovering that the Greeks did it better, the Romans switched their cavalry to the Greek style. 'For this is one of their great strengths – no other people are so ready to adopt new customs or to copy what is done better by others'.[38] Regrettably Polybius does not tell us when the Romans experienced their epiphany with regard to the cavalry, but it is probable that this was whilst fighting the cities of Magna Graecia in Italy, so that the cavalry that fought Philip was either native Greek, or similar enough to it as to be indistinguishable.

Thus the Greek cavalry that fought on both sides consisted of horsemen wearing armour which protected the upper chest. Because of the problems involved with mobility and one's seat on the horse, these cuirasses were either shorter than the infantry type, or more flared at the waist. The shorter armour often was supplemented by more flexible metal plates over the lower abdomen. The bronze helmet resembled a short-brimmed hat which protected the wearer both from the Greek sun, missile weapons dropping from a steep angle, and sword cuts to the head.

The usual cavalry weapon was a javelin and riders often carried several. Early cavalry used the 6 feet long *xystos*, which was both a close-combat weapon and javelin, and this may still have been the case among some Greek states. Others (including the Romans) had gone from no shield to a substantial round shield which left the carrier no choice but to abandon the *xystos* and opt for javelins and a sword. Like all cavalrymen in antiquity, they had no stirrups, and relied on the saddle and firm thighs to keep themselves on horseback.

In the event cavalry were significant in the war, but only in that the Roman generals had to be careful not to allow them to play too great a part. This meant ensuring that supply lines were well protected and that battles were not fought in areas which allowed the Macedonian cavalry the freedom to sweep on to the Roman flanks and rear; a freedom which had disastrously been afforded to the Carthaginian cavalry at Cannae. The Second Macedonian War was above all a contest of infantry.

Chapter 5

The Road to Cynoscephalae

The Roman declaration of war left Macedon diplomatically isolated. In theory, Philip could call on his powerful Seleucid ally, but in practice Antiochus was preoccupied with Egypt. Even had he not been, it was probable that the Seleucid ruler would have stood aside from the war, and waited to see if Philip was weakened enough by the Roman onslaught to be vulnerable to a follow-up attack from the east.

The Achaeans, generally faithful allies of Macedon, were suffering from internal political troubles, as Philopoemen had stood down from his command, and a resurgent Nabis of Sparta was threatening to take revenge for Mantinea. Furthermore, what the Achaeans had seen of the Romans in the First Macedonian War had discouraged them from wanting to face them during the second. Nor were those urging that Achaea stay with its traditional alliance helped by the arbitrary and undiplomatic handling which Philip had afforded them in recent years.

Thessaly, naturally, was loyal since much of it was now a Macedonian province in all but name, but the rest of Greece was neutral, or openly hostile.

Galba had evidently spent some of his time away from Greece brooding on his earlier campaign. He had reached the conclusion that the best way to defeat Philip was to stretch his resources. If the Macedonian army was strong enough to face any threat whilst concentrated, Galba would make it fight divided. Accordingly he sent raiding parties to hit Macedon from the east and west. The western force advanced up the River Apsus from just north of Apollonia (which city Galba made his base) and raided a number of towns just within the Macedonian border, the largest of which was the fortress town of Antipatreia at the headwaters of the Apsus. Rome received support in region from Macedon's inveterate enemies, the Dardanians, and further south from Amynander, the political weathercock who reliably allied himself with whatever power was strongest in the region at that time.

Yet Philip was unable to respond to this assault in the west, as Galba had ensured that he had even more serious problems in the east, especially at Chalcis in Euboea. The Roman fleet, under the enterprising Gaius Claudius Cento had been sent to guard the seas off Attica, as Athens was suffering considerably from Macedonian-sponsored raids by pirates based in Chalcis. Claudius went straight to the root of the problem and hit Chalcis itself. The sloppily guarded city was taken before most of the inhabitants were aware that there were even Romans in the vicinity. Since there was no way that he could hold the city, Claudius razed the place, paying particular attention to the destruction of the stocks of grain and the arsenal of war materiel that Philip had laid up there. All males of military age were massacred, apart from those prisoners of Philip who were rescued from the dungeons.[39]

By the time Philip had rushed to the scene, the booty-laden Romans were long gone, leaving the furious Macedonian king master of a smoking ruin. Ever the opportunist, Philip decided to convert his presence in the area into a lightning assault on Athens, which his spies informed him was as carelessly guarded as Chalcis had been. Philip might have succeeded in his surprise attack had not his army been spotted by the soldiers manning one of the many watch-towers dotted about Attica, and a runner arrived in Athens in time for the gates to be slammed almost in Philip's face.

That dawn, the Athenians were emboldened to offer battle in front of their city. However, they withdrew within the walls when Philip advanced, though not before Philip hurtled into their midst with a small body of cavalry and vented his fury on those soldiers he caught up with. Though vastly outnumbered, his cavalry force came out of the melee intact, because the sudden assault panicked the Athenians and those on the walls did not get a chance to fire missiles before Philip was among the Athenian ranks.

With Athens secure behind its formidable walls, Philip turned his fury on Attica. The unfortunate hinterland of Athens had been so repeatedly devastated that there was little left for Philip to spoil, so he vindictively set his men to smashing the very stones of destroyed buildings so as to make reconstruction harder. The Macedonians also probed the defences of nearby Eleusis, but found that the recent alarms had put the garrison there onto full alert.

Hearing that Achaea and Sparta were now openly at war again, Philip took himself to a meeting of the Achaean League, and promised to help against the Spartans, but the Achaeans were unwilling to accept the aid of so dangerous an ally. Philip returned to Attica, and probed hard at the defences of Piraeus, Eleusis and Athens itself. Eventually however, he had to accept that conquering Attica would involve greater effort than he was prepared to commit, especially as the Romans were taking an interest in the city's plight and sending ever-stronger reinforcements.

Consequently Philip pulled back to Macedonia, and the war shifted to the diplomatic front. Galba lobbied the Greeks and Illyrians hard in an attempt to have Macedonia completely surrounded by foes, and Philip's ambassadors tried energetically to prevent this. Galba had the force of two legions to lend heft to his arguments, but he was also fighting against his own lacklustre record and earlier brutality during the First Macedonian War. And if anyone had forgotten how in that war the Romans had pulled back to leave the Aetolians to face Philip's vengeance unaided, Macedonian ambassadors were quickly on hand to jog memories.

In these opening rounds of this second war the Romans had acted more as raiders than conquerors, hitting Macedonian strongpoints, but then pulling back before the threat of the Macedonian army. This was not conduct that indicated a serious long-term commitment to the region, and Philip's treatment of Attica was a stark warning that should Rome withdraw her interest from Greece once more, those who had taken the Roman side could expect little mercy.

All of Greece watched with interest the proceedings of the Aetolian council, since if any one Greek state was likely to ally itself with the Romans, it would be the Aetolians. Philip's ambassadors to the gathering briefly pointed out Rome's untrustworthiness as an ally, and that those who allied with the Romans had a habit of unaccountably becoming, within a few years, Roman subjects. If the Aetolians took the Roman side, Philip's envoys said, Aetolia and Greece would eventually be subjugated, and Roman rule would make that of Macedon seem mild in comparison.

The Athenians made a cameo appearance bewailing Philip's devastation of their lands (something which the Macedonians were probably keen to have publicized in any case), and then the Roman ambassador delivered a short speech. His message was brutal. Rome had conquered Hannibal. Rome would conquer Philip, and anyone who stood with him. The Aetolians were being given 'a fair chance to restore themselves to the friendship with the Romans. Either conquer with them, or perish with Philip'.[40]

The following spring, Galba (who would have known this was his last year in command of the campaign against Macedon) decided to end the war with a decisive thrust. Consequently he made a drive with his legions for the Macedonian heartland, taking the most direct route from Apollonia; the path which was later to be the Via Egnatia. This twisting passage through the mountains ran along the banks of the River Genesus, but also required the crossing of several high passes before reaching the Macedonian plain.

Galba had mobilized his allies to ensure that Macedon was assailed on several fronts at once. Attalus of Pergamum took once more to the sea and threatened Euboea, whilst the Dardanians prowled the Macedonian border forts looking for weaknesses. Leaving his son Perseus to hold the line against the Dardanians, Philip moved to meet Galba with the bulk of the army. There was a period of confusion during which each side desperately tried to establish the location of the other; no easy task in broken landscape in which two armies in adjoining valleys could pass each other unawares. But once each had established the whereabouts of the other, Roman and Macedonian settled down to a prolonged and grim confrontation. However, Galba received welcome news that the Roman initiative had paid immediate dividends. His advance had finally tipped the Aetolians into throwing their lot in with the Romans, and their army had opportunistically joined the general advance on Macedonia, taking a more southerly route by way of plunder-rich Thessaly.

Philip was not prepared to risk a pitched battle with Galba, since even if he destroyed the Roman army, it would be at the cost of his own, and there was a queue of other enemies waiting. Instead, he played to the strength of the mountainous terrain. His cavalry and Cretan mercenary bowmen caused havoc among the Roman foragers, only coming to grief on those occasions when they followed up too enthusiastically and ran into the supporting Roman maniples.

Galba found himself short of supplies and forced to fight for every pass and ridge, whilst Philip constantly feinted, threatening to get to the rear of the Roman column, or moved off in an unexpected direction, causing delays whilst Galba worked out where his elusive enemy had got to. However, Philip did not have everything his own way. Through his cavalry and local knowledge his men were well supplied, but the Macedonians tended to get mauled when the Romans did manage to get to grips with them. This was both a literal mauling, in that the Macedonians were appalled by the damage that the Roman *gladius hispaniensis* did to the human body, and metaphorical. Against the more flexible legionaries Philip's phalangites were trying to hold mountain passes with tactics and equipment not designed for the job. For example in the woodland pass at Erigonus, 'The phalanx was at an immense disadvantage since the soldiers could not push their wall of pikes forward – this needed open country, and the Thracians were hindered by their lances which were likewise too long'.[41]

After five slow months of painful progress, Galba finally reached the last passes by Celatrum, a town on one of the two lakes which are the largest bodies of fresh water on the entire peninsula. However, the campaigning season was at an end, and if a fragment from the historian Zonarus is to be believed, Galba may well have fallen sick during the campaign. Realizing that a successful Macedonian defence of the final passes would leave the Roman army stranded in the mountains to be destroyed by the approaching winter, Galba pulled back, arriving in late October at Apollonia, back where he had started.

Relieved of the threat of a Roman invasion, Philip made short work of the other invaders. His son, Perseus, had been pulled back from garrison duty against the Dardanians to bring his troops to help with his father's final defence of Macedon, and this had brought the Dardanians rushing on to the Macedonian plain. Now they rushed away again, with Philip's cavalry at their heels cutting down the stragglers.

It appeared that no-one had warned the Aetolians that the Romans had pulled back. The Aetolian army was making leisurely progress as it looted its way unopposed through Thessaly, secure in the knowledge that Philip was elsewhere fully occupied with Galba. Their first update on events was the appearance of the Macedonian army moving through their disorganized ranks like a knife through butter.

A feeble attempt to rally failed, and the Aetolian force ran for their lives. They took heavy casualties and would have suffered worse had Amynander not manfully resisted the temptation to change sides yet again. Instead he led the Aetolian remnants home by a series of little-known trails through his native land.

Meanwhile, news came through that Attalus had achieved little on his summer cruise of the Aegean. He had been accompanied by a Roman legate and some legionaries, and the people of the little town of Gaurioun on Andros were the first Greeks west of Athens to see legionaries in action. The combined Roman and Pergamene naval force suffered a bloody nose in a failed attack on Cassandreiea, but took and sacked the town of Acanthus in Chalcidice. This minor success aside, the campaign of 199 BC, which was intended to see Macedon collapse from an assault from all sides, had finished with the Macedonian hedgehog basically intact and the attackers bloodied and discouraged. Galba's advance and subsequent retreat had deeply disillusioned the Roman soldiery. It will be recalled that many had joined on the promise of plunder, and the total lack of profit from their summer in the mountains had left them downright mutinous.

It did not help the Roman cause that Antiochus of Seleucia, having gained possession of much of Coele Syria, now decided to turn his troops against Attalus of Pergamum. This was probably less to help the beleaguered Philip than because Antiochus too felt that the ambitious Attalus needed taking down a peg or two. Attalus appealed to the Romans who had to agree that defence of his realm took priority. The Pergamene king now bowed out of the Macedonian War, leaving Philip's eastern seaboard clear of enemies.

For the Romans it was evident that a new approach was needed. Galba would not be the man to supply this, as his term in command was now completed. He returned to Rome, leaving his successor P. Villius Tappulus with a restless army which felt strongly that it should have been going home with Galba. With his army demoralized, Villius wisely decided to give the troops a chance to recover from their mountain exertions before he made another attempt on Philip's securely-entrenched defences. He mercilessly punished some Greek states which he considered either hostile or insufficiently enthusiastic to his cause and thus (apart from reinforcing the Greek concept of the Romans as violent barbarians) had achieved little of note before the startlingly-early arrival of his successor, a young man called T. Quinctius Flamininus.

Flamininus

Though young, Flamininus came from an ancient family and included among his forebears the noble Cincinnatus who had been called from the plough to save the Republic. Flamininus was both a typical Roman aristocrat of his day and also one of a new generation of Romans, who like Scipio Africanus before him, admired the Greeks and their culture. Like almost all Romans of the senatorial class, Flamininus was deeply ambitious, and his ancestral nobility gave him a confidence which bordered on arrogance. This was demonstrated by his decision to stand for the consulship in his early thirties and without first holding any of the usual offices of the *cursus honorum*, as the succession of Roman magistracies was known.

Whilst he might have been expected to have first been an *aedile* and then a *praetor*, Flamininus had in fact only held the offices of military tribune in the Hannibalic War, and the governorship of Tarentum. However, in the latter office Flamininus had founded colonies in the cities of Narnia and Cossa, and could count on the votes of the grateful veterans whom he had given land there. Much has been made of the wisdom of the Roman Senate in allowing the choice of a young man steeped in Hellenic culture to take the helm of the war in Greece, but in truth, chance was as great a factor.

Firstly, Flamininus was pretty much an unknown quantity, both as a general and as a diplomat, insofar as he had held only a relatively minor office, albeit with some distinction. Secondly, there was in fact strong opposition in the Senate to his appointment, and the senate did not actually appoint Flamininus, but merely agreed to overlook his lack of qualifications and let the people decide. Finally, the consuls received their provinces by lot, and it was pure chance that the Hellenistically-minded Flamininus did not spend his year in office fighting the Gauls.[42]

Nevertheless, once he was given the Macedonian command, it soon became apparent that young Flamininus had already given considerable thought to the situation there, and he assumed the consulship with a clear idea of what to do next. Firstly, he intended to do it at once. This was somewhat unusual for a Roman consul, who generally spent much of his early period in office dealing with civil matters in Rome, and only set out on campaign late in the season. Generally, once established in the field, the commander would then have his authority as a general prolonged by the Senate in the form of a proconsulship, and in this position he would wage war for the next year, and if successful, perhaps even longer.

Flamininus broke with this precedent by waiting only for the enrolment of new recruits to his army before he went east. These recruits were new only in the sense of being well rested; generally Flamininus tried to select the flower of Scipio's African veterans for the coming campaign. With the levy successfully accomplished, and with reinforcements now available to the tune of some 8,000 legionaries and 800 cavalry, Flamininus left Italy immediately. It is partly because of Flamininus' early arrival in Greece that Villius was unable to do much in his brief time in command. The new commander did not want to lose someone who had both the trust of the troops and experience of campaigning in the region, so Flamininus kept Villius on as an advisor.

Philip had spent the winter of 199/8 BC in furious activity. He had fortified his defences against the Dardanians and the Illyrians, mustered new troops and above all, prepared for whatever the Romans were going to throw at him over the coming year. He had decided, correctly, that a repeat attempt to cross Illyria from Apollonia was unlikely. If the Romans were going to come, the attack would be through Greece, and given that the most accessible bit of Greece nearest Rome was Epirus, it was likely that the Romans would make their next attempt at Macedon by this route. That is, by going up the Aous Valley from Epirus to Pella via northern Thessaly, thus bypassing the strong fortresses which guarded access to Macedonia further south at the passes from Thessaly. At the same time, if the Romans did try Galba's northern route once more, Philip wanted to be situated to move directly across the Roman supply lines and trap their army in the mountains. Realizing that it would be impossible to hold his Greek possessions in the face of a Roman army, Philip entrusted these strongpoints to the Achaeans, a move which he also hoped would help to bind that confederation more closely to his cause.

He then moved his army to the vicinity of the fortress of Antigoneia in Epirus.[43] Antigoneia commanded the gorge of the River Aous, a river which ran south of and parallel to the River Apsus, which both Macedonian and Roman had travelled up and down several times already in the course of their various wars. Antigoneia was situated near one of the few possible crossing points of this often-torrential river, near its confluence with the River Drin. According to Plutarch, the river

> makes its way between vast and lofty mountains which all but meet above a single deep ravine in the middle. It is somewhat like the River Peneus in its general appearance and fast-moving current. It leaves only a craggy, narrow path cut out beside the stream. An army would find it barely passable at any time, but not at all when guarded by an enemy.[44]

His experiences against Galba in the mountains had convinced Philip of the need for light troops, and he had both trained his own and recruited mercenaries, and these men, under his general Athenagoras, now commanded the passes leading to the fortress. The royal camp was on one side of the gorge on a mountain called Meropus. Philip had here constructed a formidable rampart and had made sure that access was guarded by fortifications and covered by artillery.

Given the strength of the Macedonian position and the difficulties involved in forcing it, Flamininus owed it to the troops who would have to make the assault that first he should at least appear to negotiate with Philip. Indeed, there appeared to be very little option. Flamininus could, perhaps, have attempted to go around the Macedonian strongpoint, but this would have involved a very long journey through hostile territory, harassed by Philip's cavalry, and with the very distinct possibility that Philip would simply then decline to fight and pull back, leaving Flamininus master of Epirus but with little else to show for a long and expensive campaigning season.

So Philip had to be winkled out of his redoubt. The problem was that Flamininus had no idea of how to go about it, and his troops kicked their heels for over a month as possibility after possibility was examined and discarded. Talking appeared to be the only avenue of approach left unexplored.

Philip was always happy to talk, and throughout his series of wars with the Romans he never turned down a chance to engage in discussion. So with the local worthies of Epirus acting as intermediaries, Flamininus and Philip met on opposite sides of the River Aous to discuss a possible peace settlement. Philip was looking for a genuine settlement of a war he knew he could not win, and readily agreed to give up those cities which he had conquered. However, he insisted that he be allowed to retain those conquests which had long been part of his patrimony. Appearing to accept this, Flamininus then demanded that Philip pay compensation to those cities which he had devastated during his recent campaigns. Again Philip assented, quibbling only as to who should arbitrate on the degree of compensation required. Philip then asked which cities he would be withdrawing his garrisons from and Flamininus began by listing the cities of Thessaly.

Since Thessaly had been so long under Macedonian rule that it was practically integrated with Macedon, this demand was evidently intended to be intolerable to Philip, and it so proved. The king shouted furiously across the river: 'Titus Quinctius, you could impose no heavier demands if I were in fact a defeated enemy!' And in fact he was correct: later, when Philip's position was much worse and he sought peace, the terms Flamininus was prepared to offer were lighter than this. But Flamininus had come to Greece in search of glory, and if he could not get it in the field it would be through forcing Macedon to accept a diplomatic defeat of major proportions. Later when he had won his glory, he was prepared to be more generous in making a peace which gained him the distinction of having won the war.

Therefore Flamininus was not deeply upset by Philip's initial rejection of his terms, though at the time of the discussion, tempers between Roman and Macedonian flared to the point where their subordinates had to intervene to prevent the pair from having a minor missile skirmish across the river then and there. Though the negotiations failed, they also had the advantage that Flamininus was able to put before the Greeks in the audience the purpose of the Roman mission in Greece in a statement known to later historians as the 'Aous Declaration'. Rome, announced Flamininus grandly, had come not to conquer Greece, but to defeat Macedon. Macedon was only a threat to Rome so long as Philip commanded the resources of Greece, and therefore Rome would be satisfied, not with the subjugation of Greece, but its freedom from the hegemony of both Rome and Macedon. This was the same message that Flamininus had been giving to those Greeks whom he had met privately. The Roman's polished manners and fluent Greek were winning him diplomatic conquests among the neutrals of Greece, and his public commitment at the Aous to Greek freedom produced an unexpected bonus in winning the trust of one Charpous of Epirus.

This minor aristocrat came to Flamininus and announced that his shepherds were familiar with the area in which Philip was entrenched, and they knew of an unguarded path by which the Macedonian flank could be turned, rather as the Persians had turned the Greek defences at Thermopylae. Desperate for a breakthrough, Flamininus put his trust in the man and sent 4,000 infantry and 300 horse to follow the shepherd who was sent to show the route. Meanwhile, to keep Philip distracted, the Roman started operations as though he intended to force the crossing of the river by brute force.

For three days Flamininus kept the pressure up, knowing that his flanking party could move only at night so as to escape detection. On the third day, a smoke signal arose signalling to the general that the outflanking force was now behind the Macedonian lines. Flamininus now divided his forces into three columns and attacked up the river valley. This attack with his entire force overcame the Macedonian outposts, and swept against the main rampart where it started to take heavy casualties.

At that moment, with perfect timing, the outflanking force raised a clamour and made its presence known at the Macedonian rear. Panic resulted and the Macedonian position was overturned. However, Philip was a canny fighter with a well-founded tendency towards pessimism. Whilst not knowing how his position could be forced, he had prepared for the eventuality, and pulled his army back with the loss of some 2,000 men. He also lost almost all his baggage, but could draw comfort from the fact that forcing his position had at least cost the Romans somewhat in terms of casualties on their side.

Indeed, Flamininus' victory in this battle, which came to be known as the Aoi Stena achieved very little in military terms. Philip fell back toward Thessaly, and selected another defensive position from the dozens which the Greek landscape so generously offered. Flamininus, whose caution in following up his victory had greatly helped Philip to pull his army out largely intact, followed up only as far as the 'camp of Pyrrhus', barely a day's march away. In fact, having achieved his immediate objective (a military

A legionary (*top left*), Roman officer (*bottom left*) and cavalryman (*top right*) from the altar of Domitius Ahenobarbus, discovered in the Campus Martius in Rome and now in the Louvre, Paris. The altar depicts a military census at the end of the second century BC and though the carving probably dates to 122 BC the Roman soldiers depicted here are supposedly contemporary with the events described. (*Adrian Goldsworthy*)

The site of ancient Sparta and the remains of the walls of Sparta; view showing the north gate of the acropolis. In their glory days, the Spartans boasted that the strength of their armies made walls redundant. However, by the second century BC the Spartans definitely required the sanctuary of strong walls, and were not too proud to take shelter behind them. (*Jackie Whalen*)

Macedonian cavalryman: The armour and equipment of Philip V was probably a more elaborate version of this style. Supply was a constant preoccupation of Roman generals because the superior Macedonian cavalry made foraging difficult. (© *Johnny Shumate*)

Skirmishing: A Roman cavalryman in a stand-off with a Greek peltast. Peltasts were used to keep the enemy off the flanks of the phalanx and to defend broken ground. They were often mercenaries and acquired their equipment from a variety of sources, as this soldier's Gallic sword and shield indicate.
(© Johnny Shumate)

ulture clash: A Roman *hastatus* at Pydna finishes off a Macedonian phalangite. Once the ranks of a
halanx were broken, the individual Macedonian soldiers were no match for the greater ferocity
nd superior equipment of the legionaries. (© *Johnny Shumate*)

Numidian elephant riders on campaign in Greece: It is a matter of some controversy whether Hannibal's elephants had towers, but it is more probable that these were fitted as standard by the time of the Macedonian Wars. (© *Johnny Shumate*)

A view of the stoa of Attalus. This stoa was a gift to Athens by Attalus II of Pergamum who ruled from 159 to 138 BC, and it reflects he continuance of the good relations between Athens and Pergamum which were forged during the Macedonian Wars. (The stoa is a reconstruction, as the original was destroyed in the third century AD). (*Avi Shah*)

The mountains of Thessaly as seen from the Nevropolis plain to the southwest. Such panoramas were commonplace to Romans campaigning in Greece, and rapidly lost their scenic appeal for those soldiers who were expected to march over them and dislodge well-fortified garrisons in the process. (*Jackie Whalen*)

View of Thermopylae looking northwest along the end of the Mount Kallidromos range with the Trachis plain on the right. Because Mount Kallidromos squeezed any army marching southwards along the east coast of Greece on to a single narrow strip of coastal plain, Thermopylae has been the scene of repeated battles through the ages. (*Jackie Whalen*)

The tip of Euboea as seen across the Malian Gulf from mainland Greece. Because Euboea was so close to the mainland yet separate from it, the island made a useful base for naval forces seeking to command the eastern seaboard of Greece. (*Jackie Whalen*)

victory over Philip) it appears that Flamininus realized that his men would have little appetite for repeating the process (assuming co-operative shepherds and outflanking mountain passes could be found) all the way up the Aous Valley into northern Thessaly.

Instead, Flamininus turned his forces south back into Epirus. Though Epirus was technically enemy territory, Flamininus made a major diplomatic production of ostentatiously ordering his men not to ravage any part of it. This deference to Greek sensibilities was not in fact a new policy, for Galba too had made a point of being nice to any Greek states which might switch allegiance to Rome. Nevertheless, Flamininus wanted to overcome the Greek prejudice against Roman 'barbarism', and so tried to make it clear that his conduct to the Greeks was driven by his inherent philhellenism, rather than Galba's realpolitik. It was Flamininus' genius that he recognized that the war against Philip was as much a war of perceptions as of actual events, and indeed, it was for that reason he had fought for his victory at the Aoi Stena; not because it mattered in strategic terms, but because it showed both the Greeks and the Roman people that Flamininus was the man to defeat Philip.

The war now reached Thessaly. Philip had prepared as best he was able, reinforcing some fortresses, and destroying such forts and towns as could not be defended. He also took what crops he could and destroyed the rest so as to give the invaders as little as possible in the way of supplies. Philip was in no doubt that, once they were aware that the Macedonians had been forced from Epirus, the Aetolians would come flooding back into Thessaly, and he was not mistaken. With the Aetolians came Amynander, who undertook the siege of the vital fortress of Gomphi, and Flamininus, who drove directly north in the hope of overcoming the Thessalian forts there and sweeping on into Macedon. It was precisely because an advance up the Aous Valley would have taken the Romans north behind these forts that Philip had taken up his defensive position there. Though defeated at Aoi Stena, he had nevertheless made the point that the valley could not be used to approach Macedon whilst a hostile army held it. If Flamininus wanted victory in 198 BC, he would only get it by taking the more southerly route and breaking the defensive series of Macedonian fortresses at Gomphi, Phaloria and Atrax.

Once Amynander and Roman engineers had taken Gomphi, next in the firing line was Phaloria, defended by 2,000 Macedonians. These men were overwhelmed by the sheer energy of the Roman attack which went on day and night until the garrison collapsed as much from exhaustion as anything else. Flamininus had pushed the attack here with vigour, as he felt that what happened at Phaloria would set the tone for the rest of the Thessalian campaign. In this he was mistaken.

Phaloria was plundered and put to the torch, an action which showed clearly that whilst Flamininus offered liberation to those who welcomed him, he offered destruction and slavery to those who did not. With Phaloria flattened, the Romans turned on the smaller and less strategic, but even better-situated fortress of Aeginium. This fortress however was so manifestly impregnable that Flamininus soon abandoned the siege and moved on to the larger and more militarily significant redoubt of Atrax, which was manned by elite Macedonian troops. If Macedon could make a stand anywhere, it would be here.

The opening attack went well for Flamininus, and the Romans quickly smashed a substantial breach in the walls. However, when the assault party went into the breach, they found the Macedonian pikemen waiting for them. With the pikes before and behind the broken ground of the wall preventing a quick retreat, the Romans took a nasty beating. This was the first time the Romans had taken on a phalanx on ground which suited it, and they found the experience deeply unpleasant. As Livy relates of a further attack: 'the Macedonians in tight formation thrust out their tremendously long pikes, whilst the Roman *pila* could make no impression on a formation where the shields were so close packed as to resemble a *testudo*. When the Romans drew their swords they could neither get to grips with the enemy nor damage the spears which formed a virtual palisade, in which even a broken spear was effective'.[45]

Flamininus next tried a siege tower of immense size and strength. Sadly, this monster was unable to cope with the irregular ground, and almost tipped over at one point, to the huge consternation of the legionaries within. Since the walls on each side of the breach were still very competently manned by Macedonian defenders, it became apparent that even if the tower did reach its objective, this in itself was by no means certain to win the siege. And it was already autumn.

Admirable as the continence of his army in Epirus had been, this self-restraint came at a price, in that the army was dependent on its supply trains to keep it fed. Philip was well aware of this, and had taken care to devastate the farmlands of Thessaly for exactly this reason. The Romans were initially dependent for their food on the efforts of Lucius Quinctius, the brother of Flamininus, who was in charge of the fleet. Together with Attalus, Lucius had concentrated his efforts on Euboea, where the pair had attacked Eritreia and eventually forced the surrender of the garrison and plundered the city. Their command of the sea allowed the combined Pergamene and Roman fleet to bring supplies to the Romans en route to Thessaly, but the location of Atrax was such that there was no harbour within range where sufficient materiel to supply an army could be offloaded.

Consequently the attack on Atrax would not have been possible had not Amynander and the Roman reinforcements with him taken the fortress of Gomphi, which opened a further supply line running from the Gulf of Ambracia through Athamania and Gomphi to Thessaly.

The capture of Gomphi had thus made possible the attempted advance toward the plain of Larissa and the sustained effort to crack the obdurate Atrax. But with the winter closing in, the stubborn defence of that fortress meant that any advance on Larissa would have to be postponed. With great reluctance, Flamininus was forced to conclude that there would be no swift conquest of Macedon in 198 BC. He pulled his troops back from the siege of Atrax, and took his army down through Thermopylae (which had enthusiastically surrendered to him on the way up) and to Phocis, with the intention of capturing a port where his army could receive sufficient supplies to pass the winter.

The Diplomatic Struggle

The Roman conquest of Phocis relied partly on diplomacy, though it was not so much the smoothly fluent Greek of Flamininus that carried the day but rather the readiness of his legionaries to make a horrible example of anyone (such as the unfortunate inhabitants of the town of Elatea) who refused to listen to him.

Furthermore, the presence of the Roman army next door concentrated the minds of the Achaeans, who were now forced to get off the fence of painful neutrality on which they had so far been perched. On the one hand, Macedon had done well by her ally of the past quarter century, helping the Achaeans against Sparta and Aetolia, and when, for example, the Romans had captured the town of Dymale, Philip had ransomed the population from slavery. He had also, in a gesture of good faith, handed all his southern possessions to the Achaeans for safe keeping. On the other hand, Philip's savage temper and contemptuous treatment had alienated many Achaean aristocrats and, over and above all else, there was a large and barbaric Roman army between Achaea and Macedonia. This army was in itself capable of flattening Achaea, leaving aside the fact that in the event of hostilities it would be vigorously assisted by the Spartans and Aetolians, with Attalus and

Lucius Quinctius ready to provide naval transport to whatever Achaean city was top of the list for destruction.

Perhaps, the more cautious of the Achaeans argued, the alliance with Macedon was in fact more a marriage of convenience, forced on them by their over-mighty protector, from which Achaea would do well to escape whilst the chance offered. Rome under Flamininus was offering the hand of friendship (with a bloody sword barely concealed in the other hand should that friendship be refused). Perhaps now was the time to consider a change of patrons and abandon Philip to his fate. Once the Romans offered the Achaean assembly mastery of Corinth (which they were currently poised to attack), the League agreed to throw its support behind the Romans.

The decision was far from unanimous. Representatives of several cities walked out of the meeting in disgust at this betrayal of Philip's cause, and the city of Argos went even further by withdrawing from the League altogether and welcoming a Macedonian garrison. The obstinacy of Argos inspired the Acarnanians to keep to their traditional alliance with Philip, which they did even as the Romans attempted the same degree of violence with which they had threatened the Achaeans. However, Acarnania was simply too small and far away to be more than a minor side-show to the Romans who were well aware that Flamininus' struggle with Philip would determine the fate of the rest of Greece. In fact even the Achaean vote was not considered so important that Flamininus felt he needed to take time off from running the war to attend the conference.

Given the importance of the Roman offer of Corinth in swaying Achaean opinion, it came as something of a shock to the southern Greeks when the Romans proved unable to deliver on their offer. Corinth stubbornly refused to be taken. The city had a substantial population of deserters from the Roman army who had fought for Hannibal and were desperate to avoid the brutal punishment of Roman justice. Even Romans supporting the Achaean troops were unable to overcome their fanatical resistance. When Philip managed to get a supporting garrison into the city, the Romans were forced to raise the siege and accept that Corinth and Argos, two of the most important cities of southern Greece, were firmly in Macedonian hands; no little compensation to Philip for his setbacks over the summer.

The Conference at Nicea

Philip had certainly been researching the violent barbarians who were currently assailing his land. Indeed, it would have been foolish not to have done so, and even his worst enemies had to concede that Philip was no fool.

The reason for the rapid changes of Roman command in recent years would not have escaped him. The men leading the legions against him were exercising consular or proconsular power which was renewed on an annual basis. Flamininus' term in office was coming to an end.

On the positive side, the Roman could show the Senate that he had crafted or maintained an anti-Macedonian alliance that included Pergamum, Athens, Aetolia and Achaea. He could point to the subjugation of Phocis and Epirus and successful raids on Euboea by his brother. However, Thessaly was back in Macedonian hands, and the heartland of Philip's kingdom had not even been touched. The Romans had been given a bloody nose at Atrax, and had seen Corinth and Argos fall squarely into the Macedonian camp. So the question being pondered by all the protagonists in the Macedonian war was: had Flamininus done enough to warrant having his command prolonged by the bestowal of proconsular power? Given that Rome liked quick, spectacular results, especially with a large and expensive force such as that which Flamininus commanded, the issue was certainly in the balance.

Philip reasoned, and correctly, that if he could not have the honour of crushing Macedon, the glory-loving Flamininus would not want that privilege to go to his successor. Rather he would settle for a diplomatic victory, and the honour of having brought Rome's war to a satisfactory, if not a glorious end. After the bruising campaign just past, Philip was prepared to offer more, and rightly believed that Flamininus would settle for less than he had demanded at the Aous. Consequently, ambassadors were sent to sound the Romans out about peace talks.

In fact, the Senate had already decided to prorogue Flamininus in his command 'until a successor should be appointed', but word of this had not reached the Roman commander, who took up Philip's offer of talks 'leaving himself the option of continuing the war if he stayed, or of making peace if he was to be superseded'.[46]

The conference took place at a small seaside city called Nicea on the Malian Gulf, not far from Thermopylae. Flamininus, Amynander and the leaders of Aetolia and Achaea were already present when the royal flagship gently ground on to the beach, and Philip came to the prow to open negotiations. Livy has reported the opening words of their meeting:

> 'If you would come down' suggested Flamininus, 'we could talk and listen to each other more conveniently. After all, what are you afraid of?'

> Philip replied 'I fear the Gods, and nothing besides. But I don't for
> a moment trust some of the people down there with you.'
> 'Surely the risk is the same for them as it is for you?'
> 'Indeed so. But the rewards are not. If it comes to treachery
> Phaeneas [the Aetolian leader] is not an equal exchange for Philip.
> The Aetolians will find themselves another chief magistrate soon
> enough. I would be harder to replace.' [47]

This brisk repartee reduced the conference to momentary silence, and
thereafter all concerned settled down to hard bargaining with Philip still
looking down from the prow of his ship. Flamininus stated those conditions
which were non-negotiable. Philip should withdraw all troops and garrisons
from Greece (though, significantly, this time Thessaly was not mentioned).
He should restore all captives he had taken and deserters he had received,
and give back to Rome those parts of the Roman protectorate in Illyria he
had seized since the Peace of Phoenice. (Another significant mention, as
Macedonian gains there are not described by any ancient narrators of the
war, yet were evidently substantial enough to have caused the Romans pain.)

Thereafter, the Roman allies stood in turn and one after another listed
their demands for reparations. Some Philip accepted, with others he stood
firm. To Attalus he pointed out that the Pergamene king had taken it on
himself to wage war on Macedon, and he should take the consequences for
his actions. However, he was prepared to help with the restoration of those
sites of religious significance devastated during the war. 'And thus', he
commented in a pointed aside to the others 'do kings speak with kings'.

The conversation with the Aetolians was predictably somewhat sharper.
When they repeated that Philip should pull his garrisons from Greece, the
king replied with the barely veiled threat that much of Aetolia was not,
technically speaking, part of Greece. Phaeneas roughly replied that he was
not interested in Philip's smooth evasions and linguistic traps. 'You must
submit to your superiors, or overcome them in battle'.

'That is evident, even to a blind man' replied Philip. (Phaeneas was blind,
and his mocking observation causes Livy to comment irritably in his text
that Philip was more satirical than suited the dignity of a king, and allowed
his humour too free a rein even in serious matters.)

That he was going to have to agree to the Roman demands sooner or later
was probably evident to Philip, in so far as he was straining his uttermost to
hold the Romans at bay, and had not yet even needed to engage with the
Achaeans, as he undoubtedly would have to if the war went on. At least these

had few demands to make of him, and Philip further played on Achaean consciences by having read aloud to them all the decrees passed by their people honouring him and his ancestors. Some of the areas Philip offered to withdraw from were already lost to him. For example, he had no hesitation in offering to restore to Ptolemy those Egyptian possessions he had seized in Thrace. His need for manpower had forced him to withdraw his garrisons from there already, and if Ptolemy wanted his possessions back he would have to fight the Thracians for them.

Philip initially refused to turn up for the next day's conference, claiming that he had been so grieved by the insolence and demands of Rome's allies he was unsure whether he wished to continue discussions at all. By this stratagem he was able to avoid talking till late in the day, and then, to speed up discussions, he talked to Flamininus alone. Philip was amenable to meeting all the other demands of the Greeks, but was determined if at all possible to hang on to the fortresses of the Acrocorinth (the citadel of Corinth), Demetrias and Chalcis.

Eventually, and despite the initial misgivings of the allies, it was agreed to submit the matter to the Roman Senate and abide by its decision. By way of surety, Philip agreed to withdraw his garrisons from those cities which he still held in Phocis. Given that in the event of war recommencing he would probably lose these garrisons anyway, and it was impossible to safely withdraw them with a hostile Roman army in the field, Philip's sacrifice here was hardly the diplomatic victory that some later historians seem to imagine. In fact the real losers at the conference were the allegedly-free cities of Greece which agreed to have their fate decided by the Roman Senate; an acknowledgement of a lost autonomy which, despite fine Roman words on the topic, they were never to regain.

In a shrewd move, Flamininus included Amynander in the delegation to Rome. His envoys contributed greatly to the future of Greece and Macedon by giving the senators a geography lesson which showed the strategic significance of the fortresses which Philip wished to retain. With ownership of these 'fetters of Greece' (as he himself described them) Philip would be well placed to recoup his past losses should the opportunity ever present itself. After their grim experience of the Hannibalic War, most senators had developed a keen appreciation of military strategy, and accordingly interrupted the presentation by Philip's delegation with a single question. Was Philip prepared unconditionally to give up these fortresses? The Macedonian delegation was unable to give this commitment, and the Senate accordingly rejected the peace terms.

Flamininus had sent private messages with the public delegation. If he was to be replaced in command, he urged his friends in the Senate to move for the acceptance of peace with Philip. If the Senate wished him to continue in office, then the terms should be rejected. Thus the blunt approach of the Senate to Philip's envoys showed that Flamininus' party had carried the day. He would retain his command, the peace would be rejected and the war would resume.

Even with this determined, there remained further diplomatic efforts before the renewed campaigning season. Philip needed a protector for Argos, rather as he had put his Greek possessions into the hands of the Achaeans at the start of the Roman assault. For Argos, he chose Nabis, the erratic king of Sparta, on the grounds that the Spartans and the Achaeans were already hostile. This proved an even worse choice than Achaea had been for other Macedonian holdings and protectorates, for Nabis not only treated Argos as a captured city to be despoiled at his pleasure, but also went on to obtain an accommodation with the Romans in any case.

Meanwhile, Flamininus launched a charm assault on Boeotia. Thebes was no longer the mighty city of yore, but having been devastated by the Macedonians and then settled with colonists from that country, it could be assumed to be thoroughly pro-Macedonian in its sentiment. Flamininus camped 5 miles from the city and on being met by the city fathers he accompanied them back to the city. At no time did he allow a decent pause in the conversation and pleasantries for the Thebans to bid him a polite farewell, and the embarrassed Thebans found that they had the choice of allowing Flamininus and his entourage within the walls or giving mortal offence to the man with the most powerful army in Greece.

Not that Flamininus appeared to have noticed that he was now in de facto possession of the city. He called a meeting of the council for the following day. At the meeting he argued that the Boeotians should join the anti-Macedonian alliance and did this so sincerely that he almost seemed to believe that the Thebans still had a choice. King Attalus also attended the meeting, but halfway through his address to the council he seemed to lose the thread of his speech and collapsed. It appears from reports of his condition that the king suffered a stroke. Partially paralysed, he was carried from the meeting, and later taken back to Pergamum where he died.

The Decisive Battle

News of the disability and later death of the man who had been a constant irritant for the past decade would have been cheerful tidings to a

Macedonian court which was currently short of good news. The envoys had returned from Rome with the Senate's rejection of the peace, and almost all of the Greek peninsula up to Thessaly was now firmly in the hands of Flamininus and his allies. Only Corinth and Chalcis remained in Philip's power, together with the Acarnanians who were still stoutly resisting the best efforts of Lucius Quinctius to bring them into line.

With Macedonian resources stretched to the limit, Philip knew that even holding the Romans off for another year would not be enough to save his kingdom. As Polybius remarks: 'The Macedonians had already used up the greater part of their resources'.[48] Whilst Rome had the power to keep fighting for year after year, Philip had barbarian tribes constantly probing his defences and threatening to overwhelm his ever-thinning border defences. And even if he did, by a heroic effort, manage to throw Flamininus back across the sea, all would have been for nothing if it left Macedon so weak that it was helpless before the predatory power of his fellow Hellenistic monarchs of Egypt and Seleucia. One way or another, Philip was determined to bring matters to a head in 197 BC.

He would give the Romans the head-on battle they so evidently desired. If he won, hopefully he would be able to negotiate peace from a position of relative strength. If he failed, then he would be at the mercy of the Romans, but unless he tried, this would probably happen anyway.

Even with his back to the wall, Philip planned to make the best of his diminished resources. He called virtually every male in his kingdom to arms, including 16-year-old boys and men well past military age. He thus collected an army which together with mercenaries and allies came to some 23,000 men. A goodly proportion of these were untried and untrained, something Philip tried diligently to remedy in the time available at his camp at Dium, where he mustered his army just after the spring equinox. He did not, however, recall the garrisons from his forts in southeastern Thessaly, since (as has been cogently argued) his intention was to force any Roman force driving toward Macedon to move inland rather than attempting to take these fortresses one by one.[49] Atrax had probably put Flamininus off Macedonian fortresses in any case, making the route of the Roman advance relatively predictable.

Flamininus meanwhile waited at Thebes, at first to care for his friend Attalus in his illness, but also to await the arrival of the Aetolians and Amynander. The 6,000 or so Aetolians and 2,000 Athamanians brought the Roman forces to about 26,000 men. Flamininus had also an innovation with which the Romans had been experimenting since the wars with Carthage.

Massinissa, king of Numidia, had sent the Romans ten elephants, and though somewhat nonplussed as to how to use the beasts, Flamininus had incorporated them into his army. With elephants and Greek allies, the Roman army was almost equal to the forces that Philip had at his disposal (though Philip's only pachyderm was his general Nicanor 'the Elephant', who was so nicknamed for reasons now lost.)

However, parity in numbers could not hide the fact that Flamininus' legionaries were veterans of the previous season's campaign and the war with Hannibal before that. On the other hand many of Philip's soldiers were about to see action for the first time, or had believed that they had seen it for the last time over a decade ago. As Flamininus moved up from Thebes, Philip moved down from Larissa, with both sides believing that they would meet near a minor city in Thessaly which, confusingly, was also called Thebes.

In the event, the two sides made contact even further north, near the town of Pherae on a pass in the Karadag mountain range. This was bad news for Philip, as he had counted on getting somewhat further south where he could receive supplies from both Thessalian Thebes (which remained loyal to Macedon despite Flamininus' best efforts to get the town betrayed to him) or from the fortress of Demetrias to the east.

In fact neither Flamininus nor Philip were particularly pleased with the site of their prospective battlefield, as Pherae abounded in broken ground and dry stone walls. The lightly-armoured Aetolians were in their element, and they distinguished themselves in the fierce opening skirmishes with Philip's Thracians, whilst both sides sent cavalry into the fight where they could. However, with neither phalanx nor legions able to properly deploy or fight, neither commander was prepared to risk a full-blown battle.

Philip took the initiative, breaking off and moving west towards Scotussa, on the headwaters of the River Platanorrema (Onchestus). Once he had resupplied himself there and secured his supply line to Larissa, he could pick a defensive position to suit himself from the multiplicity of potential sites in the Karadag range, and wait for Flamininus to come on to him. Flamininus had been waiting for some such move from the Macedonians. He could not move before Philip did, as this would leave Philip free to get to Demetrias, but as soon as he knew which way his cat was jumping, Flamininus mirrored the move so precisely that the two armies moved off 'almost as if by prearrangement'.[50]

That evening saw the Macedonians camped near Scotussa, with the Romans just over 10 kilometres to the south at the town of Eretria, with the hills of the Karadag range between them. Hereafter, matters become somewhat confused, as the ancient triumvirate of Polybius, Livy and Plutarch offer slightly contradictory accounts. And none of these accounts seems to bear much relation to the geography of the terrain which puzzled historians have later tramped over in an attempt to locate the exact site of the battlefield. The whereabouts of the epic confrontation between Philip and Flamininus is still uncertain, but certainly lies on one of the passes between Eretria and Scotussa.

Having watered his cavalry and fed his men, Philip moved southward cautiously from Scotussa, even as Flamininus moved north. Consequently, both armies finished camped on either side of a ridge called Cynoscephalae in that some of the rock outcrops topping the ridge resembled dog's heads if seen from the right angle.

Whatever the exact location, the two armies were not now far from the site of Pharsalus, which conforms to the fact that in the course of history most Greek battles are fought in a limited number of venues, as the constraints of strategy and landscape allow for little option. It is quite possible that both Philip and Flamininus would have chosen the relatively flat ground near Pharsalus as the site of preference for their decisive battle, but the closeness of their camps, combined with a sudden change in the weather meant that matters were taken out of their hands.

Philip, according to Plutarch, had been intending to make a decisive move the day before, and climbed on to a rise in the ground to address his men. However, he had barely launched into his oration before he was informed by horrified aides that he was standing on a grave tumulus, something which was both a terrible omen and an insult to the dead. Unsurprisingly, the king decided upon reflection to let things calm down before he committed his forces. Accordingly he posted light troops near the 'dog's heads' at the top of the ridge and waited for the weather to clear. The previous day had been damp, and the new morning (a few weeks after the vernal equinox according to most sources, though Livy, almost certainly mistakenly, seems to think the battle was fought in autumn) saw the hilltop blanketed in heavy mist.

Flamininus was eager to find what the Macedonians were up to and accordingly sent light infantry backed with slingers to scout the hilltops and to report back on the Macedonian dispositions, especially if Philip was moving east or west. Instead, the scouts ran into the Macedonian picket lines, and a vicious series of skirmishes broke out. The Roman light troops acted according to their orders, which was to find out where the main body of the Macedonian army was. It was, after all, quite possible that Philip had moved off and left this force to cover his retreat, but the only way to find out was to push the light troops aside. Accordingly the Romans sent back for reinforcements and began to push the Macedonians backwards off the hill. The Macedonians responded by sending to their commanders for reinforcements of their own, and once these arrived, they pushed the Romans back in their turn.

By now it was plain to both commanders that a major engagement was brewing, and they began frantically to muster their troops. Here, the advantage lay with Flamininus, as his troops formed up in maniples, literally 'handfuls' of men, with the maniples forming up three lines deep with about five feet of frontage between each man. It was a relatively loose tactical formation that could be drawn up swiftly.

Philip on the other hand, had to muster his men into their phalanx. This massive body of men was sixteen deep, and each soldier had only 3 feet of frontage. When assembled, the phalangites presented five rows of spears to the front, with the back ranks holding their spears at an angle to deflect missiles. It was a tight, inflexible formation that meant that every legionary in the advancing Roman ranks would face ten separate spear-points, but first the wielders of these spears had to be lined up and neatly put into their rows. With each man holding a 16-foot spear in a very confined space, the initial organization had to be precise, and could not be rearranged later.

Just to make matters worse, the hillside was not a perfect battleground for either the Romans or the Macedonians. The Romans had the unenviable job of fighting uphill against an advancing phalanx, and the phalanx had never yet been beaten in such circumstances. The Macedonians had their own problems, because the ground on their left was somewhat broken, and Nicanor, the general commanding that wing, was having a diabolical job getting his phalangites lined up.

Time was not on Philip's side; already the cavalry on both sides were engaged, and Philip was desperate not to lose the advantage of the sloping hillside to the advancing Romans. He also needed to take the initiative before the more flexible Roman force adapted to the terrain, spread out, and started working around his flanks. Consequently, he ordered the troops on his right flank to advance down the hillside, giving orders to Nicanor in no uncertain terms to follow as soon as he possibly could.

Coming downhill at the advancing Romans, the phalanx must have been absolutely terrifying. The Romans launched their *pila* but they were throwing uphill at tightly-packed armoured men who could and did use their hedge of spears to knock some of the missiles aside. With their missile weapons spent, all the Romans could do was to try to get within the hedgehog wall of spears. Once past the tip of the first rank of spears, the soldiers in the Macedonian front ranks were dependent on the men of the second rank to defend them, and if the Romans ever managed to get shield to shield with the Macedonians, they would be fighting nearly-defenceless men. However, getting there was easier said than done, and instead the Romans legionaries took hundreds of casualties and were forced to give ground.

Flamininus summarized the situation swiftly, and made the strategic decision to leave his men to it, and to concentrate on the Macedonian left, where Nicanor, though he was now advancing, had not got his men properly formed up, and the rough terrain was causing the phalanx immense difficulty. The phalanx, as Plutarch comments, was designed to fight as a single organism and the rough ground prevented it from doing so. The Roman elephants were also deployed against this discomfitted phalanx along with as many reserves as Flamininus was able to muster. Though elephants were not particularly effective against formed infantry, they did have a discouraging effect on cavalry, which needed careful training before the horses would approach them.

This meant that Philip's cavalry, already at a disadvantage on broken ground, were unable to prevent the Romans getting to grips and holding their own against Nicanor's phalanx, or possibly even forcing it to give ground. At this point the battle was finely balanced. Philip was clearly winning on his right, and keeping the Romans in check on the left. If he continued to press, eventually the Romans in front of him, already giving ground, would break, and he could begin the ponderous business of wheeling his phalanx to crush the Romans on his left between his men and Nicanor's. Flamininus in his turn was gambling on the strength and tenacity of his veteran soldiers, hoping that though they would give ground they would not break, whilst eventually his pressure on the Macedonian left produced results.

The different fortunes of the two wings produced the inevitable result. A gap opened up between the Macedonians under Philip pressing on downhill, and the already tardy forces of Nicanor, struggling to hold the Romans on broken ground. The connection between the two phalanxes had literally become unhinged. This was noted by a nameless but quick-thinking military tribune on the Roman side. Every legion had about half a dozen of these tribunes, often young aristocrats in their first military command, or experienced soldiers with previous experience in commanding auxiliary soldiers. This commander suddenly noticed that when looking left he was looking at the backs and shoulders of Philip's men as they advanced downhill.

In battle, military tribunes were expected to use their initiative, as this man decisively did. He pulled together a scratch force of some 2,000 men from the reserves and the right-hand portion of the forces fighting Nicanor's phalanx and took them in a charge across the centre of the battlefield to fall on the left flank and rear of Philip's phalanx.

This attack was a cruel thing to do to a tight-packed body of men intent on moving forward. The last thing a phalangite with a 16-foot pole wedged between the ranks of his fellow soldiers wanted to feel was the presence of a much more heavily-armed legionary at his back. And sadly, due to the unplanned nature of the battle, Philip had been unable to put in place the peltasts who usually had the job of guarding a phalanx from such assaults.

The Roman flanking force was fighting virtually-unarmed men, and though their force was tiny, it caused consternation out of all proportion to its size. The phalangites in the front rows were aware that something horrible was happening behind them, but could not even turn to find out what it was. Those further back saw the Romans chopping their way towards them and came to the only logical conclusion – there was no point in standing facing forward when death was closing in behind. If pikes were useless, then the best thing to do was to drop them and run. As soon as Philip's phalanx began to lose formation the legionaries at its front were able to push their way into the wall of pikes and close with the front ranks, thus fighting almost-defenceless men there as well.

Out-manouvered and clearly facing massacre, Philip's phalangites surrendered. This they did in the traditional way by raising their pikes to the vertical, thus signalling that they had taken themselves out of the battle. Either no-one had explained this to the legionaries, or they did not care. Accustomed to fighting barbarian Celts and Spaniards, the Romans fought by less-civilized standards than the Greeks, and were unaccustomed to the concept of whole units surrendering en masse. Their tradition did not allow for surrender in mid-battle, nor did they know how to accept it. Consequently they continued to slaughter men who were now making no attempt to defend themselves.

Once this dawned on the appalled phalangites, they took the only other option available, and ran for their lives. This meant that the Romans now overtook the flanks of Nicanor's plalanx, and they fell on that in turn. The battle dissolved into a manhunt, with the legionaries bounding after Philip's broken army, killing thousands, but finally taking prisoners to the tune of several thousand more. Flamininus had won his decisive victory, and the power of Macedon was broken.

Chapter 6

The Seleucids Come

The Coming of the Seleucids

The massive defeat at Cynoscephalae meant that Philip was forced to surrender. He could console himself that his position could have been even worse. The Aetolians followed up the success of the legions and came very close to capturing Philip, but chose instead to go on to plunder the Macedonian camp. This they did so comprehensively that there was nothing left for the Romans when they got back from chasing the last Macedonian remnants from the field. Unsurprisingly, this caused a certain amount of tension between Romans and Aetolians, and this ill-feeling got considerably worse over the following weeks.

The Romans might be a military superpower, but they were well behind in the arts. A pro-Aetolian epigrammist called Alcaeus of Messene, produced a verse which was soon current throughout Greece:

Naked and tombless see
Thirty thousand dead in Thessaly
Slain by the Aetolians and the Roman band
... Alas for mighty Macedon, and oh,
King Philip fled, fleet as a roe!

Whilst Philip replied briefly in verse:

Naked and leafless, passer-by, you've spied
The cross where Alcaeus will be crucified.

Flamininus had no such response at his disposal. The Aetolians, whose major contribution to events at Cynoscephalae had been to let Philip escape, appeared to be credited in the popular imagination with having won the battle, albeit with Roman assistance. To a dedicated glory-hound such as

Flamininus this was an affront of major proportions, and one for which the Aetolians were to pay dearly.

Philip retreated only as far as 'Tempe', a generic name for all the passes to Thessaly, but in this case referring to a town in a specific pass which he had strongly fortified before his advance into Thessaly. There, he set about rallying and organizing the survivors of the battle. Livy (who explicitly tells us he is quoting Polybius here) says that the Macedonians lost 8,000 men with another 5,000 captured. Assuming that a goodly number of other Macedonians had decided to abandon their military careers, one might estimate that Philip had some 7,000 remaining men immediately to hand, as well as others scattered about on garrison duty in Macedon and northern Greece. In short, he had been severely wounded, but was not yet down and out.

As if to prove this, the indomitable Acarnanians rejected a secret agreement that their leaders had made with Lucius Quinctius and pledged to remain at Philip's side, and the Corinthians launched an unexpected sally, though this was repelled by the Achaeans. In Asia, the garrison at the fort of Stratoniceia held off the Achaeans, though Perea was lost.

Philip was further encouraged by the message he received when he sent envoys to Flamininus to see about burying the dead.[51] The Roman commander, now at Larissa, granted Philip a truce of fifteen days, and told him to 'take heart'. This outraged the Aetolians, who indignantly assured Flamininus that there could be no peace in Greece until Philip had been killed and his kingdom ground into the dust. The politically-astute Amynander sniffed the wind and confined himself to the brief comment that perhaps the coming settlement should ensure that Greece could defend itself even if the Romans were absent. Flamininus agreed, and remarked that until now no-one had been talking about a war of extermination against Macedon, as though Philip's making war was an unforgivable crime. When Phaeneas, the chief Aetolian magistrate began to expostulate further, Flamininus curtly told him to 'stop ranting'.[52]

Worse was to come. Philip now announced that he was prepared to unequivocally accept the terms which the Romans had proposed at Nicea, and would prepare to hand over his fortresses and the cities he had taken from the Aetolians. Flamininus said that he would accept the surrender of these cities to Rome, thus taking Pharsalus, Enchinus, Larissa and a host of minor towns as Roman spoils of war. The Aetolians could take Thessalian Thebes, since that town had been so reluctant to surrender to him. When an appalled Phaeneas pointed out that Aetolia had only allied itself with Rome in order to regain the territory that the Romans had now annexed for themselves, he was curtly told that Aetolia had lost all rights to the area when it made peace in 206 BC. These cities had surrendered to Rome, and under Rome they would remain.

As to the rest, Philip should, for a start, pay an indemnity to 200 talents, and send his son Demetrius to Rome, partly as a delegate to urge the senate to confirm the peace terms, and partly as a hostage. A truce was declared for four months, and if the Senate rejected the peace, Philip would get his son and money back. However, as Rome was having major difficulties with the Gauls in Cisalpine Gaul, and had a major rebellion in Spain to contend with as well, Flamininus anticipated little difficulty in getting the Senate to see things his way.

Flamininus also argued that Macedon was needed as a bulwark in the north against barbarian tribes and did so as convincingly as anyone could who had so recently allied himself with the barbarian Dardanians, Illyrians and Thracians. Fortunately, the Dardanians proved his point by invading Macedon as soon as they heard about Cynoscephalae, but discovered that Philip's army still had teeth when he crushed them near Stobi.

All depended on what the Senate would decree and it escaped no-one that the Greeks, whose freedom from Macedon Flamininus claimed to have been fighting for, were now waiting for their fate to be decided in Rome.

The decision from Rome came with the accompaniment of ten commissioners who were to see that the terms were carried out. Macedonia had to pay a fine of 1,000 talents; half at once and the rest by instalments. Philip was to give up his fleet apart from five warships and a few minor ships. He was to surrender the Greek cities under his rule, and also withdraw his garrisons where he had these. These cities were to be handed over to the Romans before the Ismithian games. The senate also gave a list of cities in Asia from which Macedonian garrisons were to be withdrawn. The key phrase followed: 'All the rest of the Greeks were to be free and governed by their own laws'.

Given that Macedon was by and large at Rome's mercy, the terms were relatively mild. Freed from her substantial and expensive commitments in Greece, Macedonia could dedicate the reserves of the silver mines in the east to paying off the Roman indemnity, and Philip would have noted with relish that there appeared to be no restrictions on the size of his army. Though he had been forced to abandon some of his recent conquests in Illyria, Rome had not set any explicit limit to the nastiness he could inflict on the Illyrians, Thracians, and Dardanians. Nor, for that matter, if the Aetolians became too aggressive, was there anything to prevent him stamping hard on any part of their forces which ventured beyond the hazily defined borders of 'Greece'.

The Aetolians had noticed this too, and were vociferous in their complaints, pointing out that whilst the Romans had listed those towns in Asia which were to be free and autonomous, no such provision had been made for individual cities in Greece. It seems that the senate had intended that this was to be determined by the ten commissioners, but this did not stop the Aetolians from loudly proclaiming that the Greeks had been sold down the river by Rome. Since the Romans intended to keep the strategic fortresses formerly manned by Philip, the Greeks 'had merely exchanged masters'.

Meanwhile the Boeotians began to energetically test the bounds of their freedom even before it was formally proclaimed. As the region had been resettled by Macedonians after an earlier and bloody conquest, the towns of the region were not unexpectedly pro-Philip. So much so that many volunteers from there had gone to fight in the Macedonian army. When these returned after the war, the small but energetic pro-Roman party arranged to have their leaders massacred. Enraged, the people of Boeotia turned on the pro-Roman faction and drove them out.

This kind of vicious internal faction fighting was indeed, for Greece, the resumption of the status quo ante bellum, and the Greeks waited with bated breath to see what Flamininus was going to do about it. To their relief, he did virtually nothing apart from fining the Boeotians thirty talents for killing some Roman legionaries who had ventured into Boeotia to see what the fuss was about.

Better was to come. Polybius says that before the Ismithian festival it was a standard game among the chattering classes of Greece to try to foresee how the Romans would arrange the balance of power in Greece. Which cities would they free, which cities would they garrison, and which would they formally annex to Rome? It was no secret that the commissioners themselves were debating the very same questions, and their verdict was awaited with suspense. When it came, the news was better than the most optimistic Greeks had forecast.

The herald announced: 'Having defeated King Philip and the Macedonians in battle, the Senate of Rome, and the proconsul Titus Quinctius Flamininus leave free and without garrisons the following cities and peoples, which are to keep their ancestral laws and pay no tribute'. Into a breathless hush, the herald read the names 'Corinth, Phocis, Locris, Euboea, Phthiotic Achaea, Magnesia, Thessaly, and Perrhaebia.' As soon as the name 'Corinth' was read out, a hubbub arose that almost drowned out the names of the rest. Eventually the herald had to reread the list to reassure the incredulous listeners.

Essentially it meant that Greece as a whole was left free and autonomous, without being subject to Rome or Macedon in any way. Small wonder that the cheers were so deafening that 'crows fell dead from the sky' and that Flamininus came closer to being torn apart by adoring Greeks than he ever had been endangered by hostile Macedonians.[53]

Yet it must have crossed the minds of the more thoughtful Greeks that Rome (a state not famed for its altruism) must have had a reason for both treating Philip with relative leniency and allowing total autonomy to both mainland Greeks and their fellows in Asia. After all, Roman soldiers had fought and died for the freedom that Flamininus' herald was now proclaiming, and it took a very trusting nature to believe that such sacrifice had been based on a selfless love of liberty.

Nor did the cynical have far to look for an alternative explanation for Rome's conduct. This reason could be summarized with a single word - Antiochus.

Before going on to expand on this, it is necessary to recap what Antiochus had been up to whilst Rome and Macedon had been fully occupied with one another. The Romans had originally gone to war to prevent Philip and Antiochus tearing apart the Ptolemaic Empire between them. With Philip out of the picture, Antiochus had continued with this project on his own. He had defeated the Egyptians in a number of minor engagements and in a major clash at Panion. By 198 BC he was master of most of Phoenicia, Palestine and Gaza. He made the pragmatic decision that an invasion of Egypt proper was beyond his current resources, and began swiftly mopping up Ptolemaic possessions in Asia Minor and Thrace.

As Philip's difficulties increased, Antiochus began also to absorb cities and peoples once allied with Macedon, effectively abandoning any pretence of maintaining his former alliance. Even as Rome and Macedonia prepared to square up for their showdown at Cynoscephalae, Antiochus was mustering his forces in Antioch. That spring he drove northward and westward with his army, at the same time sending ambassadors ahead to assure the Romans that his advance in their direction was in no way intended to bring succour to Philip. To sweeten the atmosphere even further, Antiochus announced that he had not even any hostile intentions toward the Ptolemaic possessions in the area. This was also partly to assuage the fears of the Rhodians who had no wish to see trade in the region disrupted further than it had already been.

Instead, the ruler of the Seleucid Empire claimed to be reasserting his authority over those parts of his western dominions which had been allowed to go their own way whilst Antiochus and his predecessors had been otherwise engaged. This was a transparent diplomatic fiction which neither persuaded nor reassured anyone. However, the Rhodians were brought over to Antiochus' point of view by being allowed to take several minor cities on the Anatolian mainland under their 'protection' and also do the same with the far-from-minor prizes of the city of Halicarnassus and the island of Samos. Other cities were pacified by the fact that all Antiochus seemed to want from them for now was acknowledgement of his suzerainty.

However, neither Pergamum nor Bithynia, both former Seleucid possessions and now minor but flourishing kingdoms in their own right, could see the Seleucid presence in the region as anything but a major threat. As a loyal ally of Rome, Pergamum appealed for Roman support, and it was partly to create a buffer zone between Pergamum and Antiochus that Rome had listed those cities of Asia which it explicitly declared to be free and autonomous.

That the Romans were prepared to make a similar buffer zone out of the whole of Greece shows how seriously they took the Seleucid threat. The relatively-mild treatment of Philip showed Roman understanding that, now he was severely weakened, Antiochus was as much - or more - of a threat to Macedon than he was to Rome, and that Macedonian and Roman interests were currently aligned in wishing to see Antiochus kept as far to the east as possible.

Plutarch claimed that Rome had timed its aggression in the east perfectly, 'defeating Philip's last hopes in Greece before Antiochus developed his first', a statement which blandly overlooks the fact that were Philip not solidly defeated, Antiochus would probably not have developed any ambitions in that direction anyway. But with Macedon on the ropes, Antiochus seems to have scented an opportunity in Greece. It did not help the fast-growing Roman paranoia about Antiochus' intentions that the Seleucid ruler had recently acquired a new advisor: Hannibal. The great Carthaginian general had been driven from his homeland when jealous rivals complained he was conspiring against Rome, and he had found shelter in the court of Antiochus. The thought of Hannibal's genius combined with Seleucid military might sent shivers down more than a few Roman spines.

Meanwhile the Roman settlement of Greece went on apace. Freedom for the Greeks evidently did not include the freedom to arrange their own affairs. Aetolia was outraged to find that Thessaly was made an independent state, and that Larissa was included within Thessaly's boundaries. The Aetolians were confirmed in certain minor conquests; notably the cities of Dolopia and Thessaliotis. Rather than being satisfied with this, the Aetolians indignantly pointed out that Amynander had received proportionately far more, including the strategic fortress of Gomphi which he had captured with Roman help in 198 BC. Nor had the Aetolians been granted Pharsalus, or Echinus, a town which they insisted had been promised to them by the Romans as long ago as 212 BC.

The Romans had not in fact ruled on the fate of these towns, partly to avoid inflaming Aetolian sentiment any further. They needed peace in Greece, for the next diplomatic crisis was already looming. Antiochus and the Seleucid army had landed in Europe.

Rather like Philip before him, there seems little evidence that Antiochus had any personal animus against Rome. Like any Hellenistic monarch, Antiochus was pursuing every Hellenistic ruler's basic opportunistic, expansionist policy, and he had seen in Philip's embarrassment a chance to consolidate his position in Anatolia and points west. The Roman insistence that Antiochus respect the freedom of the Greek cities in Asia Minor was regarded as an unwarranted interference in Antiochus' sphere of influence, but not as a major impediment to his actions, in that there were plenty of other cities to which his empire had a legitimate claim, albeit a claim which had gone without enforcement for generations.

One such city was Lysimacheia in Thrace. Antiochus' claim on this city was solid, in that it had been founded by Lysimachus, one of the generals of Seleucus, the man after whom the Seleucid Empire was named. As late as the 230s BC the city had been under Seleucid control, until the Macedonians had taken it over during one of their more expansionist moments. With the withdrawal of Philip's garrisons due to the crisis of the Roman invasion, the Thracians (who strongly objected in principle to Greek cities on their territory) attacked and devastated the city.

Now Antiochus was busily rebuilding the place, whilst his army cleared the indignant Thracians from the hinterland. Antiochus could blandly claim that he was restoring an ancient part of his empire's heritage, leaving free every city the Romans had told him to leave alone. At the same time he continued to build Lysimacheia into a staging post for a potential invasion of Greece and Macedon.

If anyone was taken in by Antiochus' disingenuous propaganda, Philip certainly was not. Well aware of the predatory intentions of his former ally, he was well prepared to discuss the matter of the Seleucid presence in

Europe with the head of the Roman commission for the settlement of Greece, a man called Gnaeus Cornelius. As has been noted before, even during those moments when their armies were poised to slaughter one another, Philip and the Roman aristocracy got on rather well. When Roman and Macedonian interests came together, the meeting was positively cordial. So well did it go that the two sides, which just the year before had been locked in combat, agreed to become allies. That this news would cause collective apoplexy amongst the Aetolian leadership was no doubt a welcome bonus to Philip.

Philip was probably also extracting some enjoyment from watching someone else now getting drawn into the snake pit of Greek politics. Problems began almost at once as Flamininus' enforcement of the freedom of Greece drew Rome inexorably into conflict with Philip's enemy, Nabis of Sparta. Nabis felt he had earned Argos fairly and squarely by stabbing Philip in the back after being given the city for safe keeping, and he was furious when the Romans quite literally told him to get out of town. Nabis refused, and pointed out he was a free Greek exercising his freedom. He was gambling that Flamininus was itching to get back to Rome and celebrate his triumph and would not be prepared to waste his time in a minor Peloponnesian War.

That Flamininus was prepared to remain in Greece to sort out Nabis shows how seriously Rome took Antiochus' occupation of Lysimacheia. With a war against the Seleucids looming, the last thing Rome wanted was the treacherous and unpredictable Nabis interfering with the stability of Achaea and Roman supply ships as they made their way east along the already-tricky route around the Peloponnese.

The start of 195 BC was thus spent in edgy diplomacy. Nabis was seeking a confederation of Sparta, Aetolia and Antiochus against Rome. The Aetolians appeared willing, but Antiochus was waiting for the Romans to make good their promise to depart from Greece before he made any further moves. Consequently, when the Roman commissioners came to see him, the Seleucid monarch was polite but unyielding. When the Romans demanded the freedom of the Greeks in Asia, he asked how much discretion this allowed him in deciding the liberty of Italian cities. Anyway, the question was moot, as Antiochus himself had decided, independently of the Romans, that the Asiatic Greeks should be allowed their liberty. And, no, he would not withdraw from his ancestral city of Lysimacheia just to please the commissioners.

The Romans then turned to the subject of Antiochus' aggression against

Ptolemy, and received their most stinging setback yet. The Seleucid ruler blandly informed them that Egypt had no complaint to make against him: indeed, Antiochus' daughter Cleopatra was about to wed Ptolemy V. As part of the wedding settlement, Egypt had agreed to relinquish her Syrian, Asian and Thracian dependencies to Antiochus. In compensation the Egyptians were to receive the revenues, but not the suzerainity, of their former possession of Coele-Syria. That Ptolemy had been forced to these terms by sheer exhaustion after years of Seleucid pressure was neither here nor there. The Romans were forced for the moment to leave Antiochus be, and turned their frustration upon Nabis.

From Laconian War to Seleucid War

In May 195 BC Flamininus called a meeting of Greek states and asked them what was to be done about Argos, from which Nabis militantly refused to depart. The Aetolians, practically foaming at the mouth, demanded to know whether the liberation of Pharsalus and Echinus was also up for discussion. However, flattered to be asked their opinion, the other Greek states applied themselves to the question, and concluded that Nabis was a blot on the bright landscape of liberated Greece, and ideally should be removed altogether.

Sparta traditionally had two kings at one time, but Nabis had assassinated his colleague, and launched a campaign of terror against the state's other leading citizens. By plundering the temples he had assembled a large mercenary army which he supplemented with freed slaves and helots. He had used this force as an instrument of domestic terror and foreign expansion, and was, by some margin, Greece's best-hated man.

Consequently a virtual pan-Hellenic army mustered against the recalcitrant Spartan leader. The Achaeans, inveterate enemies of Nabis, made up the bulk of the army, but most other states (with the notable exception of Aetolia) furnished contingents. There were even 1,500 Macedonians present as representatives of Philip's enthusiasm for the project. Lucius Quinctius, still commander of the Roman fleet, began the naval blockade of Sparta. He was joined by Bithynian and Pergamene ships, and also eighteen warships from Rhodes. It is interesting that the trading state of Rhodes, currently aligned with Antiochus, was joining the attack against Sparta, a potential Seleucid ally. This demonstrates the veracity of Roman claims that Nabis was sponsoring wholesale piracy in the Aegean Sea.

Whilst the land forces of the coalition ineffectually besieged Argos, the naval force attacked Gythaeum (which served as a port to inland Sparta rather as Piraeus did Athens). The attackers went about their business with considerable vehemence, and captured the port despite a spirited Spartan defence. This forced Sparta to the negotiating table, where the Greeks, rather as the Aetolians had done with regard to Philip, insisted that nothing but the total eradication of Sparta was required. Even the far milder terms of Flamininus were rejected by the Spartans, who prepared to stand siege.

Flamininus was not prepared for a drawn-out campaign, and decided to skip the siege in favour of an all-out assault on the city with the Greek forces supplemented by the rowers from his navy. Some 50,000 men flung themselves against the walls of Sparta. It had once been Sparta's boast that the only walls of their city were the men who defended it, but prudence and recent events had added to these walls of stone defending all the accessible points of approach. These the Romans attacked in three divisions, using a *testudo* formation to defend against missiles thrown from the rooftops as they pushed into the city. In desperation, the Spartans set fire to the buildings through which the Romans were advancing, and so forced at great cost a temporary Roman withdrawal. Flamininus began to muster for another attempt on the city, this time with the help of his siege train which had just arrived. However, a second assault was not required, for a chastised Nabis announced himself prepared to submit to Flamininus' terms.

These were not unduly harsh, though they required Nabis to give up almost all his conquests and territories apart from Sparta itself, pay a 500 talent indemnity, and hand over his son as a hostage and guarantor of the peace. Argos was not included in the peace. Tired of waiting for the Romans to do the job, the citizens had liberated themselves almost as soon as Nabis' son-in-law, the tyrannical Pythagoras, had left Argos with reinforcements for the Spartans. The Romans now delivered on an earlier promise by making Corinth a full member of the Achaean League, whilst the Laconian coastal cities once subject to Nabis were to be administered by the League without actually becoming members of it.

One by one, Roman garrisons pulled back from the great strategic fortresses of Greece. Demetrias in Thessaly was the last to be evacuated, and once Flamininus had put Thessaly and Philip's other former possessions on a stable and independent footing, he bade an emotional farewell to Greece, leaving not a single Roman soldier behind him. He took great satisfaction in thus disproving Aetolian claims that Rome intended to permanently occupy Greece, remarking that all men could now see that lying was not a Roman habit, but an Aetolian speciality. In fact Flamininus left Greece considerably freer of Romans than when he arrived, for many of Hannibal's prisoners of war had been sold by the Carthaginians in Greece, and Flamininus had conscientiously sought these out and liberated all he could find. These men (at least 2,000 of them) returned with him as further ornaments to the splendid triumph which Flamininus intended to be the high point of 194 BC in Rome.

Flamininus landed in Brundisium, and marched his army up through Italy in what amounted to a huge triumphal procession. Outside Rome (for a general under arms was forbidden to enter the city itself) he met the Senate and gave them a personal account of the campaign. His triumphal entry into the city took three days. Day one displayed captured statues of marble and bronze to a populace still awed by the superiority of Greek skills in the arts. This was accompanied by a parade of the armour and weapons captured from Philip's soldiers. Day two saw the booty of the campaign, gold and silver weighing tens of thousands of pounds, in every form, from coins to statuettes to vases and simple heaped piles of ingots. On the third day came 114 gold crowns donated by grateful Greek cities, and a parade of prisoners and hostages, including Demetrius, son of Philip, and Armenes, son of Nabis. Finally, to an ecstatic reception, came Flamininus and his army, together with the freed Roman ex-slaves. It was probably the kind of return that Flamininus had dreamed of when he set out for Greece in 198 BC.

But the Greece which Flamininus had left 'free' behind him was founded on a fundamental cultural misunderstanding. The Greeks understood freedom as *eleutheria* – liberty to do as they wished. But in liberating the Greeks from Philip, the Romans felt they stood in relation to the Greek states as a patron to a freedman; that is, the latter's freedom was constrained by strong obligations owed to the liberator. Also, a number of Greek states did not feel particularly liberated. The harshness of Philip's rule had been felt unevenly, and some states, forced to be pro-Macedonian by Philip's garrisons, had been thoroughly despoiled by the Romans collecting the money and statues which had so adorned Flamininus' triumph.

And of course, despite having brought many of their problems on their own heads by their undiplomatic handling of Flamininus, the Aetolians felt, with some degree of justification, that they had been hard done by. No other state in Greece had fought the Macedonians so long or so hard, and few had suffered so much as a result. Yet the Aetolians had benefitted less than most from the peace. They were further irked to discover that the Romans, admiring the obdurate support and loyalty of the Acarnanians for Philip, had made a particularly lenient peace with this people and guaranteed their territorial integrity against Aetolian aggression.

Matters rested in this uneasy state for two years. Flamininus' settlement of Greece had been even-handed, in that almost every major state felt that in some way it had been short-changed in favour of the others. However, the country was too bruised from the experience of hosting the recent contest against Macedon to do much. Philip himself was quiescent, diligently rebuilding his resources against the inevitable clash which he foresaw between Macedon and Rome, Antiochus or both.

Antiochus was consolidating his recent gains, and the Romans had their hands full with the Gauls in northern Italy and absorbing their recent gains from Carthage in Spain. The eastern Mediterranean was calm, but everyone knew it was the calm before the storm.

The first cracks in the peace came with renewed diplomatic contact between Antiochus and Rome. Antiochus was becoming irritated at the continued presence of free cities within his domains, and wanted the Romans to withdraw their sponsorship of these cities. Rome was amenable, but the Senate's price was higher than what Antiochus was willing to pay; namely that the Seleucids withdraw from Thrace and quit Europe altogether. Both Romans and Seleucids were peacefully inclined towards each other, but the issues between them forced them apart. Hannibal was also a factor. He is said to have asked Antiochus for 10,000 foot and 1,000 cavalry. With these he would raise Carthage against Rome, reinvade Italy and forever put an end to Antiochus' problems.

Antiochus, now 50 years old, was no longer an impetuous youth. He needed to decide whether to push his luck in Europe, or rest content with his many accomplishments so far. He appears to have settled for testing the waters in Greece, where many of those dissatisfied with the Roman settlement looked to the Seleucid Empire as a counterweight to their over-mighty protectors. The Aetolians, naturally, took the lead with their anti-Roman sentiments, and even suggested to Philip and Antiochus that the pair should ally with Aetolia against Rome; a suggestion which Philip rejected with incredulity. The Aetolians were received more sympathetically by Antiochus, and with enthusiasm by Nabis of Sparta. Despite Philip's reluctance, the Aetolians felt that they had the foundations of a handy anti-Roman coalition in place.

Nabis was in fact already jumping the gun somewhat. He had reclaimed several of the coastal cities officially under Achaean administration by the simple method of paying for pro-Spartan revolts in each, and now he pushed his luck even further by attempting to retake Gythaeum by an outright attack on its Achaean garrison. Led by Philopoemen, their great commander, the Achaeans rose to the challenge and flung themselves into conflict with Sparta, despite the best efforts of Flamininus who had returned to Greece in an attempt to hold his settlement together.

With another war against Nabis inevitable, the Romans dispatched a fleet under the praetor Atilius Serranus. Romans and Achaeans quickly retook Gythaeum whilst a furious Philopoemen proceeded to ravage everything Spartan outside the city's walls. With the wings of Nabis once again clipped, the Romans again enforced the status quo ante bellum by ordering the Achaeans to respect the Roman peace, though well aware that this added the Achaeans to the ranks of those simmering against Roman interference.

In fact the only state in the region which enjoyed ever-warmer relations with Rome was Macedon. From being a hostage Demetrius had turned into a charming and persuasive advocate for the Macedonian cause, and their own difficulties with what they considered the fractious and ungrateful peoples of Greece could only make the Romans more sympathetic to Philip's previous experience as hegemon of the region.

All this was noted with interest by Antiochus who now sent a delegate called Menippus to the Aetolians. In the spring of 192 BC, Menippus announced to the Aetolian assembly that, like the Romans, Antiochus too stood firmly by the principle of Greek liberty. Also like the Romans, he was prepared to back his support with military force if need be. This put the Romans in something of a quandary, since they could hardly object to someone else agreeing so enthusiastically with their own stated objectives. At least, not without explicitly admitting that it was their own interference with Greek liberty that Antiochus might object to.

Nevertheless, at this point the Romans seem to have accepted that war with Antiochus was inevitable. Given that Hannibal was in the court of Antiochus, the first step which the Romans took was to look to the defence of Italy, and to secure it against a Seleucid invasion which would see Hannibal back in his old stamping-grounds of southern Italy.

The Aetolians were confident that Antiochus would come to their aid in any confrontation with Rome. Now they set about engineering that confrontation. First they sent reinforcements to Nabis in Sparta. Then, when it appeared that Nabis was unwilling to go another round with the Romans and Achaeans, these reinforcements killed the king and attempted to set up their own government in his place. However, the killers had deeply misjudged the popular mood, and the Aetolians were ejected by the infuriated Spartans amid wild rioting. In the end, after months of near-anarchy and constant clashes with the Achaeans, Philopoemen and his army took advantage of the chaos to occupy the city, which they immediately set about de-Spartanizing by replacing the city's distinctive institutions with those more standard elsewhere in the Achaean League.

Despite this initial setback, the Aetolians continued to follow their master plan. They recognized that Corinth and its formidable acropolis were firmly in Achaean hands, but attempted lightning strikes to seize both Chalcis and Demetrias. Their strikes were double-edged, with Aetolian troops backing up the subversion of the leading figures within these great strategic fortresses. The attempt on Chalcis failed, but the Aetolians were able to take control of Demetrias, perhaps the greatest prize of all. Antiochus had now a magnificently furnished and equipped fortress, perfectly positioned to receive him into Greece from his jumping-off point in Lysimachaea in Thrace. If Appian is to be believed, the Aetolians also encouraged Antiochus by exaggerating the size of their own army and adding that Philip of Macedon was angry with the Romans and eager to join the anti-Roman coalition.[54]

However, the Aetolians had forced Antiochus' hand, and his army was simply not ready. It had a number of lively rebellions in Thrace to keep it occupied, and the majority of the Seleucid host had yet to be mustered. Yet there was no time for delay. Autumn was fast approaching and the Aetolians could only hold Demetrias by themselves for a limited period. A decision had to be made and the opportunity to make himself master of Hellas was irresistible to a Hellenistic monarch. Gathering his nerve and 10,000 infantry, together with half a dozen elephants and 500 horse, Antiochus set out at once for Greece, landing near Demetrias, and making his way from that fortress to Lamia in southern Thessaly, where he joined forces with his Aetolian allies. Like the Romans before him, Antiochus loudly proclaimed that he had come to give support to the freedom of Greece. But were the Greeks ready for another liberator?

The Thermopylae Campaign

Even the Aetolians were less than united on this topic. A more moderate faction argued that Antiochus should be kept as a counterweight to Rome, and that now the Seleucids were physically present, the Romans would have to listen to Aetolian grievances and renegotiate their settlement of Greece. However, the war party, led by a hot-head called Thoas, argued that the Romans had betrayed Aetolia time and again, and only war would see them thrown out of Hellas forever. Sentiment against Rome was high in Aetolia and the views of Thoas carried the day.

The garrison of Chalcis, still bitter about the Aetolian attempt to take the fortress by stealth, coolly informed Antiochus that they welcomed him, and the Aetolians, as friends. While they thanked both parties for their concern, they currently had no-one they needed liberating from. Now, could both Antiochus and the Aetolians please demonstrate the sincerity of their friendship by going away? Even Thessaly, currently hosting the Seleucid king and his army, adamantly refused to recognize him.

Boeotia temporized, perhaps because its citizens were waiting to see how Philip would react. Its people informed the Seleucid king that if he came to them personally, they would consider what he had to say. Athens wavered until the leader of the pro-Seleucid party was banished, and then came down firmly on the Roman side. Antiochus knew he could never persuade the Achaeans to take on the Romans and he asked only their neutrality. So important was the Achaean decision that Flamininus was there in person. When the Seleucid ambassador listed all the horsemen, bowmen and infantry the king had at his disposal, Flamininus remarked that this reminded him of a dinner he had been at recently where the meat had many different flavours, but in the end it was all pork. The enemy were just Syrians, he told the assembly, and Greeks and Romans together could defeat them.

Thus, despite Aetolian assurances that Greece was ready to rise against its oppressor, the only outright supporter of the new arrivals apart from the Aetolians themselves was Amynander, who inevitably changed sides to align himself with those he judged as the probable victors.

So far Antiochus was not committed to the point where some frantic diplomacy might not have extracted him. However, despite the lack of enthusiasm he had encountered so far, he now began liberating Chalcis by force. Once again he was being hurried by events, as it was necessary to act before Achaean reinforcements could reach there. A small Roman force was already at Delium in Euboea, and as war was not declared, they were taken completely by surprise when a pro-Seleucid force fell upon them and massacred them. Antiochus arrived outside Chalcis soon afterwards with his entire army and the garrison reluctantly opened the gates to him. The rest of Euboea followed the example of Chalcis and submitted to the invader. When Antiochus turned up there personally, Boeotia also abandoned its reservations and declared for his cause. However, even the defection of Boeotia was not enough to force the Epirots off the fence. They declared their enthusiasm for Antiochus' mission, but said that they were first in the firing line when the Romans came, and would prefer not to endure the consequences.

For no-one doubted that when news of these developments reached Rome, war would be declared and the legions would return. Consequently Antiochus began to consolidate as much of Greece into his power as he could before the Romans arrived. (In fact the Romans had already sent a small force to Macedonia under the praetor Marcus Baebius to reinforce Philip's army and ascertain the Macedonian king's intentions.) It was now late in the campaigning season, but the energetic Antiochus immediately commenced operations in Thessaly with the intention of bringing at least this region under his control before winter.

This was the last straw for Philip. Despite the worries of the Romans there was no way he was going to ally himself with the annoying Aetolians and the monarch who was pre-empting the dominance of Greece which he considered Macedon's natural right. Seleucid incursions in Thrace he endured because he could not do otherwise, but Philip regarded Thessaly as almost an adjunct to his own kingdom, and interference there was intolerable. It did not help that the Seleucids advanced to Cynoscephalae and gave a magnificent burial to the Macedonian dead, something Philip had not been able to do himself. It was probably this last humiliation which pushed him squarely into the Roman camp. Accordingly, he received hospitably such Romans as fled from Thessaly, and assured Baebius of his firm support, both diplomatic and military. In return the Romans guaranteed that Philip would do his utmost for them by promising him that whatever towns he conquered from the Seleucids, he could keep. (This incidentally also provided those towns which were not keen to return to Philip's rule with an incentive to resist the Seleucids for as long as possible.)

Larissa held out against attempts by Amynander and the Seleucids to seize control of the city. It helped that a large Roman force had appeared nearby, and its camp fires both encouraged the Larissans and discouraged the attackers. In fact this was a small Roman force detached from Marcus Baebius' troops in Macedonia which had lighted a large number of fires to make its numbers seem greater. By the time the ruse was discovered, the season had closed in and operations ceased for the winter of 192/191 BC. Antiochus had found himself a new wife in Euboea, and the Romans spread the propaganda message that he was gambolling through the winter whilst he should have been organizing for war. The reality was that both sides were preparing to bring in substantial armies. It seemed certain that the coming summer would see a decisive battle for the control of Greece.

Campaigning started early that year, with the bemused Thessalians treated to the sight of the soldiers of the Macedonian king and Roman praetor fighting shoulder to shoulder. The pair had retaken several minor towns and the important fortress of Gomphi when their campaign was abruptly given massively-extra heft by the arrival of 20,000 men, 2,000 horse and 15 elephants under the command of the consul Acilius Glabrio. Amynander's desultory siege of Larissa came to an abrupt end, with many of his soldiers captured in a sudden swoop by Philip's Macedonians. In the same raid, Philip also captured his namesake, a Philip whom Amynander had been hoping to set up as a puppet in Macedon. This man Philip treated with elaborately sarcastic courtesy, referring to him as 'brother monarch' before shipping him off in chains to the Romans. Amynander's men also received every courtesy, being freed without ransom and told to make their way home to Athamania, where they were assured that the Macedonian army would shortly be coming to visit them.

Philip delivered on that promise soon afterwards, taking Amynander's kingdom from him almost without a fight. The Athamanian king did not trust the loyalty of his subjects sufficiently to even muster a defence, but fled into exile with his family and treasure as soon as he heard of Philip's approach. The Romans under Glabrio were able to dispense with Macedonian assistance as Antiochus was only managing to get reinforcements across the stormy Aegean Sea in dribs and drabs. So far, the 5,000 or so men Antiochus had received from Asia Minor barely served as replacements for the garrisons he had lost in Thessaly.

Almost all of Thessaly had fallen to the Romans in less than three weeks. It was now apparent to Antiochus that if he was to stop the Romans from conquering all of Greece, he would have to do the job with the forces currently at his disposal. Fortunately there was one point where an attacker coming from the north could be held at bay, even by fewer defenders than he had available: the pass at Thermopylae, where the Spartans had famously held back the myriads of the Persian king.

Antiochus appealed for help to the Aetolians, not unreasonably pointing out that they were the reason for his difficulties in the first place. However, there was now a strong Roman army in the field. Many Aetolians had seen this army fighting from close up, and were deeply unwilling to face it head-on. This led to a certain cooling of Aetolian martial ardour, and the fact that Philip's army was now settling into neighbouring Athamania also meant that the Aetolians were unwilling to commit troops to the other side of Greece. Having pillaged the country twice before, Philip was well acquainted with the route to the principal cities of Aetolia, and the Aetolians were understandably keen not to have him back there yet again. All they could do for Antiochus was to send 4,000 men. Antiochus correctly interpreted this lukewarm Aetolian response as a lack of enthusiasm for the coming clash, and put the Aetolians on garrison duty. So, 2,000 men were sent to guard the western approaches to Thermopylae by way of Heraclea at Trachis, and the others were put in highly defensible positions around Mount Kallidromon, the mountain which dominates the passage between Thermopylae and the sea. At Thermopylae itself, Antiochus' own men were entrenched behind a double line of fortifications supported by siege engines.

For a while, it seemed that what Leonidas had done with his 300 Spartans, Antiochus and his 10,000 were going to do more easily. The Romans were attacking the Seleucid phalanx on a narrow frontage with no chance of outflanking it. In fact the opposite was the case, as the Aetolians and Antiochus' light troops held the heights and bombarded the attacking Romans with rocks and javelins as they tried vainly to force the Seleucid line. For a while, indeed, the Romans were in danger of being encircled, with the immovable phalanx before them, the sea to the left, and the light troops of the enemy closing in on the right. The Aetolians at Heraclea, scenting opportunity, were also moving from their position to threaten the Roman camp from behind.

However, the Romans had read their history and knew that the way to win at Thermopylae was to turn the pass with a force that made its way by night through the paths over Mount Kallidromon. This task was entrusted to two separate groups. One was led by Lucius Valerius Flaccus, who attempted to displace the Aetolians from Mount Tichius. The other group was led by Marcus Cato, the man who was later to make his name with Rome and posterity as Cato the Censor, who was to take the route over Kallidromon itself. For a while it seemed as though the outflanking forces' efforts would be a complete disaster. Valerius appears not to have even managed to reach his objective, and Cato's guide got lost. After hours wandering in circles through the dark, his men were becoming downcast and disillusioned.

In the end, Cato and one of his lieutenants scouted the way personally, and as the dawn came they received extra guidance from the noise of the main Roman force making another attempt on the pass. Cato with his 2,000 men swarmed over a defensive position held by 600 Aetolians, and fell on the rear of the Seleucid force. At the same moment Antiochus lost his teeth to a well-hurled stone, probably flung by one of Cato's soldiers on the heights. With their general somewhat distracted by his injury and the Romans pressing on all sides, the Seleucid army broke and fled, hounded by the enthusiastic and vindictive Romans. Now the same narrow passages that had made it difficult for the Romans to advance made it hard for the Seleucids to escape, especially as the Seleucid elephants chose this moment to become obstinate, and blocked some of the few exits remaining. In the panic and crush that resulted, as many of the Seleucids were trampled to death by their own side as fell to Roman swords.

The Romans had all day and the following night to follow up their victory, and first legionaries and then cavalry pursued the remnants of the Seleucid army as far as Scarpheia, some 8 miles away in Locris. Apart from some 500 men whom he kept with him as he fled the battlefield, Antiochus lost his entire army. The king paused briefly to assess the situation at Elatea, and realized that as far as his Greek adventure was concerned, his position was undoubtedly hopeless. The loss of 10,000 men was a painful blow, but far from a fatal one to a king who could call over 100,000 men to arms should the need arise. However, those 100,000 were in Asia Minor, and Antiochus had not even enough men in Greece to mount a decent rearguard action. Indeed, even now the Romans were manoeuvring to cut off his retreat. Antiochus did the only thing possible. Pausing at Chalcis only long enough to pick up his bride, Antiochus fled back across the Aegean Sea to Ephesus.

With magnificent opportunism, the Aetolians took advantage of the Roman distraction with their victory over the Seleucids at Thermopylae to try to loot the Roman camp. This attempt seems to have been initially successful, but a swift Roman reaction forced the Aetolians to withdraw. In the weeks that followed, Phocis, Locris and Boeotia fell back under Roman control without a fight. The Achaeans had now mustered their army and were commencing operations against the Aetolians even as Philip started to move against Aetolian positions in Thessaly. With Antiochus chased out of Greece, 20,000 Roman soldiers had the rest of the summer to concentrate on the last remaining enemy state in Greece. Once again the Aetolians were friendless in a very hostile world.

Chapter 7

After Philip

The Aetolian War

The Romans decided that they may as well start right where they were, and turned their attention on Heraclea, to which city the Aetolians had retreated after their attempt on the Roman camp. There was a considerable amount of rivalry in the siege which followed, for not only were Glabrio's lieutenants, Baebius, Appius Claudius and Tiberius Sempronius competing with each other for glory (Cato was out of the race as he had been sent to Rome bearing the good news about Thermopylae), but the Romans were vying with the Macedonians. These were attacking the nearby city of Lamia, and the position of Heraclea on the foothills of Mount Oetia meant that each set of besiegers was distantly visible to the other.

The Romans were using siege artillery and battering rams, whilst Philip went for his favourite technique of undermining the enemy walls. However, the hard, flinty stone on which Lamia was built proved more stubborn than the Aetolian resistance at Heraclea, spirited though that was. With Heraclea captured, Glabrio ordered Philip to leave Lamia alone, as the isolated city would fall into Roman hands of its own accord. Negotiations for a more general Aetolian surrender failed, as the Romans insisted on the surrender of those men whom they felt had been most hostile to their cause, including the treacherous Amynander. With the war still on, Glabrio moved his army to besiege the Aetolians at Naupactus.

In turn, the Aetolians sent to Antiochus for help. Their envoys explained that they were now, through their support of him, alone in Greece and beset on all sides by foes. The king gave the Aetolian delegates a sympathetic hearing, not least because it was well in his interest that the struggle in Greece should be prolonged. This would give him more time to prepare his next move, and the longer they hosted a Roman army, the more disillusioned the Greeks would become with Rome. However,

Antiochus was not prepared to back his sympathy with troops, though he did promise the Aetolians a considerable sum of money.

The delegate returning to Aetolia with the news from Antiochus was too optimistic in his guess of how far the Aetolians had been forced back, and wandered into a camp, not just of Macedonian soldiery, but one which included King Philip himself. To the Aetolian's bemusement, Philip was delighted to see him, and treated the envoy to supper as his personal guest. Philip pointed out that the Aetolians had been responsible for bringing both Rome and Antiochus down on Greece, and in each case they had lost mightily thereby. He bade the envoy to ponder on this and then sent the man on his way once more totally unharmed. Like Antiochus, Philip was more than happy with the Aetolian resistance. So far this had allowed him to take back a good deal of Thessaly and northern Greece, and whilst the Romans sat at the gates of Naupactus, the Macedonian king cheerfully helped himself to Larissa and a number of minor towns, and also to the fortress of Dolopia, and (especially sweet) the fortress of Demetrias.

That the Roman victory at Thermopylae seemed mainly to have benefitted Philip was not lost on the Romans either. Flamininus, who was now with Glabrio, was quick to point this out. Flamininus was also annoyed that the Achaeans, who had started with some promising attacks on Aetolia, had turned instead to empire building in the Peloponnese. Their army was currently besieging Messene, a free city in the region which had refused to surrender to them. Flamininus told the Achaeans to take their army away, and then negotiated the entry of Messene to the League on terms. Flamininus also gently but firmly removed the island of Zacynthus from Achaean control. The sea, he told the Achaeans, surrounded their lands as its shell does a tortoise. And like a tortoise, if the Achaeans stuck their heads too far out of the shell, they risked getting it cut off. So much had changed in recent times that the Achaeans meekly agreed, when two decades ago they would have been stunned and indignant with such arbitrary Roman interference (they had, after all, purchased Zacynthus honestly by bribing its governor to surrender the island).

Aware that the Aetolian war was taking time and soldiers that could better be spent dealing with Antiochus, Glabrio (at Flamininus' urging) was disposed to be gentle with the terrified Aetolians. These were granted a truce and allowed to send a delegation to the Senate to present their case.

Philip sent a delegation at the same time. This was ostensibly by way of being a friendly greeting, and congratulations to the Romans for their win at Thermopylae, with these messages accompanied by the sacrifice of a large golden crown to Jupiter. The Romans were so pleased by this evidence of Philip's goodwill that they ordered the hostage Demetrius to be escorted back to his father.

It is highly possible that Philip's delegation had a more devious purpose: that of persuading the Roman senators in private meetings of the iniquity of the Aetolians and the advisability of continuing the war. Money may have changed hands.

In any case, the Senate imposed impossibly harsh terms on the Aetolians, demanding that they surrender all freedom of foreign policy and (possibly because the senators had heard of the donation of Antiochus) 1,000 talents of bullion to the Romans. The Aetolians decided that they could not meet the Roman conditions for peace and, to Philip's undisguised satisfaction, the war went on.

However, the Romans had bigger than Aetolian fish to fry: they had Antiochus squarely on the menu. A victory at sea had left the way clear for an invasion of Asia Minor, and the consul for 190 BC was given the freedom to cross the Aegean and take on Antiochus if the situation permitted it. That Greece itself was something of a sideshow to the coming Roman attack on the Seleucid Empire was clearly indicated by the choice of commander for the Seleucid campaign. This was Lucius Scipio, who came east accompanied by the man who was in virtual command, the brother of Lucius, Publius Scipio Africanus, the man who had beaten Hannibal in Africa. As Hannibal was reputed to be in command of some of Antiochus' troops, Scipio now intended to repeat the feat in Asia Minor.

First though, there was the nagging business in Greece to be finished off. Lamia had, as predicted, fallen relatively easily to the Romans, who were now bogged down before the citadel of Amphissa. Meanwhile, Philip continued merrily making the most of the situation, and had added the area of Amphilochia to his rapidly re-expanding domains. At Athenian urging, the Scipios agreed to let the Aetolians send an appeal to the Senate for easier peace terms, and with a ceasefire in place, turned their attention to Asia Minor.

The plan was to go through Thrace via Macedonia, a choice of route which meant that the security of Rome's army was very dependent on Philip's being the steadfast ally he had been until now. The Scipio brothers decided to send a herald to Philip with no forewarning, so that the herald might better report on Philip's true disposition. For this they chose Tiberius Sempronius Gracchus, a man with a glowing career ahead of him, who was later to marry Scipio Africanus' daughter and produce two famous sons.

Gracchus found Philip at a dinner party, half-drunk and overwhelmingly benevolent. The king cheerfully promised to help the Romans against Antiochus to the best of his ability, and delivered magnificently on that promise. He was after all, sending one potential enemy to crush or be crushed by another. Whatever happened, Macedon would be relatively stronger as a result, and without risking a single soldier. For Philip, Rome versus Antiochus was a win-win situation, and the more the two sides hurt each other the better. Therefore he was more than happy to do all in his power to make such a happy outcome possible.

Once he had waved a fond farewell to the Scipio brothers, Philip had to hasten south, where an Aetolian-sponsored rebellion in Athamania was threatening his newly-gained territories. The Aetolians made it plain that they did not see their armistice with Rome as extending to the Macedonians, and with the Romans gone Philip's weakness after Cynoscephalae became apparent. He was unable to hold Dolopia and lost a couple of other towns besides. Aetolian hopes began to rise.

Then came news that Aetolia's principal ally, Antiochus, had been crushed by the Romans at Magnesia in Asia Minor. Furthermore, the Senate, annoyed by Aetolian aggression against their ally, had rejected their peace delegation so violently that the delegates were told to be out of Rome that day, and out of Italy within two weeks. Worse, a consular army under Fulvius Nobilior followed the Aetolian envoys to Greece with the express intention of sorting out the Aetolians for once and for all.

The Romans began by attacking Athamania, and received considerable help in this from Amynander who had discovered that the Aetolians had wrested the kingdom from Philip for themselves rather than their former ally. Macedon meanwhile began to advance once more under the generalship of Perseus, the son of Philip, and quickly regained Dolopia. However, the rugged terrain of this part of Greece, combined with the vigour of the Aetolian defence, made progress slow and hard-won. To make things harder for the Aetolians, the Illyrians joined the war against them, but since Aetolia was not particularly stretched at sea, the invading Illyrian ships were easily forced back by the Aetolian navy.

It became apparent to the frustrated Nobilior that he was going to make more progress by diplomacy than by force of arms. With Amynander's help he was able to negotiate the surrender of the city of Ambracia, which he had spent much of the campaign besieging without success. (As part of the surrender terms, Ambracia, which had once been a capital of King Pyrrhus, was stripped of its treasure of statuary and fine art for Nobilior's planned triumph. However, Nobilior's enemies in the Roman Senate made him give it all back.)

The Aetolian garrison which had fought so hard was allowed to leave unharmed, and this gesture of Roman goodwill was enough to bring the Aetolians cautiously back to the negotiating table. By now the chastened Aetolians were prepared to accept almost any terms short of outright surrender and dismemberment of their confederacy, and were readily persuaded to surrender by Nobilior's decision to lighten their fine to 500 talents. (In fact it is highly unlikely that the Aetolians even had that much, which is why they managed to persuade the Romans to accept 200 down and the rest in instalments over the next six years.)

Diplomacy was further smoothed by the presence of the son of that Valerius who had first brought the Aetolians into alliance with Rome during the first clashes with Illyria and Macedon. Nevertheless, the Roman terms were harsh. Aetolia had to give up her conquests, and the island of Cephallonia (which was a pirate base that the Romans wanted to conquer separately). They had to surrender forty hostages to Rome along with any independent foreign policy. Henceforth, Aetolia undertook to have the same friends and enemies as the Romans. However, they did get to keep Amphilochia, despite a plaintive request from Philip to have it handed back to him. That the Romans showed even this much favour to the defeated Aetolians marked their recognition that Aetolia was now effectively a Roman dependency, every bit as much as was the protectorate which they had maintained about Apollonia for the past fifty years. It also signalled clearly that the Romans felt Philip had reconquered quite enough of northern Greece as it was.

Souring Relations

The year 187 BC set the tone for much of the future of Rome and her neighbours. With the trouncing of Antiochus and his army at Magnesia, Rome had become the dominant power in the Mediterranean world. From an Italian power that seemed on the verge of being crushed by Hannibal in 216 BC, Rome had gone on to crush Carthage, take Spain, defeat Philip, take control of Greece and push Antiochus back into becoming a purely Asiatic kingdom, all in the space of thirty years. Now the fate of entire kingdoms rested, not on the outcome of clashes of arms in the field, but on battles between different power blocs and shifting alliances in the Roman Senate. The Scipios, though victorious over Antiochus, fell to the political machinations of Cato, and Scipio Africanus was exiled.

The Senate, which had made much of 'the freedom of the Greeks' as its watchword in the confrontations with Philip and Antiochus, seemed less interested in the term once the struggle with the Hellenistic powers was won. Those Greek cities in Asia which had their freedom staunchly defended against Antiochus were casually informed by the Roman Senate that henceforth they fell under the rule of Pergamum. Many of the cities of northern Greece had already lost their 'freedom' to Philip's armies, and the Macedonian and Pergamene kings were already coming to blows over the control of the formerly-Ptolemaic possessions in Thrace which Antiochus had been forced to abandon.

Antiochus was no longer a threat to Rome, and the removal of this counterweight caused the Romans to look hard at the loyal ally who had helped in the defeat of Antiochus – Philip of Macedon. Philip had benefitted greatly from Antiochus' mere existence. First, the threat of Antiochus had caused the Romans to give him easy terms after Cynoscephalae, and then the actual invasion of Greece by Antiochus, botched as it had been, allowed Philip to regain much of what he had previously lost. Nor was Philip himself planning henceforth to depend for his security on Roman generosity. Livy remarks:

> He was intent on bringing the population back to its former levels after the disasters of war ... as well as insisting that the native Macedonians increased their numbers as greatly as possible, he forcibly moved populations from Thrace to Macedonia. During the length of time in which he now had a break from warfare, he spent all his energy in building up the resources of his kingdom.[55]

Unsurprisingly, the prospect of a revived and powerful Macedonia caused considerable disquiet in Rome, and a subsequent deterioration in Romano-Macedonian relations.

Matters were not helped by the fact that when the victorious Roman army which had conquered Antiochus was returning through Thrace, it suffered substantial casualties in a series of raids from well-equipped and well-informed Thracian war bands. These raids hit the Romans in narrow mountain valleys where they could not properly deploy and there was a suspicion – never proven – that they were sponsored with money, equipment and intelligence from Macedon. The Romans recalled that it had always rankled with Philip that he had not been allowed to complete the conquest of Lamia, and the king felt that he had been given less than his due in the settlement after the Aetolian War.

Now, a series of embassies from Greek cities went to Rome complaining – with greater or lesser justification – about Philip's conduct after the war, and to Philip's mounting fury, the Senate showed itself sympathetic to the plaintiffs. A commission, headed by Q. Caecilius Metellus, M Baebius Tamphilus and Tiberius Sempronius Gracchus was sent to Greece to investigate the various complaints against Philip. The principal issue was a number of Thessalian towns which Philip had seized from the Aetolians. The question was whether these were Aetolian cities in Thessaly, in which case Philip was entitled to them, or Thessalian towns which the Aetolians had conquered earlier, in which case they should be fully restored to Thessaly. 'Fully' was important here, as the Thessalians wanted not just the towns, but also the populations and everything movable which Philip, distrusting the commission's partiality, had already removed to Macedonia. The Athamanians had similar complaints, and the Thessalians also wanted Philip to stop using what remained of his navy to forcibly reroute naval trade to his newly reacquired port and fortress of Demetrias.

As Philip expected, the commission found against him. It did not help that whilst defending himself against the charges he lost his temper, and exclaimed ominously: 'The evening of all [my] days is not yet come' a phrase which indicated that Macedonian military power was not yet extinct, and Philip might yet fight to hold the possessions of his resurgent kingdom. When the question moved on to possessions in Thrace to which Philip had an even clearer claim, the commission equivocated, and clearly preferred the rival claims of Pergamum to the disputed territories, though the matter was referred back to the Senate. Deeply embittered, Philip realized that he was no further use to Rome as an ally and as his support was no longer needed, the Romans intended to chip away at Philip's possessions until he was safely confined once more within Macedonia. Once, just after Cynoscephalae, the king might have accepted this. But now the population of his kingdom was growing, and, as a new generation replaced the dead of the previous war, so his army was growing too, funded by recent conquests and the gold and silver mines which the king had reopened.

The king's mood was so dark that he massacred the population of a town which celebrated too soon and too enthusiastically the withdrawal of Macedonian troops. A Roman commission came to investigate this, and to check that Philip had indeed withdrawn his garrisons as ordered. However, the commissioners found that Philip's massacre (which he blandly attributed to civil strife) had left the few survivors too terrified to testify against him. Though suspicious and frustrated, the commission had no time to investigate further as its members had to turn their attention to the Achaeans and their treatment of Sparta, where the walls had been thrown down and the population ordered to abandon their traditional way of life.

The Achaeans mounted a spirited defence of their actions, but concluded with a significant comment. They argued their case, they claimed, not as equals, or allies of the Romans, but as slaves before their masters. Liberated they may be, but it was a liberty dependent on Roman favour. Let Rome decide as it willed and the Achaeans promised that they would obey. They asked only that the Romans would not treat their enemies with more consideration than those who had served them so well. Perhaps embarrassed that the glorious declarations of freedom by Quinctius at the Isthmian Games in 196 BC had come to this just a dozen years later, the commissioners declined to make any significant changes to the status quo with regard to Sparta. Nevertheless, that the Achaeans had joined the Aetolians in their disillusionment with Rome would have been noted with interest in Macedon.

The Romans had now to cope with an unexpected side effect of their favourable reception of those with complaints against Philip. A veritable flood of plaintiffs swarmed to Rome hoping for a favourable judgement against Macedon on charges of everything from boundary disputes to cattle rustling. In response Philip sent his son Demetrius, who had so favourably impressed the Romans during his earlier sojourn in Rome, as a hostage after Cynoscephalae.

Demetrius made his usual excellent impression before the senators, appearing unsophisticated and so flustered that he was asked to read directly from his father's briefing notes. These said that Demetrius was to grant the Romans whatever they demanded, but to point out that Philip was doing his best to comply with the orders already given to him by the commissioners (blatantly unjust though he felt them to be). In many cases, Philip informed his son, the difficulties in compliance were being created by the very people come to Rome to complain about him. Perhaps because these notes were (allegedly) not meant for public revelation, and because Demetrius exploited his earlier friendships to the maximum, Rome moved toward a more sympathetic view of Philip's position. The Senate announced that they would still investigate the claims, but thanks to the friendship they felt for his son, decisions would automatically be in favour of Philip unless there was overwhelming evidence against him.

As the decade of the 180s BC drew to an end, there was a feeling of change in the air. In Rome the men who had struggled to victory against Carthage were replaced by a younger, more confident generation which looked on Rome's domination of the Mediterranean as the city's natural right. Hannibal himself had taken refuge in the court of Prusias of Bithynia, and committed suicide when Rome demanded that he be handed over. Antiochus of Seleucia also was dead, killed in 187 as he tried to expand his empire in the east to compensate for his defeats in the west. Philopoemen, who had guided the strategy of the Achaean League for decades, was killed in one of the interminable inter-city disputes which still racked the Peloponnese. Philip was coming to the end of his fourth decade on the throne of Macedon, and attention was turning to the question of who would succeed him.

The Rivals

The Romans made no secret of their preference for Demetrius, and the favour shown to him by the Senate may have been intended to reinforce his position. There were rumours that Demetrias had spent long hours in private discussions with Flamininus, and even that Rome had promised Demetrius support should he make a bid for the throne. Not unexpectedly, such reports did not go down well with Philip's older son, Perseus. Two factions were forming in the Macedonian court, with Demetrius enjoying considerable popular support and the favour of the Romans who came east to keep an eye on Macedon and to make sure Philip was complying with the various judgements handed down by the senate. Philip himself made some irritated comments about Demetrius keeping a royal court whilst his father was still alive. When Philip led his army into Thrace (both to keep it exercised and to extend his dominions in a region where the Romans could not possibly object) the fortress-town which he founded to hold down his new conquests was pointedly called Perseis as a compliment to his older son.

Demetrius and Perseus represented radically-different foreign policy options with regard to Rome. The Romanophile Demetrius naturally attracted to his following those who believed that Macedon's best interests were inextricably linked to friendship with Rome, whilst Perseus seemed to be urging his father further toward a policy of confrontation. Indeed, there was a strong belief in Rome (at least in later years) that Philip was certain that war with Rome was inevitable and was actively preparing for it. This policy included major shifts of those peoples whom Philip felt he was unable to defend. Not unexpectedly, the suffering involved in such population movements made Philip more unpopular, and a failed expedition to the Balkans did little to help the king's stock with his people, many of whom openly yearned for Demetrius to take over.

Perseus may have been the older son, but this did not automatically make him Philip's successor. The Macedonians were not rigidly attached to the rule of primogeniture, and Perseus was allegedly born of one of Philip's concubines, whilst Demetrius was the son of Philip and his queen. The rivalry between the sons grew to the point where Perseus accused his brother of attempting his assassination in the festivities which followed the purification of the army (a ceremony which involved the army and its standards marching between the two severed halves of a female dog, and thereafter participating in a series of games and military exercises.) Nothing came of the accusation, but Philip was already suspicious of Demetrius because of his good relations with the Romans, and kept his son under constant surveillance. Aware of this, Demetrius began to conduct himself more circumspectly, even to the extent of asking his Roman friends to stop writing to him.

Demetrius also took the precaution of discreetly making arrangements for flight to Rome should matters ever come to that. This move too was betrayed to his enemies, and the information was taken to Philip. This intelligence was speedily followed by devastating proof of the young man's intentions. Philip's agents presented their royal master with a letter from Flamininus, apparently in reply to a letter which Demetrius had managed to smuggle out undiscovered. In this letter Flamininus laid out his position to a proposal from Demetrius, saying that he was sure that the young man's ambition would not cause him to do any harm to his family, and that he himself could not condone such an action if it did happen.[56]

Since Demetrius was not with him, Philip had done the next best thing and seized the best friend that Demetrius still had in his father's court. Now, even under torture so severe that he died of it, the friend said nothing of any plot, so Philip still had no direct evidence against his son. Nevertheless, it was determined to put an end to the matter, though not by an open trial and execution. Philip was probably aware that such events would not go down well with either his own people or the Romans, and therefore attempted something which at least allowed him a semi-plausible denial of any involvement. Didias, a courtier who was working for Philip but who had the confidence of Demetrius, invited the young man to a banquet. As soon as he had taken a cup of wine, Demetrius felt sharp pains and was taken from the room complaining loudly that he had been poisoned. He continued to do so in his rooms, implicating his father, until he was silenced - permanently - by a pillow over his face.

Philip's health was already in decline, and he was hit hard by his son's disloyalty and death. Perseus was now his uncontested heir, and conducting himself almost as if already king. In such a situation it helped not at all when those opposed to Perseus eventually managed to bring out the truth – that the letter of Flamininus was a forgery, cooked up by Philip's agents who had been suborned by Perseus. Demetrius was apparently, after all, innocent of the charges that had led to his death. It was fortunate for Perseus that he was not present at the royal court when the sorry story emerged, and when news reached him of his father's anger he made sure to keep well away.

However, Perseus kept his nerve. He was aware that there was no credible successor to the throne apart from himself, and Philip was almost prostrate with rage, grief and illness. The old king did what he could to disinherit his son, and even a few months earlier the result would have been fatal for Perseus. But Perseus had built up his own power base whilst he enjoyed Philip's favour and the position of heir apparent, and too many powerful men were committed to his cause to readily allow him to fall.

Philip promoted as his heir Antigonus, the son of Antigonus Doson, the man who had been his guardian in the years before he assumed the kingship. He spent his remaining reserves of physical strength and mental energy touring the cities of Macedonia promoting his new heir, but had reached only as far as the city of Amphipolis in the east of his kingdom when he died.

Thus, at least, is the story of the final months of Philip's rule as given by Livy, the only detailed source we have for events in Macedon at this point. How much is fanciful, how much is informed rumour and how much is pure guesswork combined with anti-Perseus propaganda will probably never be known. This much is at least certain: Demetrius died in 180 BC, and with him went the last good chance of Macedon and Rome remaining at peace for much longer. Philip died the following year (179 BC) at the age of 59 and, if Livy is to be believed, it was only his death that prevented war with Rome breaking out in that same year.

Such a claim is frankly incredible. To support his opinion, Livy claims that a tribe called the Bastarnae were to be allowed to march across Macedonia, exterminate the Dardanians, and then go on to ravage Italy whilst Philip reclaimed his lost mastery of Greece.[57] There seems little doubt that Philip had managed to persuade the Bastarnae to attack the Dardanians, as they made a confused attempt to do just that even after Philip died, but to assume that a minor Thracian tribe might go on to succeed where Hannibal had failed beggars the imagination. So too does the idea that Philip believed that a weakened Macedon could do better against Rome in 179 BC than it had done twenty years earlier, when Rome had been much weaker, and Philip and his kingdom much stronger.

Such a claim does little credit to the man who fought two wars against the Romans, and who by canny diplomacy, vicious and unscrupulous use of force, and careful use of his kingdom's resources had steered Macedon through violent and turbulent times for four decades. The physical integrity of Macedonia was intact, there was potential for limited expansion in Thrace and the Balkans, Rome was losing the propaganda war for hearts and minds in Greece, and the army and economy were growing stronger by the day. Beyond doubt, Philip expected and was preparing for another war with Rome. But that he would precipitate it at the age of 59 whilst in failing health and so risk all he had rebuilt after Cynoscephalae is improbable in the extreme. Rather, as a military expansionist himself, Philip recognized kindred spirits in Rome. He knew only too well that, once freed of their current commitments in Spain, it would only be a matter of time before the Romans turned their attention once more to war with Macedon. Like a conscientious king, he had done all he could to make sure that his land and people would be ready when that day came.

King Perseus

News of Philip's death was initially hushed up by courtiers who favoured Perseus' cause, and this allowed the king's scapegrace son to race back from his semi-exile using relays of fast horses. It is not known whether Antigonus ever attempted to sit upon the throne of Macedon, but if so his reign lasted only a few days, although it also lasted for the rest of his life.

With Antigonus disposed of, Perseus immediately sent to Rome to renew his father's treaty and to confirm that the Senate recognized him as king. The delegation to Rome was only the most important of a number of such diplomatic missions which were also sent to the Hellenistic powers of Seleucia and Egypt. The Seleucid embassy proved particularly fruitful, as that empire was now ruled by Seleucus IV who promised Perseus the hand of his daughter Laodice in marriage.

The propaganda of Macedon's new king made much of the land now being under a ruler not soured by forty years of betrayals and setbacks as Philip had been. Perseus portrayed himself as being liberal, generous and forgiving where his father had been vicious, vindictive and arbitrary. Perseus was helped by the usual raid by which the barbarians tended to test the mettle of any new Macedonian monarch, and handily thrashed the Thracians who attacked the silver mines in the east of the kingdom. The people of Dolopia had been restless about being reabsorbed into Philip's kingdom in 185 BC but Perseus calmed them by arriving with his army and quelling the secessionists in no uncertain terms. With these successes adding a recent gloss to a military reputation already established in the war with Antiochus III, Perseus then made a trip to Delphi to allow the southern Greeks to meet Macedon's new sovereign. This trip marked a thawing of relations between many southern Greek states and Macedon, particularly with the Achaean League, who began to reconsider their ban on Macedonians crossing their territory.

If Perseus made a mistake, it was in cultivating the friendship of Prusias of Bithynia in Asia Minor, to whom he gave his sister in marriage. Bithynia was a bitter rival of Pergamum, and Eumenes II Soter, king of Pergamum, had many friends in Rome. To those friends Eumenes kept up a stream of reports attributing the worst possible motives to everything Perseus did, and making unwarranted claims as to what Perseus was intending. The Romans believed that the Macedonian throne was occupied by a man who had killed off Philip's pro-Roman son in the course of getting there, and were deeply suspicious of Perseus in any case.

Given the attitude of the Romans, there was little that Perseus could do right. His attempts to cultivate more friendly relations with the cities of Greece were seen as efforts to sway these cities from their allegiance to Rome. Eumenes took himself on a mission to Rome where he laid out a set of charges showing that Perseus was committed to, and actively preparing for, war with Rome, and this report found a ready audience. In fact the historian Appian believed that the Senate secretly committed itself to war at this point; 'not liking to have on their flank a sober-minded, laborious, and popular king ... they decided to make war with Perseus, but kept the matter among themselves for the time being'.

When Eumenes was returning to Pergamum by way of Delphi, he was struck by a heavy rock which rolled down the hillside and injured him so severely that for a while it was reported that he had died. No-one believed that this was an accidental rock fall, and the blame was squarely attributed to Perseus. Others had a motive for wanting Eumenes dead, as the

Pergamene king was thoroughly unpopular in Greece and positively hated by the Rhodians, but this was ignored by the Romans who were now set on making a case for war against Macedon.

Further charges against Perseus were not lacking. The Aetolians were currently engaged in fighting a civil war as enthusiastically and savagely as they had formerly attacked their neighbours. Roman ambassadors, unable to broker a lasting peace, and given the long-standing animosity between Aetolia and Macedon, not unnaturally suspected that agents of Perseus were keeping the pot boiling. Thessaly too was restless, and again the Romans suspected the malign hand of Macedonian intrigue. Livy does admit that debt was a problem in Thessaly, and it would be interesting to discover if these debts were to Romans or their agents. Certainly in later years influential Romans were in the habit of forcing loans on Greek communities and not allowing these to be repaid until the debtors had also paid several years worth of exorbitant (and compound) interest. It may well be that some of the restiveness which the Romans attributed to Macedonian meddling might be traced to the beginnings of the dishonourable tradition of Roman financial rapacity in the east; misconduct which only ended with the Roman Republic itself. Such exploitation was already common in Spain, where Roman rapacity and corruption had aroused the hatred of the natives and prolonged the war.

So, to add to Rome's grudges against Perseus, the young and charismatic Macedonian king was beginning to make the 'liberators' of Greece seem unattractive in comparison, as Livy explicitly admits in a speech of Eumenes, saying that the Greek communities were in awe of Perseus and revered him, though what he had done to deserve it, Eumenes was unable to say other than that this might be a reaction to the Romans' own unpopularity.[58]

Perseus had done little to provoke the gathering storm, and certainly nothing more than Philip had done as a matter of course during the last decades of his reign. The more cynical members of the Macedonian court might have noted that young Tiberius Sempronius Gracchus (last seen in Greece as a surprise envoy of Scipio to Philip) had gone on to fight a highly-successful war in Spain, and with that war coming to a conclusion, Rome would soon have two glory-hunting consuls and an unemployed army looking for new worlds to conquer. There is a case for arguing that now that Spain had been dealt with, Macedon was next, and nothing that Perseus could do short of outright surrender would stop war from happening.

Now a man called Praxo stepped forward. This man was friendly with both Perseus and many influential Romans, and he publicly proclaimed that during his confidential chats with Perseus, the Macedonian king had suggested that he take advantage of his links with the Romans to poison as many senators as possible. A moment's reflection would be enough to make clear the improbability of such a scheme being successful and of the risks to the perpetrator if it was even begun. Either Praxo did indeed so reflect, and so make Perseus' scheme public, or idle dinner chat was blown up into a major conspiracy for propaganda purposes.

For there seems little doubt that Rome was on the brink of committing itself to war with Macedon. A worried Perseus had sent envoys to the Senate requesting a renewal of the friendship officially existing between Rome and Macedon, and these received no reply. A senator called Marcus Philippus, who had been a friend of Philip, persuaded Perseus to try again and, according to Polybius, he later boasted that in so doing he had postponed the war for six months to allow the Romans to complete their preparations.

In part, these six months were taken up in the usual Roman practice of canvassing Greek opinion before going to war with Macedon. It transpired that the Aetolians were so wracked and weakened by civil war that they were no use to anyone. The Achaeans, despite a strong pro-Macedonian faction, would remain loyal to Rome on the implicit understanding that Rome would not question the legality of recent involuntary additions to their League, especially the Achaean takeover of Sparta. Eumenes of Pergamum was positively chafing at the bit in his eagerness to get at the Macedonians, whilst Prusias had no intention of tangling with Rome, and regretfully informed his Macedonian brother-in-law that he intended to stay neutral. The Rhodians were wavering. They had no intention of being associated with any enterprise which involved the much-loathed Eumenes, but could be expected to remain neutral rather than hostile if Eumenes and Rome attacked Macedon.

Nor did the marriage alliance with Seleucus IV prove of any great worth to Perseus. Seleucus was dead, and his successor was once more engaged in hostilities with Egypt. Both Hellenistic powers signalled their friendly intentions toward Rome, and pointed out that their present commitment to war against each other precluded their getting involved elsewhere.

The Illyrians were doubtful, as they loathed both Romans and Macedonians impartially. The minor kingdoms of Thrace had both pro- and anti-Macedonian elements which seemed likely to cancel each other out in any coming conflict. Overall, as Perseus would have noted without any great surprise, the coming conflict would once again find Macedon in a world bereft of friends.

All that remained was the formal sending of an embassy to 'demand reparations' from Perseus. As with similar delegations to Philip, this embassy was essentially to explain that Rome was determined on war, but for religious reasons preferred the other side to declare it first. Otherwise the ambassadors would simply keep making ever-more-outrageous demands until they finally came up with something even the most determined pacifist could not swallow.

The delegation included the illustrious names of an Appius Claudius and a Servilius Caepio, and on their return to Rome these men declared that preparations for war were going on furiously throughout Macedonia. Perseus himself, when he had finally consented to see the embassy, had been angry and hostile, accusing the Romans of greed and warmongering. The Romans were given a written reply to their charges in which Perseus allegedly said that though the treaty with Rome had been made by his father and was nothing to do with him, Perseus accepted that he had inherited its terms along with his throne. The Romans were welcome to make another treaty if they wished, as long as they treated with the Macedonians as equals.

After handing over his written reply, Perseus now showed unmistakeable signs of leaving the room. Therefore the commissioners hastily launched into a denunciation of the treaty and repudiated Rome's friendship with the king. In reply Perseus told them to get out of the country within three days, which the ambassadors did, subsequently complaining to the Senate about Perseus' lack of courtesy and hospitality.

After the long build-up and diplomatic manoeuvres, it was almost an anti-climax when, in 171 BC, the newly-elected consuls called an assembly of the Roman people on the Field of Mars, and laid before them the charges against Macedon. Perseus was accused of aggression against the allies of Rome (i.e. his defeat of the Thracians who had attacked the Macedonian silver mines) and planning full-scale war against the Roman people. The assembly voted for war, a declaration which was surprising only in its suddenness. Perseus' ambassadors were still pleading the Macedonian cause to the Senate when they were told to leave at short notice and to take with them all the Macedonians now resident in Rome. This was apparently a goodly number, whose sudden eviction caused considerable distress.

The Third Macedonian War: Macedon

It would be fair to say that the outbreak of war found the Macedonians about as prepared as they could be. As the Roman delegates had noted, preparations had been under way even as the ambassadors went to visit Perseus. However, despite the claims of Roman propagandists, there seems no reason to suppose that these preparations were for anything but a defensive war in the face of long-expected Roman aggression.

It is uncertain to what extent the Romans genuinely believed that Perseus was planning the reconquest of Greece, or even an attack on Italy. But he was very definitely preparing for war, and such a war could only be with Rome. The Roman argument was that this was a war planned by Philip and simply postponed by his death. Therefore since Rome currently happened to have the time and the armies available, they might as well fight that war at a time of their own choosing.

The Macedonians could more justifiably have claimed that this was a war planned by Rome ever since the defeat of Antiochus and simply postponed by Rome's difficulties in subduing Spain. And indeed, Spain aside, Rome was much better placed to fight Macedon immediately before Philip's death in 179 BC than it was when war actually broke out in 172 BC. What appears certain is that the mutual distrust between Rome and Macedon, coupled with the belief that each intended to go to war with the other, proved to be a self-fulfilling prophecy.

If indeed, Rome's war with Macedon was postponed by Rome's difficulties in Spain, the Macedonians owed much to Hispania's recalcitrant tribesmen. It was now twenty-six years since the Macedonian army was cut to bits at Cynoscephalae, and a new generation stood ready to replace the men lost in that battle. None of the Roman historians of the Macedonian Wars are deeply interested in economic history, yet both Livy and Polybius have commented on the strenuous attempts made by Philip to develop Macedon's economy and population specifically to fight the war which was now upon the country.

Though the figures are rough estimates, it seems that the Macedonian army now consisted of some 23,000 phalangites and 17,000 other foot, mainly peltasts. These men, it should be noted, were not hastily-recruited and poorly-trained infantry of the type which went down to defeat at Cynoscephalae. At that time Macedonia had been exhausted after years of warfare, and its army represented whatever Philip had been able to scrape from the bottom of the manpower barrel. Now, after almost a quarter-century of peace, and all the time in the world to prepare, these troops were fully-trained, and almost from the day of their recruitment none of them had any doubts as to which enemy they were eventually to fight: the Roman legions.

We have a description of the Macedonian army from Livy which is worth giving in detail. The phalangites were commanded by one Hippias of Boeotia and there were various light troops of very high calibre, each grouped in their own nationality, from an elite Macedonian unit of some 2,000 men, called the Guard, to equally-sized units of Thracians and Gauls. There were archers from Crete and a unit of 500 Spartans under the command of an evocatively-named Leonidas. The Macedonians had been researching ways to discombobulate the Romans and had added to their army slingers who fired *cestrosphendons*: basically double-pronged 9- inch shuttlecocks weighted with lead. These were developed especially with legionary chain-mail in mind, and appear to have been effective under the right circumstances.

The one arm of the Macedonian forces which was relatively weak in comparison to the historical balance of the Macedonian army was cavalry. Perseus had an estimated 4,000 horse, about half of what most ancient military theorists would have considered ideal. However, Macedonia no longer controlled Thessaly, and the Thessalian horsemen who once made up a significant part of Macedon's armies were, if anything, more likely to align themselves with Rome. The horsemen of Perseus were native Macedonians complemented by about 1,000 Thracians.

To balance his weakness in cavalry, Perseus had the strength of his economy, which had been on a war footing for most of the past decade; indeed, Perseus allegedly claimed he had sufficient materiel laid by for a decade of warfare. Arsenals had been stocked, vulnerable populations shifted out of harm's way and the areas most likely to suffer from a Roman advance had either been fortified or long abandoned. Furthermore, the loss of Macedonian influence in southern Greece meant that Macedon had no allies there to protect, and no fortresses to garrison. The whole strength of the Macedonian army could be concentrated on the defence of the kingdom itself.

The Third Macedonian War: Rome

In one way, the well-advertised thoroughness of Macedon's economic preparations told against the country. Macedon was believed to be rich, and in consequence there was no shortage of those volunteering for the legions in order to lay hands on some of this supposed wealth for themselves.

There was one drawback to these eager new recruits, and that was inexperience. Such veterans as Rome now possessed were experienced in the relatively low-intensity wars of Spain. These men knew well how to deal with guerrillas and sudden ambushes, but had little experience in fighting against the armies of a major military power. In fact, the last major action which the Romans had fought was with the soldiers who had won the Battle of Magnesia in 190 BC when these men had gone on to fight several major battles against the Galatians of central Anatolia.

It was probably for this reason that special provision was made to allow the recruitment of men of up to 50 years old. This allowed the veterans of Magnesia to rejoin the legions and impart their experience to a younger generation which had never faced a phalanx in the field. Nevertheless, the army which Rome proposed to send against Perseus was neither of the standard which had defeated Hannibal, nor even that which had defeated Antiochus. The same peace that had strengthened Macedon had been relatively debilitating for the legions.

Perhaps in recognition of this fact, the legions which were to go against Perseus were to be of 6,000 men each, whereas the usual legion strength was 5,200. Overall, with cavalry included, the Romans put some 16,000 men into the field, with their allies in Greece and Italy contributing about the same again. The Cretans, as their treaty obligations demanded, supplied a contingent of archers, but bashfully admitted when pressed that an even greater number of their compatriots had been hired to serve in the Macedonian army. This meant that the Roman attacking force was actually numerically inferior to their Macedonian opponents.

This may have reflected Roman confidence that the superiority of the legions, as demonstrated at Magnesia and Cynoscephalae, more than compensated for any numerical disadvantage. It may also have reflected a prosaic estimate, born from the previous generation's experience of campaigning in Greece, of the size of force that Rome could keep supplied whilst it was operating in inhospitable terrain. Another sign that the Romans had learned from their previous exertions in Greece was that they pressed their allies for supplies, gaining corn and barley from as far afield as Carthage, and promises of more from the various embassies which hurried to Rome to assure the Senate of their devotion to the Roman cause.

There was some jockeying amongst the consuls-elect as to which of the pair should receive the command of the Macedonian campaign, and eventually this fell to Publius Licinius Crassus, an ancestor of the man who, a century later, became a triumvir with Julius Caesar and Pompey in the dying days of the Republic. The appointment of Crassus to fight Perseus reflected the man's following in the Roman Senate and his skills as a politician, but says nothing of his ability as a general. In fact there was currently no-one in Rome with experience of commanding an army against as formidable an opponent as Macedon, and whoever was chosen was going to have to do his learning on the job.

Chapter 8

The Third Macedonian War

The Campaign of 171 BC

The inexperience of the Roman commander and his army became rapidly apparent. Perseus quickly moved into northern Thessaly and, obviously following a long-established plan, quickly made himself at home in his father's old base of operations at Tempe. There he waited for the Romans to fall upon him. The expected assault did not materialize, so Perseus conducted a series of sweeps across Thessaly to find out what was keeping his opponents. It was perhaps his greatest failing in the entire war that, both at this time and in the future, Perseus failed to keep a close enough eye on what his opponents were doing. In fact the Romans had been struggling to get across the mountains from Apollonia. They had been so battered by their battle with the terrain that it was freely admitted that had the army first encountered the Macedonians at the same time as its soldiers encountered the mountains of Greece, the war might have come to an abrupt end then and there.

The consul was forced to rest his men at Gomphi, where he received the encouraging news that Eumenes had turned up near where the Roman fleet was assembling at Chalcis, on the east coast of Greece. Eumenes had his fleet, 4,000 infantry and about 1,000 cavalry. The Romans at Gomphi were also joined by some 1,500 unenthusiastic Achaeans who represented the minimum degree of support the League thought it could get away with. The Achaeans were serving alongside an unknown number of equally depressed and demoralized Aetolians, whilst the Thessalians, as predicted, had contributed a substantial contingent to the Roman cavalry. Unlike Rome's more reluctant Greek allies, the Thessalians had much to lose if Perseus was victorious and therefore were actually prepared to fight. With his legionaries rested, and his allies mustered, Crassus finally pressed onward for Larissa, well aware that his tardy performance to date was encouraging the Macedonians and causing consternation amongst his supporters.

The Battle of Callicinus

With the Romans 3 miles short of Larissa, Crassus stopped by a hill called Callicinus and called a council of war to decide how operations in Thessaly were to be conducted. The council never reached a conclusion. Whilst its members were still debating, a messenger came with urgent news: tired of waiting for the Romans to turn up, Perseus and his army had come to them. The Macedonian vanguard was now only a few score stades away and closing in fast on the Roman camp.

Crassus immediately sent a force out to test the mettle of the advancing enemy. A brisk cavalry action costing some thirty men convinced the Romans that the Macedonian cavalry, at least, were in fine fettle and spoiling for a fight. Thereafter Crassus decided that his troops would not leave camp again until it was time to engage the main Macedonian force. So behind their ramparts the Romans stayed for the next few days, though the Macedonian vanguard tried valiantly to provoke the Romans to further action.

Perseus and the main Macedonian force pitched camp 5 miles from Crassus, and formed up for battle early the following day with the intention of engaging the Romans soon after sunrise. This measure shows considerable confidence on the part of Perseus, as a dawn engagement meant that a major defeat of either side would give the victors the rest of the day to hunt down and destroy the fleeing remnants of the defeated army.

Perseus took the centre with the Guard and his bodyguard cavalry, with a good part of the Macedonian cavalry positioned on the flanks. The remaining cavalry were deployed in packets mixed with light and medium infantry, in the expectation that the coming fight would be a series of disjointed actions across the broken ground surrounding the hill. The terrain being unsuitable for the phalanx, Perseus kept that in reserve for his army to fall back upon should the day go badly.

Because of the broken ground, Crassus too decided to keep his heavy infantry (i.e. the legions) in reserve within the camp, and deployed his light infantry and cavalry to meet the enemy. Even with the heavy troops of both sides held in reserve, the resulting battle was a substantial affair involving some 24,000 men, with approximately equal numbers on each side.

Perseus took the initiative, throwing forward his Thracian and Gallic irregulars who charged with a ferocity that dismayed the Italian cavalry facing them. Perseus took his own cavalry straight into the Greek infantry contingent and easily overwhelmed it. For the Romans, all that saved the day from total disaster was the Thessalian cavalry. These horsemen kept their formation, and by threatening to fall on any unit which became disordered in pursuit, they forced the Macedonians to rally before they could press their attack on their disordered and retreating enemies. Taking advantage of the reprieve, the Roman forces rapidly abandoned the battlefield for the safety of the camp.

Seeing the success of the light troops, the Macedonian phalanx came up of its own accord to follow up the victory. Perseus held the phalanx back, though some historians believe that by doing so he passed up the chance for a decisive victory. However, Perseus knew what had happened to his father's phalanx when it fought on unsuitable terrain, and he was well aware that the legions had not yet come into play. Furthermore, there were diplomatic considerations. Given a stinging setback or two, Roman prudence might force Crassus to decide that Macedon was too tough a nut to crack and he might consequently settle for a face-saving peace. But if dealt a crushing defeat, Roman pride would force the Senate to keep trying until the insult had been avenged on the smoking ruins of the Macedonian capital.

As it was, the Romans had lost 200 cavalry and more than ten times that number of infantrymen. The Macedonians had lost some 60 men, and showed a net gain of 540 once the number of prisoners they had taken was added to the overall tally. With the Macedonians triumphant and the Romans chastened, both sides retired to their respective camps for the day.

Negotiations

Perseus had probably not missed a trick in forbidding his phalanx to join in the day's battle, but he certainly missed one that night by (yet again) not keeping an eye on the Romans. Had he done so, he would have observed his opponents pulling back across the River Peneus. Given that he was demonstrably superior in cavalry and light infantry, Perseus would have been in a position to force Crassus to stay where he was or risk extermination as he crossed the river. As it was, his failure to keep proper watch meant that by morning the Romans were safely across the river, but deeply depressed by the progress of the war to date. At the post-battle council of war Crassus joined in the general Greek tendency to blame everything on the Aetolians, and sent five scapegoats from amongst their officers to explain the lacklustre Roman performance to the Senate.

The problem for the Romans was what to do next. Secure as the camp was, they could hardly stay in it indefinitely when they were meant to be conquering Macedonia, yet the enemy superiority in light infantry and cavalry meant that moving the army and protecting supply lines was going to be tricky.

Perseus helped by pulling his army back somewhat, allowing the Romans to be reinforced by Massinissa of Numidia, who sent his Roman allies 1,000 infantry, 1,000 cavalry and 22 elephants. Given that the Numidian light horse were considered amongst the best in the known world, this eased Crassus' cavalry problems somewhat.

The reason for the Macedonians holding back soon became apparent: Perseus wanted peace. Envoys came to the Roman camp offering the same terms as offered to Philip when he had surrendered to Titus Quinctius after Cynoscephalae. All the cities that Philip had given up Perseus would surrender once more, asking only in exchange that he be considered a friend and ally of the Romans. Such a 'surrender' would of course give Perseus a massive propaganda boost with regard to the rest of Greece. If, as has been argued here, Perseus had not wanted war in the first place, he would be more than happy to reap the prestige of making peace after having given the Romans a mild beating and sent them off home again all but empty-handed. At the very least, it might cause the Achaeans and others to rethink their loyalties.

If, on the other hand, the Romans refused terms (and Perseus must have known that Crassus faced political extinction if he ended the war without a major victory to show for it) then the rest of Greece and the Hellenistic world would be able to see clearly who the aggressor was. After all, it was a strange would-be conqueror of Greece (as the Romans claimed Perseus to be) who wanted to stop after his first minor victory, but it was perfectly consistent for a would-be conqueror of Macedon (as Perseus claimed the Romans to be) not to cry off after the first setback.

Crassus, as Perseus probably expected, rejected the Macedonian offer outright, and proposed a counter-offer that was tantamount to a fresh declaration of war. The Romans would consider peace, he said, if Perseus surrendered himself, his army, and his country unconditionally to the mercy of the Romans. The propaganda effect of these negotiations was as might have been predicted, and overwhelmingly favourable to Macedon. As Livy reports with apparent perplexity:

> The news spread across Greece, and how it was received revealed the hopes and sympathies of those who heard it. Not only were Macedonian supporters delighted by the outcome of the battle, but so too were many others who were deeply obliged to Rome,

even those who had suffered from the violence and tyranny of Perseus.[59]

The fact that Crassus, from the time of his arrival, had behaved more as though he was invading Greece than saving it from Perseus probably explained something of the Greek reaction. As did the fact that the sailors with the navy at Chalcis had raped and robbed the local citizens so extensively that the commander was later recalled to Rome and punished, after having first been instructed to locate those innocent Greeks his men had sold into slavery and restore them to their families.

The navy atoned somewhat for its misdeeds when the sailors moved inland to support operations in Boeotia, where Macedonian settlers remained sympathetic to their motherland. Eventually Thebes was captured. This was to constitute the major Roman success of 171 BC, though it was achieved at the cost of taking the navy from its proper duty of preventing the Macedonian army in Thessaly from receiving supplies from the western ports, rather than having to haul these with great difficulty across the mountain passes.

To the End of the Campaign of 171 BC

The war in Thessaly continued, though neither side achieved a great deal. This suited Perseus, whose intention through the war was evidently the same as Philip's had been in similar circumstances, namely, to make life as difficult as possible for the Romans in the hope that they might eventually give up and go home.

Even with his extra Numidian cavalry, Crassus was having trouble with supplies. This was not unexpected, and was probably the reason why the Romans had brought only two legions to Greece in the first place. So far these were staying out of trouble by consuming local supplies, and setting their camp down in the middle of a cornfield every time they had to shift it. After the Romans had been in one location for a while, the Macedonians decided that the inside of the Roman camp must be filled with husks and stalks of corn, and made a dawn raid to try to set the thing on fire.

The alertness of the Roman sentries drove the Macedonians back, but they had better luck at a place called Phalanna, where Roman foragers dispersed too widely whilst harvesting grain, and took substantial casualties from a lightning Macedonian raid. Some 800 foragers took shelter on a hill, and Perseus concentrated on capturing these. So intent was he on his mini-siege that he failed to notice that some foragers had escaped his cavalry and brought news of the situation to the Roman camp. Crassus immediately sallied out with almost his full force, including his elephants.

The Macedonians had, in the course of their methodical preparations, taken elephants into account. These beasts were formidable mainly on account of their effect on horses, which generally refused to come anywhere near them. Lacking elephants of his own, Perseus had trained his cavalry horses to confront large scale mock-ups coated with an evil-smelling substance which hopefully resembled the aroma of an enraged pachyderm. Trumpeters hidden within the dummy elephants had habituated the horses to the noise.

However, whilst the horses may have had nerves of steel, they were no match for the entire Roman army. Perseus had to make a hasty retreat to his main force, leaving it so late that the Romans managed to dispatch some 300 of the light infantry who had accompanied the Macedonian king on his raid.[60]

This action more or less completed the campaign of 171 BC. Perseus pulled back to Macedonia, where he intended to use the dregs of the campaigning season to tidy up outstanding issues with the Thracian tribes. Crassus tried to follow the Macedonians across Thessaly, but discovered that Perseus had left a number of well-provisioned garrisons in fortresses across the country with this very eventuality in mind. After trying his luck against some of these strongpoints and meeting with mixed success, Crassus eventually decided to pull back and winter with his sailors in Boeotia whilst awaiting his replacement by the next consul elected in Rome.

The Campaign of 170 BC

Perseus achieved his objective with the Thracians, and secured the defection of an important Thracian king, Cotys, from the Roman side. Now that the snow had closed the passes into Macedonia, Perseus turned his attention to the Illyrians, employing the same tactics of divide and conquer that the Romans had so far effectively employed on a larger scale in Greece as a whole.

There were minor actions fought against the Romans in their protectorate south of Illyria. Whilst neither Romans nor Macedonians achieved much in these clashes, familiarity with the local conditions meant that the Macedonians generally got the better of things. This suited the long-term Macedonian plan of making life as uncomfortable as possible for the Romans, and indeed, after a lacklustre opening year, morale on the Roman side was already sagging.

Spring saw a new consul, A. Hostilius Mancinus, and a new plan. This time the Romans would try to go west around the mountain ranges that divided Macedonia from Thessaly, perhaps along a route like that of the River Aous which Titus Quinctius had found so securely blocked by Philip V when he considered this approach during the First Macedonian War.

As Hostilius discovered, the river valleys of Greece were hard going for an army even if the route was undefended, and impossible if it was. The Roman sources give little detail of the summer campaign, which is in itself a sure indication of a lack of success. We can glean that Hostilius tried twice, once with sufficient determination and commitment for his army to take significant casualties. Plutarch, the biographer, informs that this second battle with Hostilius was at a place called Elimiae, and Perseus forced the Romans to retreat.

With his men somewhat demoralized, Hostilius pulled back into central Greece. There he discovered that Perseus, being able to defend his western approaches with a minimal force, had used the remainder of his army to once again make itself at home in Thessaly for the summer. Recognizing that there was not enough of the season remaining for another assault on the Macedonian hedgehog, Hostilius sensibly refrained from further ventures. Instead he shored up morale by giving generous leave to men who would not be needed until the following year in any case, and tried through diplomacy to undo some of the damage that the insensitivity of the previous year's commanders had inflicted on Graeco-Roman relations.

Appius Claudius, commander of Rome's forces in western Greece, brought the year in the west to a bad end by bungling an attack on the town of Uscana. He attacked with a force mainly composed of raw recruits who arrived in bad order and fled at the first sign of resistance, taking substantial casualties when the townsmen followed up their flight.

Perseus had once again had a good year, though the Roman navy had been something of a thorn in his side. In a combined operation with Eumenes, it had captured and sacked Abdera at the mouth of the Nestus River in Thrace. Unfortunately for the diplomatic efforts of Hostilius, the navy retained its rapacious habits and its conduct during the operation went a long way to lowering Rome's reputation on the eastern seaboard of Greece.

At the close of the season, Rome had kept its legions in the field for two years with very little to show for it other than Greek disillusionment with the Romans and weariness from supporting their armies. There were rumours that Eumenes too had grown disillusioned with the war, and had offered Perseus his services (for a goodly price) in brokering peace between Macedon and Rome.[61] Nothing came of this, but Roman relations with Eumenes were cool thereafter. The motives of Eumenes may have been misjudged. The legendary Roman stubbornness had demonstrably failed to wear down Macedonia's protecting mountains, and without mediation the war seemed set to continue indefinitely.

Once the senate had rejected diplomacy as an option, it was up to whoever commanded the legions in 169 BC to do something dramatic to break the deadlock.

The Campaign of 169 BC

The Romans were now taking the war with Perseus a good deal more seriously, As Plutarch remarks, so far the Romans had 'inflicted less hurt on the enemy than they had received from him'.[62] The war had so far yielded much in terms of strenuous mountain exercise, but little in the way of booty for the soldiers. Consequently the censors had to make a particular effort to ensure a good turnout of recruits for 169 BC. Nor were the Greeks happy about the continued presence of the Roman army on their soil. To pacify Greek sentiment, the senate passed a resolution that local commanders were not to levy services or goods from Greek cities without explicit permission. Since Livy remarks that some cities were being 'drained dry' by these exactions, it is fair to guess that Roman officers had been making requisitions with great enthusiasm, and keeping a cut for themselves before passing the remainder to the main army.

Partly because the mood in Greece was becoming increasingly mutinous, ambassadors were sent to calm both the Achaean League and the Aetolians. Aetolia's leaders reported ever-increasing anti-Roman sentiment among their people and asked for garrisons to be stationed in some cities to prevent them from going over to the Macedonians. This, as will be seen, was a very real possibility.

To start the new season Perseus went west again. The Illyrian King Genthius was having trouble with a number of Illyrian minor tribes, so Perseus, in keeping with his divide and rule western policy, lent the beleaguered monarch the full support of the Macedonian army. Though grateful for Macedonian help, Genthius remained reluctant to commit himself to war with Rome, perhaps because the Romans had recently commissioned a fleet to make a strong showing off the Illyrian coast.

Perseus remained in the west, but transferred his attention southwards toward the Roman protectorate, falling unexpectedly upon a town held by a mixed Illyrian and Roman garrison. This garrison, though taken aback by the appearance of the enemy, held out until the sight of Macedonian siege engines convinced them that this was no impromptu raid. The Romans yielded on condition that they be allowed to keep their liberty and possessions. (They discovered later that 'possessions' did not include their weapons, which the Macedonians confiscated as the Romans left their fortress.) The clemency shown by the Macedonians on this first occasion was instrumental in persuading a number of other strongpoints to surrender without a fight.

Perseus strongly garrisoned what he had gained to date and then went to try his luck further south. It was as well that he did leave strong garrisons, because as soon as the main Macedonian army was gone, Appius Claudius made an unsuccessful attempt to reverse Macedonian gains in the area.

Perseus advanced as far as the Aetolian border in the vain hope that the city of Stratus was ready to come over to him. However, the Romans had evidently heeded the Aetolian ambassadors and the city had recently received a fresh garrison whose Roman commander acted quickly and decisively enough to forestall any pro-Macedonian coup by the citizenry. Obviously, Perseus had been told of the Aetolians' increasing disillusion- ment with Rome, for he hung around hopefully at the border to see if he would receive any further delegations from would-be rebels. When these were not forthcoming he took himself home.

Spring saw the arrival of Marcus Philippus, a man with considerable experience of getting into Macedonia, having been both a friend of Philip V and a former ambassador to Perseus. The question was whether Philippus was capable of getting into Macedonia whilst bringing an army with him. No-one, Macedonian, Greek or Roman, doubted that the energetic and ingenious Philippus would certainly give it a good try. Philippus had brought substantial reinforcements with him, and wasted no time in joining his predecessor, Hostilius, at Pharsalus.

After finishing his campaigning season early, Hostilius had spent his time getting the army into peak condition for 169 BC. An appreciative Philippus followed the example of Flamininus and persuaded his predecessor to remain with the army as proconsul and advisor for the current campaign. Since the army was as ready as it was going to be, Philippus at once loaded his men with as much corn as they could carry and set off northwards. At that point no-one in the Roman high command was sure which of the various options for attacking Macedonia should be attempted. However, all of the most feasible choices had a common starting point near the town of Azorus at the foot of Mount Olympus, so the army took itself there.

Roman uncertainty as to what to do after reaching Azorus had at least the benefit of leaving Perseus completely in the dark. Until the Romans decided what was going to happen next, the Macedonian king did what he could by putting half of his army on garrison duty at the passes and keeping himself in reserve with the rest.

In a campaign which was to set high standards for the display of military ineptitude, Perseus soon showed that, as had been the case throughout the war, he was culpably lacking an efficient system of military intelligence. This lack prevented him from working out what the Romans might do next. Worse, Perseus often had no idea what the enemy were doing at any particular time, or even where they were whilst they were doing it.

At the opening of the main campaign of 169 BC what the Romans were doing, with great difficulty and in small numbers, was struggling up the passes to where the Macedonians were encamped near a point called Ottolubus. Perseus was ignorant of this fact, but had through luck or foresight situated his main reserve at Dium in the Macedonian countryside just beyond this pass. Nevertheless, the Roman advance party, led by the consul's son, was able to exploit Macedonian unawareness of their location and establish a small and advantageously-situated camp overlooking not only the enemy, but also the countryside beyond. However, when Philippus arrived with the main army, the Macedonians were alerted to his presence and immediately went on to the attack.

The next three days confirmed what the Romans had spent the last thirty years discovering: it was practically impossible to get through the passes if there were enough Macedonians there to stop them. The Macedonians were easily supplied from their own hinterland, but Roman provisions were at the end of a long supply chain, and despite his foresight in ordering his men to carry extra corn, food stocks in Philippus' army were dwindling alarmingly.

This left Philippus in a precarious position. He could not go forward as the way was blocked, and he could not remain much longer where he was. However, even if a safe withdrawal could be managed with the light Macedonian infantry following up on the Roman rearguard, another humiliating retreat from Macedonia's mountain fastnesses would deal a huge blow to Roman prestige and morale.

Perhaps made light-headed by the mountain air, Philippus decided on a massive gamble. Leaving only a small rearguard to hide his intentions from the defending garrison, he set off over the mountains for Macedonia on a track more suitable for mountain goats than a fully-equipped army. At this point, had Perseus even an inkling of what was happening, it would have been child's play to block both the Roman advance and retreat, leaving the army strung out along mountain paths until it surrendered or starved. As it was, even without Macedonian intervention the terrain was a stubborn enough opponent, especially as Philippus insisted on bringing along Massinissa's elephants, which took a very dim view of the situation.

Stumbling and sliding through the peaks, the Romans made very slow progress of only a few miles a day, though once the descent began, this was accomplished considerably more rapidly. Livy, with pardonable exaggeration, speaks of virtually the entire army sliding and rolling down the mountainside, with the elephants skidding along behind on their haunches. Overall, it was a crossing of which Hannibal would have been proud.

But Philippus was no Hannibal. The result of his arduous operation was to deliver the Roman army into hostile territory whilst the enemy sat squarely across the only two possible lines of supply: the pass of Tempe, and that via Ottolubus and Dium, where the Macedonian garrisons, though bypassed, were still firmly entrenched. And the Romans were already low on rations.

The next thing for Perseus to do would be to ensure that the Romans were unable to supply themselves locally, and above all to prevent them from gaining access to the sea, where the fleet could bring supplies. All that was needed to accomplish this was to block the only way out of the valley where Philippus had ended up with his army. This valley was less than a mile wide, and made much less so by a broad river which flowed out of it. A town and an eminently-fortifiable temple precinct made the perfect cork to complete the bottling up of the Romans. With the block in place, there would be no need for a battle. The army of Philippus would either have to batter itself to pieces on securely-entrenched Macedonian positions or starve in very short order. Now that it was known where the Romans had gone from Ottolubus, it would also be very easy to order the garrison in the mountains to make sure they could not get back that way.

In short, the audacious manoeuvre of Philippus in crossing the mountains was tantamount to military suicide. Instead of the enemy surrounding him and cutting him off, he had, with huge difficulty and effort, managed to do this to himself. If the historian Polybius is particularly scathing in his report of Philippus' conduct, this is because he was himself an experienced commander who could clearly understand events. Indeed, he could understand them very clearly, since he had the misfortune to be on a diplomatic mission from the Achaeans and was present with the Roman force at the time.

All that saved the Romans from total disaster was Perseus' lack of intelligence, both of the military and the more conventional kind. The news that a Roman army had made it through Macedonia's mountain defences and camped within his kingdom hit the king like a thunderbolt. In his defence, it has to be said that no-one in recorded history had ever before broken into Macedonia from the south. Even after Cynoscephalae, Philip had held the pass at Tempe and negotiated with his kingdom intact.

In the turmoil that followed the news of the Roman arrival, Perseus appears not to have asked himself precisely how Philippus had got to where he was. Perseus was too good a general to perform a manoeuvre as idiotic as Philippus had just executed, and therefore he assumed that Philippus had not done so either. After all, the Roman commanders he had fought so far had been solid and unspectacular, not suicidally incompetent.

Therefore the only logical explanation for the Roman army being within Macedonia was that Philippus had forced one of the passes. Once that assumption is accepted, what Perseus did next was both rational and decisive. If a pass had been forced, then there was nothing but the Macedonian army between the Romans and the capital, and the next thing to do was to gather the army and gamble everything on a major battle.

Accordingly word was sent to the Macedonian garrisons in the passes that the men should leave their positions post-haste and join the main army. By acting so promptly that he failed to check exactly which pass had been forced, Perseus had effectively trumped Philippus' incompetence with a blunder yet more monumental, and made what he feared the Romans had accomplished into reality. All a delighted Philippus had to do was send messengers back to Larissa and instruct the Romans there to take possession of the abandoned Macedonian positions in the passes without delay. The road to central Macedonia was wide open.

In fact, so speedily had the Macedonians abandoned the pass at Tempe that they left there the supplies of grain which they had stockpiled against a Roman attack. These supplies were gratefully received by Philippus' army which was almost out of provisions, an indication that if Perseus had in fact blocked the Romans in the valley, their situation would quickly have become desperate.

Philippus had advanced as far as Dium, but on hearing the news from Tempe, he pulled his army back to save his precious new corn supply from being transported over hostile countryside. He then secured access to the sea via the Macedonian town of Heraclea and showed unmistakeable signs of digging in there until the end of the campaigning season. One reason for this was that the Romans had now set teams of engineers working on the passes from Thessaly, and wanted to start 168 BC with a veritable highway leading over the mountains into Macedonia. It may also have occurred to Philippus that he had stretched his luck far enough already and he should leave it to an abler commander to capitalize on his achievement.

Perseus had by now had time to take stock of his self-inflicted disaster. His initial instinct had been to play for time whilst he concentrated his forces. After a while he became aware that the Romans had no intention of hurrying to battle. What he had taken as a powerful Roman force set to drive into the heart of Macedonia was in fact desperately attempting to secure a tenable position. While Perseus had been carefully trying to put off a decisive conflict until the end of the campaigning season, the Romans were gratefully consolidating their undeserved gains.

This relative inertia on the Roman part allowed Perseus to countermand some of the desperate measures he had set in motion. Treasures he had ordered thrown into the sea to keep from Roman hands were fished up again, and messengers were sent with urgent instructions to prevent the burning of the fleet at Thessalonika, for which orders had been given when it seemed the city was about to be taken. (Fortunately the man sent with orders to burn the ships had some inkling that Perseus might later rue his decision, and had delayed until the expected countermanding order arrived.)

Back in Thessaly, the fortress of Demetrias was still in Macedonian hands. The garrison not only held out against Eumenes and Philippus' lieutenants, but even launched some spirited sallies against the Romans. As it became apparent that little more was going to be achieved that year, the Pergamene king abandoned the half-hearted siege and took himself back to Pergamum.

Not only Eumenes but several other Greek states had been wrong-footed diplomatically by the dramatic developments in Macedonia. As well as the Pergamene offer to negotiate peace at a price, Prusias of Bithynia had pleaded with the Senate to bring the war to an end, and the Rhodians, exasperated by the effect of the war on their maritime trade, practically demanded it. With dispatches from Philippus in Macedonia giving them even more than their usual arrogance, the senators briskly dismissed the foreign envoys in the confident expectation that peace would indeed soon return to the region, and that peace would unconditionally be a *pax romana*.

The Campaign of 168 BC

The Macedonian boar was at bay, but it was still formidable. Perseus had been out-manoeuvred (or at least had out-manoeuvred himself), but his formidable army was still intact, well trained and well equipped. The climatic battle that everyone now expected to decide the war would certainly not be a walkover for Rome. Consequently there was considerable interest and speculation as to who would command Rome's army in this crucial year.

This turned out to be Aemilius Paulus, a Roman of an ancient family. Patricians to the core, the Aemilii had a long history of military service to Rome. Indeed, the father of Aemilius Paulus had, as consul, fought Hannibal at Cannae in 216 BC, and perished in the battle along with much of the Roman army. The son had already campaigned successfully in Spain and northern Italy and now, with the Macedonian nut cracked open by the fortuitous exploits of Philippus, he was expected to produce a similar result in Greece.

A man of mature years, Paulus was in no hurry. The first thing he did was to demand a comprehensive report on the current state of affairs in the war zone. He had no intention of repeating the mistakes of his predecessors who had hurried to war and only discovered the situation on the ground by painful experience. Rome's new commander believed that forewarned was forearmed. The situation which the report would have explained to Paulus was as follows:

Firstly, Rome now controlled access to Macedonia. However, Perseus had moved his army to a near-impregnable position on the Macedonian side of Mount Olympus. Entrenched across the River Elpeus (which was dry at this time of the year, leaving the river bed a formidable trench) he was refusing to offer battle. Since the Macedonians still had the edge in light infantry and cavalry, movement for the Romans under Paulus would be no easier than it had been for Crassus at the start of the war.

Genthius, king of the Illyrians, who had steadfastly refused to join the war whilst it was going relatively well for the Macedonians, had, now that Perseus was in trouble, joined in against Rome. This was partly because

Perseus, who was said to be careful with his resources to the point of stinginess, had waited until now to offer the Illyrians a bribe of 300 talents for their assistance. It was also partly the result of the long courtship of Illyria which Macedonian diplomacy had been conducting for the past three years, and the failure of the Romans to make any significant ground in the west.

One of the last acts of Philippus as consul had been to forbid Appius Claudius from raising further reinforcements from the Achaeans. This reflected the fact that the Achaean League was becoming increasingly restive, but it left Rome's western front in a precariously weak position now that Genthius had joined the fray. It did not help that pro-Macedonian sentiment was increasing in Aetolia, and Epirus could not be counted on to stay loyal much longer. Philippus had levied a large part of his supplies from there, and belatedly tried to assuage the ill-feeling this had caused by asking the senate for money to pay for his exactions.

Finally, even the Macedonian navy, quiescent for most of the war so far, now celebrated its reprieve from self-inflicted immolation by venturing out into the Aegean and doing what harm it could to Roman trade. As well as escorting corn supplies to Macedon, its ships fought a successful action at the island of Chios. In short, it was well for the Romans that they had secured the passes into Macedonia the previous year, as otherwise the situation might fast have become unsustainable.

Once Paulus arrived to take up his command in Macedonia, he determined by personal examination the truth of what he had been told. He quickly ascertained that Perseus was indeed dug in so securely that it would be an act of collective suicide on the part of the Roman soldiery to attempt to winkle him out. The campaign so far had consisted of the two armies regarding each other peacefully across the river bed, whilst the Romans passed their time digging wells to relieve their otherwise-inadequate water supplies.

Paulus could at least console himself that Perseus had rejected an offer of assistance from a large Gallic army which had turned up in Thrace (probably the Bastarnae), the commanders of which demanded a huge sum for taking on the Romans. Livy and other historians condemn Perseus for refusing to pay the sum demanded, and also for rejecting Eumenes' offer to mediate peace at a price. However, it should be noted that all those offering their services demanded money up front, and given Perseus' current difficulties, there was nothing to prevent his would-be helpers from simply taking the money and leaving the Macedonians in the lurch.

Rather than simple avarice, it was probably to ensure continued Illyrian loyalty that Perseus had paid Genthius only the first instalment of his 300 talents as soon as he declared war on the Romans. The rest would come once the Macedonians were sure they were getting value for money.

Genthius obligingly unleashed his privateers on Roman trade in the Adriatic. He advanced southwards with 15,000 men to where Appius Claudius girded his loins to meet him. Claudius had not had a distinguished war so far, and was now due to hand over to his successor, Anicius. The latter had already arrived at Apollonia with reinforcements, and told Appius to do nothing until the two had joined forces. Thereafter the pair marched northward and met with little resistance until they ran Genthius to ground at the city of Scodra.

Genthius had hoped for reinforcements from his brother. However, the latter evidently decided, in the spirit of cut-throat Illyrian dynastic politics, to abandon his brother to his fate. Bereft of allies (Perseus having problems of his own), Genthius surrendered at Scodra after a token resistance which fell considerably short of even 150 talents worth of value for Macedonian money.

The successful and early end of the war in the west hardly affected the Roman position on the other side of Greece. With the Macedonian army occupying the space between Mount Olympus and the sea, the obvious thing for the Romans to do was to use their superior naval ability to turn the Macedonian flank. Indeed Perseus was well aware of this possibility, and had stationed units along the coast to guard against it. Nevertheless the Roman fleet was called to Heraclea, which Philippus had secured for Rome the previous year, and a large Roman force of some 8,000 men ostentatiously prepared to board.

This was a feint, designed to convince Perseus that the Romans intended to get around his defences by sea. In fact the Romans intended to turn Perseus from the inland flank, and as soon as it was dark, the Roman force reversed direction from Heraclea and marched across the slopes of Mount Olympus. This force was commanded by Scipio Nasica, the Scipiones and Aemilii being close political allies at this time. Given the state of Macedonian military intelligence, this elaborate double bluff was probably wasted effort, as it was highly likely that Perseus had no idea of the original movement, let alone of the clandestine manoeuvre which it masked. In any case, secrecy was rendered pointless by a Cretan archer from Scipio's force. During the night, this man deserted to the Macedonians and personally brought Perseus up to speed with developments.

The Macedonians immediately dispatched covering troops to block the Roman outflankers. What happened next is uncertain, as Polybius says that these fell upon the Romans as they slept and slaughtered many. On the other hand, Plutarch claims to have seen a personal report written by Scipio which claimed that the Macedonians were thrown back, and the outflanking manoeuvre executed successfully despite the lack of surprise. Probably the latter is correct. Firstly, the Romans were probably not literally caught napping, as Paulus had recently enforced strict vigilance among sentries, to the extent of depriving them of spear and shield. He argued it was a sentry's job to alert the army, not to fight the enemy, and the sentries would be more alert if they were more vulnerable. Secondly, and more revealingly for those who feel that the outflanking manoeuvre worked despite being betrayed, Perseus did what might be expected if the enemy had got around his position. He immediately pulled his army northwards, and prepared to make his defence in front of the Macedonian port of Pydna.

The Battle of Pydna

Perseus placed his army near the town of Katerini where two small rivers, the Aeson and Leucus, flowed past his lines to the sea. In expectation of battle, he had chosen a level plain, where (unlike Cynoscephalae) the Macedonian phalanx could be deployed to maximum advantage. The sea (which came much further inland toward the mountains than is the case today) partly secured one flank, and a range of low hills suitable for peltasts and other light infantry secured the other. With Romans and Macedonians equal in cavalry at about 4,000 a side, there was no way that either infantry or cavalry could take the phalanx in the rear.

Legion and phalanx were going to have to go head-to-head. Some 20,000 legionaries faced 1,000 or so more phalangites, so neither side had the advantage of numbers. The Macedonians had about 20,000 lighter troops to the Roman 15,000, though the Romans also had Masinissa's 22 elephants. Conditions for a battle were as good as Perseus was going to get.

Accordingly, as soon as the Romans arrived, Perseus showed his intentions by offering battle. Paulus, aware that the Macedonians were rested and ready, refused to engage. His army had been marching all day under the midsummer sun, and he wanted to give it at least the next twenty-four hours to prepare. His commanders, especially Scipio Nasica, were indignant at the delay. They pointed out that the men were ready, in fact eager, to engage and the longer they delayed the more likely it became that the Macedonians might pull back from the fight. If the Macedonian army dispersed into scattered garrisons, a war that could be ended in a single battle might instead become a process of reducing Macedonia town by town. Paulus responded to his subordinates' concerns by pointing out that he was older and wiser than they. He was the commander and if he said the army was going to rest, then rest it would.

What happened next can be as precisely dated as almost any event in ancient history. We are told that it was just after the summer solstice, and that night there was an eclipse of the moon, which means the date must have been precisely 22 June 168 BC. The eclipse was reportedly seen as a bad omen by the Macedonians, who believed it portended the overshadowing of their ancient kingdom by Rome.

Plutarch alleges that Aemilius Paulus waited until late afternoon to start the battle, so that the sun would not be in his soldiers' eyes. Then he cunningly released a horse in the direction of the enemy's skirmish line knowing that this would precipitate a light infantry action that would draw in the rest of each army. Given that it was midsummer, this means either that the Roman army was facing slightly east, or that Paulus was being wise after the event.[63] Given that Perseus had already clearly indicated his intention to fight a battle, there seems no reason to loose a 'stray' horse to draw him into one. It is highly probable that if the fight did start as described (with skirmishers fighting over a loose horse) this was an accidental start to a battle for which both sides were already prepared. In fact Paulus had spent much of the morning killing oxen. After the eclipse, he had sacrificed an ox to Hercules. The omens were not favourable, so he sacrificed another one. Then another, and another, and so on through twenty oxen. Perhaps realizing that Paulus was prepared to go on all day until he got the omen he wanted, Hercules finally relented on the twenty-first ox, and signalled that the day (or what was left of it) would go propitiously for Rome.

The Romans drew up their battle line, and Plutarch gives a stirring description of the Macedonian army as it swung into action against them:

First came the Thracians... huge men with brightly polished shields, wearing black tunics and their legs protected by greaves. As they advanced they brandished their straight spears, heavy with iron, [which they carried] on their right shoulders. After the Thracians marched the mercenary soldiers, each armed in their native style, with the Paeonians mingled amongst them. The third

unit was of picked men, the bravest and strongest native
Macedonians, in the prime of life, gleaming with golden armour
and wearing scarlet coats. As these formed up, they were followed
from the camp by the troops of the Brazen Shield phalanx. The
whole plain seemed alive with flashing steel and gleaming brass;
and the hills resounded with their shouts.

As far as we can tell of the order of battle, Perseus took the right wing,
together with his guard cavalry and a special experimental anti-elephant
corps. These men apparently wore armour with spikes protruding at
angles from their curiasses, apparently in the hope that the elephants
would find attacking them the equivalent of a human walking barefoot
over a lawn of unshelled chestnuts. According to a writer called Posidonius
(quoted by Plutarch), the king was suffering from a horse kick which he
had taken so violently on the thigh that the bruising forced him to fight
without armour, spiky or otherwise.

Paulus lined himself and his legionaries against the 'Bronze Shield'
phalanx, and the second legion, under an ex-consul called Albinus,
squared up to the second phalanx, which Livy calls the 'White Shields'.

The battle began on the right wing, where the elephants made short
work of the anti-elephant corps. This success was followed by the Latin
allied troops who began to push back, and on occasion rout the opposing
Macedonians. Another set of Italian allies, the Pelignians, were amongst
the first to face the phalanx. They hesitated, nonplussed by the
impossibility of penetrating the hedge of spears, until one of their
commanders seized their standard and threw it into the enemy ranks. This
inspired the Pelignians to rush onto the Macedonian spears, where they
were promptly slaughtered.

Paulus himself later admitted that the sight of the oncoming phalanx
gave him palpitations. As the wall of spear-points bore down on the
Romans, the legionaries were totally unable to get at the enemy. They, like
the Pelignians before them, were impaled by the oncoming pikes, and were
unable to beat them aside and get to grips with the men wielding them.
Seeing the famed Roman legions slowly forced into giving ground, some of
the fainter-hearted of Rome's allies began to quietly slip away, assuming
the battle to be lost.

In the middle of a heated engagement, the son of Cato the Censor lost
his sword. Not wanting to report this disgrace to his formidable father,
young Cato persuaded a group of his friends to hurl themselves back into

the melee and help him to find it. So ferocious was this inspired charge that the Macedonians were forced to give ground and Cato retrieved his weapon. Across the battlefield similar minor triumphs and disasters were taking place, with the inevitable result that the line of engagement became somewhat ragged as the Macedonians pressed forward in some areas, and were stalled in others.

Paulus realized this gave the more flexible Roman formations an opportunity. Rather than fight legion to phalanx, he ordered his men to break into smaller units, and to concentrate upon those places where gaps had opened in the enemy formation. It is highly probable that this order gave sanction to what the legionaries were already doing, as Roman legionaries generally showed considerable initiative on the field, and some, at least, were veterans of the Spanish wars, and accustomed to fighting in small co-ordinated groups.

This revealed the essential difference between phalanx and legion. Where the legion was forced back it gave ground, losing men, but not cohesion. But once even a small party of legionaries got in among the phalangites, they caused chaos out of all proportion to their number, and created a gap into which ever more Romans could pour. At close quarters, a 16-foot pike was little use against the dreaded Roman *gladius* and, after the front rank, most phalangites were lightly armed in any case. At one point after another the spear-hedge dissolved and the Macedonian advance came to a confused halt. As soon as the legionaries had chewed their way into the phalanx far enough to start taking enemy soldiers from the side, the phalanx lost all cohesion and collapsed like a stack of cards.

Perseus had by now taken a light wound from a glancing blow by a spear to go with his horse kick. When he saw his phalanx buckle he did not need to be told that the game was up. With the day clearly lost, he pulled back his cavalry and retreated, leaving the infantry to their fate.

That fate was grim. After the scare they had been given, the Romans were in no mood to show mercy. Macedonians were cut down where they stood, and slaughtered if they tried to surrender. Some waded out to sea to escape the legionaries, and offered their surrender to the Romans who set off after them in small boats. These were either killed in the water or driven deeper until they drowned. Seeing the crush on the shore, the elephant drivers turned their mounts on the crowd, and many more phalangites were crushed either by the elephants or in the attempt to escape them.

Some 3,000 Macedonians mounted a last stand, bravely holding their ranks until the last of them was cut down. Elsewhere the battle had become a massacre so violent that it was reported that blood from the 15 to 20,000 slain made its way into a river over a mile distant. Only nightfall brought an end to the slaughter.

Macedon's army of 40,000 had in an afternoon been reduced to fewer than 5,000 men. Apart from those killed in the battle and aftermath, thousands more were taken captive. Roman casualties were well under 1,000, much of this number made up by the hapless Pelignians. Paulus was deeply concerned about his son who had gone missing, but the young man returned well after nightfall, having gone further than most in chasing and cutting down the fleeing enemy. Apart from the fact that Perseus was still at large, the day had gone as well as Paulus could possibly have hoped. His victory was total, and Macedon was totally and unconditionally crushed.

Aftermath

Pydna was purely an infantry battle. Cavalry and generalship had little to do with the outcome, which depended purely on whether the phalanx would break the legion or vice versa. It is an interesting question as to what would have happened if the Macedonians had not had morale so high that they advanced to within a quarter of a mile of the Roman camp. Had they been more defensive, and moved forward slowly enough to keep their formation intact, it is difficult to see what the legions would have done about this. However, Pydna proved one point beyond doubt, going forward, the phalanx was no match for a legion, even if it could briefly force that legion back.

Perseus and the Macedonian cavalry received criticism both immediately afterwards and from later generations for their early retreat. The truth is that Pydna would be won or lost by the phalanx, and once the phalanx had lost, all the cavalry had to decide was whether they wanted to die pointlessly or not. Perseus himself fled back to Pella, but paused only long enough to collect his family and treasure. He then headed for Amphipolis, perhaps with the intention of fleeing to Asia and throwing himself on the mercy of Prusias or another of the Hellenistic kings. Paulus rejected all efforts by Perseus to negotiate anything other than unconditional surrender. In the end, abandoned by almost all his followers, Perseus was forced to buy passage on a Cretan trader for his family. The Macedonian navy had already quickly assessed the situation and sent envoys to arrange the surrender of the fleet to Rome.

As he was no longer in a position to negotiate, Perseus had been forced to pay a substantial amount of treasure for his passage. The trader promptly demonstrated why earlier in the year Perseus had refused to pay for assistance before it was earned. The trader took the treasure and sailed, leaving behind Perseus and his family to fall into Roman hands. Within two weeks of his victory at Pydna, Aemilius Paulus had Perseus, Pella and most of the rest of Macedon under his control without the need for any further fighting. This distressed the army, since they had been looking forward to looting Macedonian cities which had never previously been sacked. It was little consolation that Paulus was personally as scrupulous as he forced his soldiers to be, taking so little from his success that later his daughters had to borrow money for their dowries when they married.

Chapter 9

Andriscus

Andriscus and the Achaean War

With the defeat of Perseus, the long drama of the Roman conquest of Macedon moved into its final act. The Third Macedonian War had represented the destruction of the last power on the Greek mainland capable of withstanding Rome. However, it would take another generation for the *fait accompli* to be recognized, and painful lessons remained to be learned before Rome's mastery became an accepted fact.

The Settlement of Macedon

Once the kingdom of Macedon had been occupied by the Roman army, Paulus took himself on a tour of Greece. His conduct was now studiously pacifistic, and he travelled with only a small retinue which included his son. He finished his tour by meeting with the ten commissioners he had sent for from Rome. (It was invariably the practice of a Roman commander who had conquered somewhere new to ask the Senate to send a commission to settle the newly-conquered lands.) En route to the meeting, Paulus was astounded to be met by Perseus and his family, all apparently perfectly at liberty thanks to loose supervision by their Roman captors. Paulus ordered Perseus to be politely but firmly taken back into custody, and after due deliberation with the commission announced the Roman settlement of Macedonia.

To the surprise of many, it had been decided not to absorb Macedon into the Roman Empire. However, if Macedonia was to be outside Roman rule, it was too powerful a state to be left intact. The Macedonians had repeatedly declared themselves to be Greek, and the Senate appears to have taken them at their word and organized the Macedonians after the fashion of other Greeks. The monarchy was dissolved, and the country was broken into four smaller republics, each based on a major Macedonian city. To make it plain that these were to be separate states, the peoples of each were forbidden to own territory or intermarry outside their own part of the former kingdom.

Livy has given us the boundaries of the four states, for which the commissioners appear to have allowed themselves to be guided by geography.

The first of these states was between the Rivers Nestus and Strymon, with its capital at Amphipolis. This area possessed the rich mineral reserves which had powered the war machines of Philip and Perseus, so the commission sensibly enough ordered that the gold and silver mines be shut down. The second state ran from the Strymon to the Axius, including the Chalcidice, with Thessalonika as a natural capital. The third comprised much of central Macedonia including its historic capital Pella, and was in the land between the rivers Axius and Peneus. The fourth and final republic took up the remainder of the west, to the borders of Illyria and Epirus. Its capital was a former provincial town of the region of Pelagonia (which town is uncertain; there are three possible candidates, the most likely being Heraclea Lyncestis).

All those who had been in the service of the Macedonian king (even as ambassadors on diplomatic missions) were without exception ordered to exile themselves from Macedonia to Italy. A similar purge was ordered in the rest of Greece, where anyone suspected of pro-Macedonian sympathies was summarily ordered out of the country. These expulsions happened even in Achaea where amongst the many exiles was Polybius, the historian whom, both directly and indirectly through later sources such as Livy, we have to thank for our detailed knowledge of these times.

This arbitrary treatment says much about Rome's new attitude to people who were ostensibly friends and allies. In part, the Third Macedonian War had come about because the defeat of the Seleucids meant that the Romans no longer needed the friendship of Macedon. In the same way, the crushing of Macedon meant that there was no longer any reason for the Romans to be nice to the Greeks, and the senate now demonstrated this fact with chilling brutality.

The Roman army was returning westward through Epirus, and it was apparently decided to show the Senate's displeasure at the surliness earlier shown towards Rome. That Epirus had been inclining toward Perseus was unmistakeable, and indeed, it is suggested that numerous cities had actually declared for his cause, though they had not apparently acted on their words. Whilst Perseus remained a threat, the Romans had done no more than seek to diplomatically soothe Epirot unrest. Now, with no need for restraint, the Senate ordered Paulus to comprehensively loot any cities which had been less than enthusiastic for the Roman cause. The same soldiers who had found slim pickings in Macedonia now had the chance to pillage some seventy cities and enslave some 150,000 Epirots, and did so vigorously whilst the rest of Greece looked on in appalled horror.

Paulus returned to Rome for a magnificent triumph with the captive Perseus and his family as the star attractions. It was customary for a captured enemy leader to be killed at the conclusion of the triumph, but Perseus lived for some two years longer. He was kept under house arrest at Alba, and apparently bullied brutally by his guards. What became of his daughter is unknown. Perseus' elder son died two years after his father and his mother about a decade afterwards, but the younger son assimilated himself into Roman society and ended up in the unassuming profession of a magistrate's clerk.

Greece

It is significant that Paulus, after his conquest of Perseus, acknowledged that Greek and Macedonian affairs were intimately intertwined, and undertook to settle affairs in Greece along with those in Macedon. The first stage of that settlement, as has been seen, was the apparently unprovoked rape of Epirus. Modern historians, unable to grasp the opaque reasoning of the Senate are flatly unable to account for it. The Roman response to what were, at most, pro–Macedonian sympathies in what was officially still a friendly state seems violent beyond reason.

Whatever the causes of the savage attack on Epirus, the Greeks failed to take from it an understanding of what henceforth passed for Roman diplomacy towards Greece. Rome's attitude would vary almost randomly between conciliation and harsh and arbitrary demands, followed by abrupt back-pedalling, and ultimately disproportionate application of savage violence.

There were several reasons for this: the first was simply that the Romans had now an extensive empire to run. The Senate was engaged in warfare with Gauls and Spaniards, and intense diplomacy with Ptolemies, Seleucids, and the states of Asia Minor, Africa and the Aegean. Senators did not have a lot of time to deal with the squabbles of Greek cities, and when they did it was not always the same senators who took an interest. Add the fact that Rome tended to be more conciliatory when her resources were stretched and more militant when an army was available. Then consider that the vagaries of the electoral process might almost randomly put philhellenes in power (who sometimes favoured an expansionist imperialistic policy in Greece) or reactionaries (who often believed in limiting Roman concerns to Italy and letting the Greeks go hang) and the near-randomness behind Roman conduct becomes clearer.

It would be clearer still, were modern readers not abandoned by Livy, whose history is missing from after the Macedonian settlement, whilst Polybius breaks up into almost-incomprehensible fragments.

Enough remains in the source material to show that Rome did have a basic overall strategy for Greece, and the settlement of Macedonia provides a clear indication of what it was. Greece was intended to be independent under Roman tutelage. Its constituent parts should refrain from fighting each other and sort out their disputes between themselves. Rome would offer guidance, advice and, in the case of crises incapable of any other solution, arbitration. Rome had declined to take possession of Macedonia because the basic function of Greece was to act as a sort of peaceful buffer zone between Rome and the East whilst the nascent Roman Empire sorted out its differences with the Spaniards and Gauls. The basic failure of diplomacy between the years 168 and 148 BC was the failure of the Romans to properly explain this concept, and the inability of the Greeks either to grasp it, or to act accordingly.

168–150 BC

With Aetolia no longer a force in Greek geopolitics, Achaea was now undisputedly the region's most powerful state. With the removal of 1,000 of Achaea's leading citizens to Italy, the League's leaders were those politicians who had shown themselves most slavishly attached to the Roman cause. At the head of the League was a man called Callicrates, whom the Romans had trusted enough to draw up the list of those to be exiled. It is difficult to draw a picture of Callicrates, as Polybius felt that the list of exiles had nothing to do with Macedonian sympathizers and everything to do with those Callicrates had exiled for personal political gain. Polybius loathed Callicrates accordingly, and is uninhibited in his invective.

Roman puppets were put in power in the smoking remains of Epirus, where a particularly unpleasant despot called Charops was installed, and in Aetolia, Boeotia and Acarnania. Athens, having been pro-Roman to begin with remained a 'friend of Rome', though the confused and fragmentary sources for this period point to the city-state as being highly impoverished by the recent war. This may be because the commander of the Roman fleet had demanded an improbably massive amount of corn from Athens during the campaign. As Athens was not a corn-producing region, the state may either have beggared itself in trying to get corn from elsewhere or spent a fortune bribing various Romans to get out of the imposition.

According to the fragmentary text of Polybius, Callicrates was universally loathed in Achaea to the extent that people were not even prepared to step into the water after he had used the baths.[64] Nevertheless, Callicrates could not have been the undisputed despot that Polybius describes, as no less than four embassies were sent to Rome in the years 165, 160, 155 and 153 BC requesting the return of the exiles, and at least one of these embassies was inspired by Thearides, who appears to have been the brother of Polybius. It is highly unlikely that Callicrates would have countenanced these embassies if it was in his power to prevent them.

The main points of friction in Greece in the years before 150 BC were Sparta, the island of Delos, and a small city-state called Oropus. How Rome dealt with these minor crises is revealing. In 166 BC Athens took control of Delos and ordered the inhabitants currently there to leave the island. Many ex-Delians settled in Achaea and took citizenship with cities of the League. Then, as citizens of the Achaean League, they sued the Athenians for the property they had lost during their eviction. Athens appealed to Rome, which simply told the Athenians to accept Achaean arbitration. The Athenians did so, but with bad grace and ill-feeling that boiled over into minor cross-border raids.

The situation did not improve when, around 160 BC, the Athenians, for reasons now unknown, decided to attack and pillage Oropus. Oropus, as was by now almost standard procedure, complained to the Senate. The Senate found that the Athenians were at fault, and delegated Sikyon, a city of the Achaean League, to fix a penalty. It did not help relations between the League and Athens that this penalty was set at a thumping 500-talent fine, which on appeal by Athens to the Senate was reduced to 100. Not liking this judgement either, the Athenians appear to have simply ignored it. The citizens of Oropus now directed their appeal to Achaea. According to a recently-found inscription, someone called Hiero was thereafter responsible for persuading the Athenians to restore Oropus to its citizens.[65]

Significantly, Rome had taken no action apart from referring the matter to the League, and, as far as we know, had failed even to protest when the League's judgement and the Roman amendment of it was flouted.

Nor did Rome show any great inclination to get involved with Sparta. Though forcibly incorporated into the Achaean League, Sparta could not forget the glories of its epic past, and yearned, if not for greatness, at least for independence. A spat broke out in 164 BC between Sparta and the neighbouring city of Megalopolis over border lands which had changed hands repeatedly according to the fortunes of war. The standard appeal was made to Rome. As it happened, Rome was about to send two envoys to the East and these stopped en route to hear the Spartan case. Polybius in a surviving fragment complains that the delegates (especially one Gallus) were insufferably arrogant toward the complainants.

There is no reason to doubt this, as the Romans after Pydna were a confident breed, certain of their place as masters of the Mediterranean world and intolerant of discussion, let alone dissent. It is probably at this period that some Romans started referring to the Greeks as *Graeculi*. This derogatory term means something like 'wretched little Greeks', and was used to distinguish contemporary Greeks from their ancestors whose art, literature and overall culture the Romans were coming increasingly to admire, absorb and emulate. Indeed, an Athenian embassy to Rome at this time was composed of philosophers, and those philosophers gave extra-curricular demonstrations of their subject which left an impression on the Romans that far outlasted the effects of the official visit.

Gallus probably regarded his Greek stopover as an annoying distraction from his main mission which was to investigate another complex and long-running dispute between Pergamum and Bithynia. His decision on the Spartan question was simply to point out that both Megalopolis and Sparta were members of the Achaean League, and to hand the problem back to Callicrates for resolution. This was enough to excite the wrath of Polybius, but seems in itself a decision consistent with Roman policy towards Greece. If the much later evidence of Pausanias is to be believed, an Aetolian city called Pleuron took advantage of the Roman presence to petition for permission to secede from the League. The request was referred back to Rome and granted.

If this did occur (and Pausanias is no trustworthy guide) then this would explain the later Achaean conviction that Rome was set on breaking up the League; a belief that clumsy Roman diplomacy was later to strengthen.

In Macedonia, meanwhile, the Roman experiment at regime change was proving a failure. The belief that a land accustomed over the centuries to rule by a centralized monarchy might instead contentedly settle down to being four autonomous republics was always somewhat naïve. And the situation was made far worse by the fact that Paulus and his commission had expelled from Macedonia almost every Macedonian with any experience of government. The result of inexperienced politicians attempting to implement an unfamiliar form of government on a resentful and unco-operative population was predictable. Corruption and factional infighting paralysed the administrative machinery of the republics, and nationalist and pro-monarchial sentiments rose accordingly.

As early as 164 BC, the Senate was concerned enough about the state of Macedon to divert a commission headed for Syria on the death of Antiochus Epiphanes. What the commission reported is unknown, but the troubles continued. In 162 BC we hear of one Damasippus fleeing from Macedonia after murdering the members of the city council of the town of Phacus, near Pella. In 158 BC the gold and silver mines were allowed to reopen, perhaps in the hope that increased prosperity might calm unrest. In 152 BC, the Macedonians invited the intervention of Scipio Aemilianus, a son of Paulus adopted into the Scipio clan. The reason this intervention was required is unknown, but it is perhaps significant that this year also marks the first appearance of one Andriscus.

This man, Andriscus of Adramyttion, styled himself Philip, and claimed to be the son of Perseus by his wife Laodice, who had recently died in Italy. There is little sign that the Romans took all this seriously, other than as a symptom of the problems in Macedonia. In fact, even the Macedonians were initially unconvinced by the pretender's claims. Failing to find much support in his native land, Andriscus sought support from the Seleucid King Demetrias. Demetrias did the sensible thing and arrested Andriscus, and believing him no more than a minor trouble-maker, sent him off to Rome.

Either the Romans were unconcerned enough not to press charges, or Andriscus escaped from his guards. Either way, he was rearrested in Miletus, escaped once more, and next turns up at the court of the Pergamene prince Athenaeus. The wife of Athenaeus was a Macedonian princess and her support gave Andriscus much-needed credibility. This was further boosted by Teres, a Thracian chieftain. Teres had married a daughter of the real Philip, and claimed to recognize his father-in-law.

By now, fuelled by Macedonian discontent with the status quo, a popular movement had grown in favour of the pretender. The Romans appear to have still considered events as an internal Macedonian affair and, consequently, the rise of Andriscus is poorly recorded. We do know, however, that at some point around 150 BC, Thracian support helped the pretender to win a battle to the east of the River Strymon. This development saw the stock of Andriscus soar among the Macedonian people, and caused enough concern among the Romans to have Scipio Nasica sent out as an ambassador to do what he could to soothe the situation.

In the same year that Andriscus won his victory on the eastern borders of Macedonia there was a significant development further south in Achaea.

This was the return of the exiles whom the Romans had sent to Italy at the end of the war with Perseus. According to a contemptuous quip by Cato, the Romans felt that the exiles were now too old to be a serious threat any longer. Supposed senility aside, it is almost certainly no coincidence that the return of the exiles saw the fall of the thirty-year-long rule of Callicrates, and the outbreak of violent political faction fighting in Achaea.

Thus 150 BC saw popular rebellion brewing in the north, whilst the political situation further south was spiralling out of control. The Senate in Rome must have been aware that something urgent needed to be done about Greece, but from its subsequent conduct it can be seen that the Senate was deeply divided about what that something should be. The mixed signals that were sent in consequence created confusion in Greece which had ultimately catastrophic results.

The Legions Return

From the confusion that followed the fall of Callicrates, one Diaeus rose to power. Like many a politician before and since, he chose to unite his people behind him by focusing their attention on a common enemy. That 'enemy' was Sparta and Diaeus' antagonism was made all the stronger by the fact that his chief rival for power was Menalcidas, himself a Spartan and the chief general of the League in 151/150 BC.

It seems (and again we must complain about the inadequacy of the evidence here) that, despite having risen to the top of politics within the Achaean League, Menalcidas was at least sympathetic to those Spartans who wanted to secede from the League altogether. The old boundary dispute with Megalopolis was brought up before the senate again. This time the Spartans did not just dispute the League's settlement: the Achaean reaction suggests that the Spartans even disputed the right of the League to make the settlement.

The Senate were not interested. The last thing they wanted was for Sparta to return to the troublemaking ways it had exhibited when last independent under Nabis. Once again, it was announced that the Spartans were, like other members of the League, subject to League rulings. The Senate acknowledged, in keeping with a previous adjudication of some thirty years before, that the sole exception to this was in trials carrying the death penalty. In such cases Spartans should either judge the case themselves or submit to independent arbitration outside the League. Nevertheless in its overall verdict, the Senate came down firmly on the side of the status quo and supported the Achaeans.

However, it is possible that there was growing impatience within the Senate at the League's failure to keep its house in order. From the Roman point of view the League existed to keep central and southern Greece quiet and orderly. If it failed to do this then it was not fit for purpose, and it might even be worth disbanding it and letting individual cites manage their own affairs. This feeling would have grown as the squabbling with Sparta continued.

Diaeus tried to keep the Romans from being bothered by forbidding constituent parts of the League from sending independent embassies, and by ordering the trial on unspecified capital charges of leading Spartan dissidents. The Spartans undertook to try the men themselves, and found them guilty. Guilty, that is, *in absentia*, as they took good care to make sure the accused were well out of the city before they passed judgement. Intense pressure had been applied to the Spartans to force even that verdict; in fact Diaeus had started mobilizing troops to ensure the Spartans got the hint about what they were meant to decide.

In 149/148 BC these Spartan exiles appealed to the Senate against the verdict and the Achaean pressure that had led up to it. In the obvious hope that the problem would go away if they neglected it, the Senate said that they would send someone to Greece to arbitrate, and then conveniently forgot about the whole thing. The Romans had other things to think about. Apart from wars in Spain and Gaul, there was an impending crisis with Carthage thanks to the agitation of Cato in the Senate. His constant demands that *Carthago delenda est* (Carthage must be destroyed) were in the process of launching the Third Punic War, which was intended to achieve exactly what Cato wanted. Meanwhile, in Macedonia things were going from bad to worse.

The claim of Andriscus to be the son of Perseus had gained credibility from recognition in two different royal courts. This was further boosted by his victory on Macedonia's eastern frontier, and by the fact that the Macedonians were so dissatisfied with the current Roman settlement that they were prepared to accept the claims of almost anyone who promised to restore the kingdom. The four republics collapsed in a popular uprising and in 149 BC Andriscus was installed as Philip VI of Macedon. His rule was marked by a savage purge of his opponents. While the evidence for this is a brief comment from a highly-biased Roman source, it would not be surprising if the chaotic state of Macedon required some arbitrary bloodletting, and Andriscus might well have done this with deliberate cruelty to discourage counter-revolutionaries. Furthermore, the corruption and inefficiency of the previous system had left Andriscus' supporters lusting for revenge which he could hardly deny them.

Those who suffered most under Andriscus were servants of the former Macedonian republics. This was natural enough but, of course, most of these men were pro-Roman placemen. Rome was not going to stand by and see its supporters destroyed, and in any case was not prepared to see its settlement cavalierly overthrown and the Macedonian kingdom restored. Scipio Nasica, who had found diplomacy unsuccessful, had already gathered a force of locally-recruited allies for an advance into Macedonia. The Romans now decided to supplement this with a full-scale legion.

Thus in 149 BC, for the first time in almost two decades, the Roman army returned to Greece with a legion commanded by a praetor called Publius Iuventius Thalna. The Romans evidently felt that if two legions under Paulus had been enough to sweep away the highly-trained army of Perseus, a single legion should disperse whatever rabble Andriscus had put together. As with a great many of the events in this period, what happened next is uncertain. However, it is quite possible that rather than a disorganized rabble, the army of Andriscus included a goodly number of veterans from the army of Perseus, and these men were both skilled and motivated soldiers. The Romans were brought to battle somewhere near Macedon's borders. Thalna was killed and his army was massively defeated, but at least a part of it managed a night withdrawal and retreat.[66] With the Romans (temporarily) crushed, Andriscus moved south and emulated his 'ancestors' by taking control of most of Thessaly.

Even allowing for their preoccupation with Carthage, the Romans had now to act decisively. Rome's consuls were required elsewhere (one in Africa and the other in Gaul), so Macedon received the attention of Quintus Metellus, who, like Thalna, was a praetor, but possibly one with consular powers and an army of two legions to match.[67] Getting this army together was quite a stretch for Roman manpower resources, since in that same year Rome already had to field at least eight other legions (four at Carthage, two in Spain, and two with Sp. Postumius Albinus in Gaul). Since another legion had already been lost (or at least badly mauled) in Macedonia, it is evident that the levy was sweeping almost every able-bodied Roman male into the armed forces, and was consequently becoming dangerously unpopular. Metellus could not afford to fail.

The Achaeans meanwhile were making life yet more complicated for the already-overstretched Romans. Their council had decided that this was a good time to deal with the Spartan issue once and for all. The question was not whether the Achaeans could crush Sparta; they quite evidently had the men to do this, even allowing for the military support which they, as good allies, had sent to join Metellus. The question was whether the Romans would permit it. However, with Macedonia in flames, and the Romans barely holding on in Spain, Gaul and Africa, the Achaeans decided that now was as good an opportunity as they were likely to get. It is probable that Sparta had already unilaterally withdrawn from the League and was preparing to make a stand with or without support from Rome.

Certainly Rome had given Sparta little reason for hope. Rome's record with regard to the city was one of non-involvement, and such decisions as the Senate had handed down invariably favoured the League. The benign indifference shown by Rome to Athenian aggression at Oropus would have encouraged Damocritus, the Achaean commander that year, to hope that Achaean action against Sparta would earn at worst a mild rebuke. And indeed, when it became clear that the League was mustering troops for military action against Sparta, Metellus sent just such a rebuke and urged the Achaeans to wait for Rome's long-delayed envoy. But Metellus had a battle imminent in Macedonia and was perhaps aware that he needed the Achaean auxiliaries in his army, so he did nothing further when it became evident that his intervention was going to be politely ignored.

Damocritus led the Achaean army against Sparta and achieved the expected crushing victory in the field. Thereafter, Achaean popular opinion was violently in favour of Damocritus going on to take and destroy Sparta itself. However, Damocritus held back. Perhaps he feared that the remnants of the Spartan army were too formidable for a full-scale assault on the city walls to be feasible; or, more likely, he feared that actually sacking Sparta might push Roman patience too far. If the latter, then this demonstrated a shrewd grasp of foreign policy, as Rome was fast running out of patience with the prevailing chaos in Greece. Sadly, the rest of the Achaeans did not share Damocritus' perception, and the general was heavily fined and then exiled for what the people saw as wilful dereliction of duty in allowing Sparta to remain standing.

Diaeus replaced Damocritus, and immediately received yet another urgent request from Metellus to keep his hands off Sparta. How events to the south relate to the campaign of Metellus further north is uncertain, but matters in Macedonia were fast approaching a crisis, and Diaeus might have stayed his hand in order to see how the campaign against Andriscus played out.[68] Certainly, despite popular clamour, he launched no further assault.

Metellus had proceeded swiftly to engage with Andriscus, and outflanked a Macedonian force sent either to meet him in Thessaly or intended to literally head him off at the pass as he tried to enter Macedon. This failure to block the Roman advance left the Macedonian army fatally split in two, with one part in Thessaly and the other drawn up near Pydna. Andriscus had evidently used his time in Thessaly to recruit cavalry, as he had considerable success in using this to blunt the speed of the Roman advance. However, the Pergamene fleet had turned up to support the Romans and this forced Andriscus to keep somewhat inland to prevent a seaborne force from being landed to the rear of his army. The unrelenting Roman pressure soon paid off. Somewhere just north of Pydna, Andriscus was brought to bay and defeated, though the pretender himself escaped and fled to Thrace with Metellus hot on his heels.

In Thrace, Andriscus and his allies gathered another army and prepared for battle, but the Romans had the momentum and attacked the rebels even as they reached the battlefield, ploughing right through the vanguard into the main force before it was ready. After this second defeat, Andriscus was turned over to Metellus by a Thracian prince who had decided on a strategic change of allegiance. What became of the force sent to Thessaly by Andriscus is unknown. Dio says Metellus 'disposed of' it, without explaining how the disposing was accomplished whilst the Roman army was engaged elsewhere. Either a *vexillation* (a unit detached from the main army) was enough to do the job, or more probably, disheartened by the news from the north, the Macedonians in Thessaly quietly disbanded themselves. Either way, Macedonia and Thessaly were once again in Roman hands. A pretender called Alexander briefly made an appearance, but lasted as long as it took the Romans to chase him into Dardania. Metellus accordingly sent word to Rome and the country again waited for the Senate to decide its fate.

Sparta likewise waited to hear what decision the Romans had come to, for the long-awaited Roman envoy had now arrived. Whilst Metellus had been wrapping up the Andriscus campaign in the preceding months, things had not gone well for Sparta. The Achaeans had respected Rome's wish that they leave Sparta alone, but had nevertheless garrisoned the rest of Laconia, leaving the city in a state of virtual siege. Menalcidas, commanding the Spartan forces, made the fatal error of attempting to relieve the pressure by attacking one of the towns held by the League, and in so doing broke the de facto truce. This allowed the Achaeans to increase the pressure on the Spartans by declaring them the aggressors, and Menalcidas was forced to commit suicide as the price for a restored peace on Achaean terms.

The Achaean War

This was the situation in the summer of 147 BC when Aurelius Orestes arrived in Corinth. The Roman legate brought with him a diplomatic bombshell. Not only had the Senate decided that Sparta could leave the League, but Corinth, Argos, Orchomenus and Heraclea were to leave as well. This effectively ripped the heart out of the League, leaving basically a rump of cities in the northern Peloponnese. It is difficult to see how the Senate expected the League to go along with this directive, especially as none of these cities, apart from Sparta, had shown any inclination towards independence. In the absence of clear information about the Senate's motivation, several theories have been advanced.

One is that, as the Epirots had discovered twenty years before, the Romans were at their most dangerous when they were annoyed and had a spare army in the region with which to demonstrate the fact. The League was intended to keep the peace in Greece, and having clearly proven itself unfit to do so, it could pay for flouting the explicit requests of Metellus to stay away from Sparta. Now the League could either disband, or face the consequences.

Another theory is that the Romans had decided to make Macedon a province of their growing empire, and concluded that they might as well take over Greece at the same time. Therefore the proposal of Orestes was a deliberate attempt to force the Achaeans into a war that would end with Greece under direct Roman rule.

Alternatively, it has been suggested that what Orestes proposed was more of a threat than an ultimatum, and that the Achaeans were supposed to be shocked at how far the Romans were prepared to go.[69] By this theory, the Romans expected the Achaeans to send tearful embassies to the Senate abjectly apologizing for flouting the directives of Metellus and begging to be allowed to keep the League intact. The Senate would agree, and the partition of Sparta from the League would then pass through with the Achaeans grateful things had been no worse than that.

If this latter was indeed the plan, it backfired spectacularly, for when the Roman directive became public there was a wave of popular outrage amongst the Achaeans that left Orestes feeling in actual physical danger. Certainly any Spartans whom the mob could catch suffered badly, and other Spartans in Corinth were arrested, including those who had fled to the Romans for protection. Orestes left hurriedly and later complained of his ill-treatment to the Senate. It is highly likely that the Senate itself was at this point undecided about what to do about Achaea. It may well be that different sections of the Senate held one apiece of the opinions suggested above, and that the only consensus was that the situation in Greece needed to be sorted out one way or the other. Certainly, Rome's next move indicated no fixity of purpose. A senior ambassador was sent (the consul of 157 BC, Sextus Julius Caesar) and his tone was decidedly conciliatory.

The Achaeans too were rather regretting their strong words and sent an equally-conciliatory embassy to Rome. The leaders of Achaea were too sensible to fall out with their mighty neighbour, and for a while they might have hoped that the issue of splitting the League was going to be quietly dropped. Unfortunately, the common people of Achaea were outraged with the Romans, and this outrage was harnessed by one Critolas to secure leadership of the League in the autumn of 147 BC. Critolas had a delicate balancing act to perform. He had to convince the Achaean people that he stood with them in their anger at Rome, but at the same time he had to try as hard as possible not to actually offend the Romans. This turned out to be an impossible task, not least because of a cultural gulf between Greek and Roman approaches to warfare. The Greeks regarded warfare as an extension of politics. When reason failed to achieve a desired object, the Greeks readily enough turned to war as a way of achieving political ends. This was not the view from Rome. The Romans had been fighting wars almost every year since their city's foundation. For them politics was a way of achieving the goals of warfare without actually fighting. When politics failed, the Romans dropped back to warfare as the default condition. Consequently, Critolas needed to be careful of bringing Rome toward a political impasse, but his own perceptions caused him (wrongly) to believe that the attempted solution to any impasse would, at least initially, be political rather than military.

Critolas invited Caesar to a conference at Tegea to discuss the Spartan issue. But, after Caesar and the Spartans had been kept waiting, Critolas eventually turned up alone without the Achaean delegation and announced that whatever decision the conference came up with would have to be ratified by the Achaean assembly, which was not going to meet for another six months. Caesar could not reasonably be expected to kick his heels in Greece for this period, and returned to Rome decidedly miffed about the whole business. This probably suited Critolas. He had now six months leeway to calm the situation before anyone committed themselves to anything, and maybe in that time negotiations with the Romans would produce a discreet deal that Critolas could sell to his people. This opinion would have been reinforced by a delegation from Metellus that arrived after Caesar had delivered his report to the Senate. Though Caesar had complained about the prevarication and high-handedness of Critolas, Metellus' delegates were softly spoken, and it appeared that, like the Achaean leaders, the Romans were looking for a way back from the brink.

Unfortunately, these delegates came into contact not just with the Achaean leadership, but also the common people of Achaea, and these made their feelings about Rome and Sparta very clear. If Critolas wanted to keep his job, and possibly his neck, he had to be seen to be doing something, and he decided that the least damaging something he could do was to make highly ostentatious moves indicating the seriousness of his intentions towards Sparta. Consequently he began to put the country on a war footing. To Roman objections Critolas made the point that he was dealing with an internal League matter, and whilst he welcomed the Romans as friends, he and the Achaeans were not in any way bound to or subordinate to Rome.

To say that this was a dangerous line to take is putting it mildly. However, little as the Romans might have liked what they were hearing, to some degree Critolas had a point. The Achaeans were friends and allies rather than subjects of Rome, and the Romans themselves had repeatedly accepted that Sparta was a part of the Achaean League. Nevertheless, in his efforts to avoid bringing his people into conflict with Rome, Critolas had greatly underestimated the danger of bringing Rome into conflict with his people. The Roman response to Critolas' vigorously-expressed opinions about Achaean autonomy was silence; from the Roman perspective there was no more to discuss. The Achaeans had been warned, and would take the consequences if they ignored the warning. However, the Achaeans may have taken the lack of response as a sign that the Romans had washed their hands of the entire business. Nevertheless, Critolas decided to play it safe. Although he had mustered his army, it seemed a good idea to test the waters of Roman opinion by first taking it not against Sparta, but against the small city of Heraclea in Otea which had, like Sparta, renounced its ties to the League. If the Romans did not object to the forcible reintegration of Heraclea, then perhaps it would be safe to move on and deal with Sparta afterwards.

Thus, in the early summer of 146 BC, Critolas marched on Heraclea. His soldiers were still some distance from the city when the army's outriders reported hostile contact. To their appalled horror, the Achaeans discovered that the hostile force was not the Heraclean militia but the Roman army of Metellus. The scale of Critolas' blunder was now fully apparent; military action in the face of Roman objections had been interpreted as a de facto declaration of war. The Achaeans now had to face the legions which had conquered Andriscus, not instead of, but as well as the Heraclean levies – and Sparta.

That the Achaeans were utterly unprepared for this development is evident from the way that their army recoiled back to Locris. Metellus followed the Achaeans there with the *celeritas* that was becoming his personal trademark, and not unexpectedly defeated them soundly at a place called Scarpheia. Critolas chose this moment to vanish from the pages of history, leaving later commentators to ponder his fate (Livy says he committed suicide by poison). Metellus brushed past the Arcadians at Chaeronea and marched against the Boeotian League, at this point an Achaean ally. After repeated setbacks and sackings in the past decades, Thebes was already in a sorely reduced state. The population simply abandoned their city to the Romans who proceeded to dilapidate the place a good deal further.

With Critolas vanished, Diaeus took over the defence of the League. It must have been plain to him that Achaea was now fighting for survival, and the chances of coming out with the League intact were minimal. News now reached the Achaeans that in addition to Metellus, the consul L. Mummius was on the way with an army of 23,000 men to fight a full-scale war. With him was the same Orestes who had delivered the unacceptable ultimatum which had sparked the present crisis. Given that Achaea had neither the manpower nor mountain defences of Macedon, or the support of allies either in Greece or overseas, it was evident that resistance would be futile. In a very real sense, the end of Greek independence came with the outbreak of war rather than with its inevitable conclusion.

This does not mean that the Achaeans failed to go down fighting. Diaeus returned to command, and tried desperately to negotiate with the Romans even as every town mustered troops and prepared its defences. Slave volunteers were added to the Achaean army, which has been estimated at about 14,000 strong. The Boeotians, who had probably joined in the war under the mistaken belief that they were simply going to terrorize the Heracleans, had already been effectively knocked out by Metellus. Boeotian aggression had also probably incited the Eritreans to declare for the Romans, practically the only city in Greece to do so. Certainly nearby Chalcis did not, and later suffered grievously for taking the Achaean side.

The advance of Metellus took him to the isthmus, where he came to a halt against the walls of Corinth. The Corinthian resistance brought to an end the participation of Metellus in the war. Mummius was consul to Metellus' praetor, and as soon as the senior politician arrived on the scene, Metellus was sent back to his province, where he stayed to help with the post-war settlement. Thereafter Metellus returned to Rome where he displayed the hapless Andriscus, who was executed after the customary triumph, and he received the *cognomen* (honorary nickname) of 'Macedonicus' for his efforts on behalf of Rome.

Diaeus meanwhile appears to have noted that Mummius had no great military reputation. Indeed, he had already sustained a slight reverse from a successful Achaean ambush on part of his army. However, this success was transitory, since when the Achaeans followed up Mummius sallied out of his camp and drove the Achaeans back to their lines. Now, with the Roman fleet getting established outside Corinth, the city could either stand a prolonged siege or the garrison could risk everything on a surprise assault on the Romans as they were digging in. Diaeus opted for the latter. It is quite possible that Achaean morale was flagging in any case and, without a quick victory, surrender would have come sooner rather than later. On the other hand, a short, sharp setback might bring the Romans back to the negotiating table, where things had looked rather promising until discussions were broken off.

Accordingly, Diaeus mustered his entire force and offered battle at Leucopetra, just outside Corinth. Heartened by Mummius' refusal to draw up his army against him, Diaeus marched into the valley leading to the Roman camp. Mummius now proved that he knew a thing or two himself about ambushes and hit the Achaeans in the flank with a surprise attack by cavalry charging down the hillside. With exquisite timing, the legions hastened out and broke the Achaean vanguard whilst it was still working out what had hit them. Thereafter the battle became a rout. Diaeus returned to his native Megalopolis, burned his house and possessions and committed suicide. Those Corinthians who could immediately fled the city in anticipation of the inevitable Roman sack.

This brief action was the last fought by an independent Greek army, for thereafter the Achaean League effectively dissolved itself, with its component cities scrambling to make peace with the Romans before they arrived in the Peloponnese. According to Pausanias the war ended in 140 BC, with the final settlement of the region by Roman commissioners, but to all intents and purposes the war was over in 146 BC. Rome, which had seemed so peripheral to Greek affairs when it had sent ambassadors to Queen Teuta of Illyria in 230 BC, was now, eighty-four years later, the undisputed ruler of Greece. Likewise Greece's former hegemon, Macedon, once all-conquering, awaited Rome's decision as to its fate.

Chapter 10

Aftermath

Corinth

Mummius had won his war in a single engagement. This engagement had been outside Corinth, the city which had been at the centre of Achaean-Roman friction over recent years. It was in Corinth that Orestes had been abused for his proposal to break up the Achaean League, and it was here that Spartans who had fled to the Romans had been unable to receive protection. It was Corinth which had baulked the advancing army of Metellus, and it was Corinth which the Romans chose to symbolize their wrath with the Achaean League as a whole.

Accordingly, Mummius called a final meeting of the League. Its constituent cities, he told them, were to be 'free' (a word the Greeks must by now have regarded with considerable cynicism). The exception was Corinth. Mummius ordered that all Corinthians at the meeting should be seized and enslaved. Many Corinthian women and children had already been enslaved in any case, but after the taking of the city many of the men who had not been put to the sword had fled to other cities for shelter.

The lands of Corinth were declared *ager publicus* - fields belonging to the Roman people (the territories of Thebes and Chalcis suffered the same fate). Corinth itself was sacked. Not just in the usual comprehensive Roman fashion, but with the same thorough determination to make the place uninhabitable for the immediate future that the Romans were also showing with freshly-conquered Carthage on the other side of the Mediterranean. Mummius did not go so far as to sow salt in the fields, as the Romans did at Carthage, but his legions made sure that hardly any stone was left standing on another.[70]

Everything of value was crated and shipped to Rome, where the populace were so impressed with what they saw, that 'Corinthian wealth' became a byword for opulence. Polybius, who was to play an important part in the post-war settlement, was at Corinth for the occasion. Though his report has not survived, the geographer Strabo says that he wrote heartbreakingly of

> the disregard shown by the army for the works of art and votive offerings; for he [Polybius] says that he was present and saw paintings that had been flung to the ground and saw the soldiers playing dice on these. Among the paintings he names that of Dionysus by Aristeides, to which, according to some writers, the saying, 'Nothing in comparison with the Dionysus', refers.[71]

Mummius himself is portrayed in legend as the archetypical Roman philistine, incapable of understanding the scale of what he was perpetrating. One story has him telling the dockers to be careful with priceless statues that he was shipping off to Rome. If any of these were damaged, he allegedly threatened, the dockers would have to replace them personally. It is quite possible that Mummius himself perpetrated some of these stories; the Romans of the day, and for some time after, liked to pose as bluff soldiers immune to the decadent influence of Greece.[72] However, what we know of Mummius shows that he was more sophisticated than this. For example Plutarch tells us that he freed a young Corinthian who movingly quoted Homer at him when he was testing potential slaves for literacy.[73] It is reasonably sure that Mummius was well aware of the historical and cultural significance of the city he was so comprehensively destroying.

So why did he do it? The Roman destruction of Corinth was an act of inhumanity and cultural vandalism which has been decried by generations since. Indeed Cicero, who visited the site in the early 70s BC, confessed himself deeply affected by the ruins. We can rule out those apologists such as Polybius who claim that Mummius acted impulsively and under the bad advice of those in his entourage. Such a far-reaching act must have been decreed by the Senate, and been carried out after due deliberation.

It was above all an act of terrorism, and as such it succeeded. Rome was prepared to utterly destroy Corinth, a city ancient before Rome was founded and from which, according to legend, came the ancestors of Tarquin, king of Rome. What then would Rome do to any other Greek city which aroused its anger? The intention was to utterly cow Greece, and so it did. If, as others have claimed, Rome acted to destroy a trading rival (Corinth was a centre of Mediterranean trade until its decease), then this too was successful. It should be noted that the two motives are not mutually exclusive, but the Roman Senate seldom acted purely from economic motives.

The Settlement

This time the Senate refrained from any social experiments in Macedonia. The Macedonians had shown that they were happiest as a single state under a sole ruler. This ruler, the Senate decreed, should be a Roman governor, and henceforth Macedonia was to be ruled as a province of Rome. In fact the province was expanded to take in Epirus, Thessaly and parts of Illyria and Thrace. Ironically, in being conquered, the Macedonians finally realized the ambition of their kings who had sought domination of these areas for centuries. Building began of the Via Egnatia, the great Roman highway which brought Macedon from its mountain fastnesses, and allowed trade with the west to flourish.

Macedon was not left entirely in peace, as it was briefly conquered by Mithridates of Pontus during the early 80s BC, and it suffered considerable disruption during the civil wars which brought about the end of the Roman Republic. However, with the accession of Augustus, Macedon became an ever more Romanized province. As with the equally once-troubled province of Hispania, Macedon became a quiet and productive part of the Roman Empire, and enjoyed centuries of peace before the Gothic invasions which heralded the fall of Rome in the west.

The rest of Greece was still 'free', but by now the Greeks had come to understand that this freedom was not *eleutheria*, or complete freedom in the Greek sense, but *libertas*, the freedom which a subordinate Roman had under his patron, bound about with duties and obligations.

The usual Roman post-war settlement commission came to Greece and Macedon in 146 to sort out matters once the dust of war had settled, and Polybius earned praise by refusing to accept any rewards for the work which he and his friends had put into ensuring that the settlement was as equitable as possible. The commissioners stayed for six months, and the main effect of their work was (as has been seen) to add to the province of Macedonia those states of southern Greece which they felt were most likely, otherwise, to cause problems for Rome in the future. Much of the commission's time would have been spent in drawing up the *lex provincia*, the set of laws under which the new province would be governed. This was a task greatly complicated by the number of non-Macedonian cities added to the new province, many of which would have needed virtually new constitutions of their own. Fortunately, Metellus had spent much of the ten months or so between his dismissal from the Achaean war zone and his return to Rome on the organization of Macedon into a proto-province, and the commission evidently built upon his work.

It is (almost) certain that the same commission that sorted out the provincialization of Macedonia was also responsible for settling affairs further south. This was guided by Mummius, and at least some cities were pleased with the result, as shown by the fact that a number of monuments dedicated to Mummius have since surfaced in Greece (and one in Macedonia).

At least some of the cities of southern Greece were made subject to tribute to Rome, and laws were passed to stop members of one state holding land in another. Steps were also taken to stop Greek cities federating once more into leagues. Henceforth, each Greek *polis* was to be on its own under Roman tutelage. Perhaps the major winner from the war was Sparta, which finally achieved its long-desired liberation from the Achaeans, though it never regained its former dominance of southern Greece. The traditional Spartan constitution was restored in a somewhat modified form, and in its declining years the city became something of a parody of itself for the benefit of the Roman tourist trade.

Later History

Unlike Macedon, which appears to have been largely peaceful apart from the disruption caused by the Pontic invasion of the 80s, life in Greece was far from relaxing over the next century. Some of the bloodiest battles in Greek history lay in the immediate future. For a start, Mithridates invaded not only Macedonia but also central Greece.

The most enthusiastic supporters of Mithridates were the Athenians, and they paid for their defection from Rome after a bloody siege by Sulla in 87/86 BC. When the city fell in March 86, the killing spree which followed was so intense that the blood was said to have run in a small stream through the gutters and out of the city gates. Thereafter Athens, like Sparta, was a shadow of its former self. Sulla went on to fight Mithridates at Chaeronea, in a battle involving over 100,000 men, and then in a rematch at Orchomenus which involved armies of the same scale. To pay for his campaign, Sulla looted the sacred treasuries at Delphi. He was by no means alone in his looting of Greece, and the country continued to suffer from the attentions of Roman senators thenceforward. Though southern Greece, unlike Asia, did not have to pay Roman taxes and largely escaped the predatory Roman *publicani* (tax gatherers), the Romans had other methods of squeezing cash even from allegedly 'free' peoples.

One favourite technique was forcing a loan at predatory rates of interest on a city, and refusing to accept the capital back until compound interest had forced the city deep into debt. Even the noble Brutus, the assassin of Caesar, used this technique of enrichment.

Before he was assassinated, Caesar too had been on Greek soil. Greece was the unhappy host of the final rounds of the civil war between Caesar and Pompey. In fact, Caesar finally won supreme power in Rome at the Battle of Pharsalus, not far from where Philip V was defeated at Cynoscephalae.

However, this victory did not settle matters, as Caesar's death once again brought Roman civil war to Greece, with a further bloody battle at Philippi in 42 BC which saw off Brutus and Cassius, the assassins of Caesar. The victors of that battle, Octavian and Mark Antony, returned to Greece a decade later for a final showdown at Actium, where Octavian, later Augustus, finally became emperor and master of the Roman world. Between senatorial depredations and the effects of armies marching and counter-marching across its territory for the best part of 150 years, much of Greece was economically devastated.

Most Greeks of any ambition or talent took advantage of the many opportunities offered by Rome's cosmopolitan empire, and took themselves either to Rome (where later poets such as Juvenal complained bitterly of their presence) or to the large and prosperous cities that flourished in Asia Minor under the *pax Romana*. A previous generation which had arrived in Rome as slaves had already helped to accelerate the fusion of Greek and Roman culture to the point where the poet Horace could remark that Greece had 'conquered her rough conqueror'.

Augustus finally made Achaea a province in 27 BC, and included in its bounds most of south and central Greece. However, by then Greece was already a backwater in geopolitical terms.

Illyria and Dalmatia

Ironically, the last part of the peninsula to fall under Roman control, was where it all had begun: in the Balkans. Since the capture of Genthius, the fortunes of the northern and southern Illyrians had varied. The Romans had divided Illyria into four regions, rather as they had attempted with Macedonia, and with about the same degree of success. By and large, the southern areas abutting the long-established Roman protectorate were readily absorbed and partially Romanized, but the northern areas were more strongly influenced by the Dalmatians, and any control exercised by Rome tended to be transitory and limited to the ground that Rome's soldiers stood on at any given time. Caesar was assigned Illyria as a province at the start of the 50s, but the word 'province' was used here in the old sense of 'area of military operations', rather than that of 'administrative region'.

This was clearly demonstrated by the northern Illyrians and Dalmatians who took an opportunistic role in the civil wars. A Roman army under Julius Caesar's henchman, Gabinius, was passing through Dalmatian territory when the Dalmatians trapped the soldiers in a narrow gorge and gave it a severe mauling which resulted in the near-total loss of the army and its standards. Caesar, preoccupied with his intentions to invade Parthia, was not prepared to undertake an Illyrian war of revenge. Therefore, he accepted Illyrian submission once he had gained power, and sent a small force of legionaries across the Adriatic to enforce that submission. However, when news of Caesar's assassination reached the north, the locals rose up in arms once more and destroyed most of Caesar's cohorts, with only a small force reaching safety in the south under the command of Vatinus, a general who was later to campaign successfully in Syria. This provoked a Roman response, but this was diluted by the contingencies of the civil wars raging at the time, and the weakened army which was finally dispatched was wiped out in Pannonia.

Thereafter, the Romans decided to leave this recalcitrant part of the peninsula alone until they had time to deal with it properly. Once he was emperor, Augustus started the project by an attack on the Segestani, a people in the far north of Greece. Having established a bridgehead there, he pushed southward against the Dalmatians and Illyrians. He soon found that whilst conquests were hard to come by (the terrain was both wooded and mountainous) the fractious and rebellious peoples of the area ensured that any gains were very easily lost.

Campaigning in the 30s saw several minor sieges and battles, resulting, eventually, in the return by the Dalmatians of the standards that had been captured from Gabinius. The area was still not subdued, and rose again in a major revolt a generation later. It was in this region also that Augustus' successor, Tiberius, learned his military skills. It was not until AD 9 that the northeast was finally settled (though the difficulties of campaigning there inspired a mutiny in AD 14).

However, expansion from Rome's bases at Dyrrhachium and Salona steadily pacified the wilder parts of Illyria, especially the obdurate Taulanti tribe of the central interior. By 27 BC, at the same time as Achaea was made a Roman province, the northwest was divided into the provinces of Illyricum and Dalmatia.

The long military tradition of the Balkans meant that when its peoples finally became reconciled to rule by Rome, they took enthusiastically to service in the legions. As Rome grew ever more cosmopolitan, Dalmatians and Illyrians were found at ever-higher ranks of the army. In the third century AD these men came into their own. Rome was beset by a series of barbarian invasions and found salvation under the guidance of a series of 'Illyrian' generals and emperors such as Aurelian, Diocletian, and the family of Constantine the Great. It was Constantine who founded the Roman Empire's second capital, Constantinople, on the Bosporus, a capital which stood firm even when the western empire was overwhelmed.

Consequently Greece and Macedon remained part of the empire for hundreds of years after the fall of Rome. While barbarian cowherds grazed their flocks in the shadow of the Senate house, the Greeks and Macedonians still considered themselves Romans. One wonders what the ghosts of Queen Teuta and King Philip would have made of that.

Notes

Chapter 1

1   Liati, A. et al 'The age of ophiolitic rocks of the Hellenides (Vourinos, Pindos, Crete): first U–Pb ion microprobe (SHRIMP) zircon ages' *Chemical Geology*, Volume 207, Issues 3-4, 16 July 2004.
2   There have been, for example, at least six battles of Thermopylae, and an archaeologist digging up a helmet there can date it anywhere from Persian (480) to Gallic (279) to British (1941 AD).
3   Even the Romans, as will be seen, sent their troopships across the Adriatic to ports they already controlled.
4   Here the convention is used of referring to the political entity as Macedon, and the geographical location as Macedonia.
5   Herodotus, *Histories*, 5.22.
6   Plutarch, *Life of Philopoemen*.
7   Each region is treated separately in this survey, and consequently there is some overlap as events are described from a different perspective. However, it is a testament to the fragmented nature of Greece that there is too little overlap to form a single coherent narrative.
8   Polybius, 2.70, says the invaders were Illyrians.
9   Appian, *The Illyrian Wars*, 1.1 (translation from the Perseus website). For a more modern view see Wilkes, J., *The Illyrians* (Wiley-Blackwell 1995).
10 Polybius, 2.45-46, *passim*.
11 *Fragmenta historicum Graecorum* II, fr 59.

Chapter 2

12 Plutarch, *Life of Pyrrhus*, 16.
13 This follows Polybius' more complete version of events. Appian, writing much later, claims that Agron was alive through what followed, and that Teuta only took over just before the actual commencement of hostilities.

Appian, *The Illyrian Wars*, 7.

14 Dio, 12.19; Appian, *ibid*.

15 Polybius, 2.2.

16 cf. Eckstein, A. 'Polybius, Demetrius of Pharus, and the Origins of the Second Illyrian War', *Classical Philology*, Vol. 89, No. 1 (Jan 1994), pp. 46–59 for one of the best modern discussions of the topic.

17 Appian, *The Illyrian Wars*, 8.

18 Polybius, 3.19.

19 *Ibid*, 4.3.

20 *Ibid*, 5.104.

Chapter 3

21 Polybius, 7.9.

22 Livy, 23.38.

23 Livy, 24.40. Livy is our only source for this story, and many modern historians find this particular incident frankly incredible.

24 *Ibid*, 25.23.

25 Livy, 26.26, talks of this city as being in neighbouring Locris, where there is no record of such a place. He is generally considered to have been in error.

26 Valerius went on to command in Sicily, and in 206 was among those who took the war to the Carthaginians in Africa.

27 Polybius, *History*, 9.41

28 Polybius fragment 10.25.

29 Livy, 28.11.

Chapter 4

30 Anyone wanting a flavour of the academic debate on this topic should start with McDonald, A. H. & Walbank, F. W., 'The Origins of the Second Macedonian War', in *The Journal of Roman Studies*, 27 (1937), and Balsdon, J. P. V. D., 'Rome and Macedon, 205-200 B.C', in *The Journal of Roman Studies*, Vol. 44 (1954), pp 30–42.

31 Dorey, T. A., 'Macedonian Troops at the Battle of Zama', in *The American Journal of Philology*, Vol. 78, No. 2 (1957), pp 185–187.

32 Livy, 31.29.

33 Who said what to whom and when has never been satisfactorily resolved, and what follows is a rough synopsis of the generally accepted positions. The reader is warned that here the story strays into an academic brawl

which had been rumbling for the past half century. For a flavour of the academic dogfight, readers are referred to the appropriately named Valerie M. Warrior, *The Initiation of the Second Macedonian War: An Explication of Livy Book 31*, and Briscoe's partial rebuttal in *HISTOS* 1997.

34 Polybius, 16.34.

35 *Ibid*.

36 Polybius, 6.23.

37 Estimated at about 20,000 foot and 2,000 cavalry.

38 Polybius, 6.25.

Chapter 5

39 Livy, 31.23ff claims rather disingenuously that the fire started by accident, and the massacre happened in the general confusion. It is more probable that the Romans started with the set intention of putting Chalcis out of use to Macedon to as great an extent as possible, at whatever human cost.

40 Livy, 31.32.31.

41 Livy, 31.40.

42 It has been suggested that the *sortitio* (lottery) of the provincial command was rigged to ensure that Flamininus received the Macedonian front. However, the contemporary record shows that consuls apparently qualified for one type of warfare were often allocated to other operations according to the chance of the lot, and there is no reason to believe that Flamininus was anything but lucky. Cf Eckstein, A. M., 'T. Quinctius Flamininus and the Campaign against Philip in 198 BC', in *Phoenix*, 30 (1976).

43 For a full description of this fortress and surrounding territory see Hammond, N. G. L., 'Antigonea in Epirus', in *The Journal of Roman Studies*, Vol. 61 (1971).

44 Plutarch, *Life of Flamininus*, 3.

45 Livy, 32.17.

46 Livy, 32.32.

47 *Ibid*.

48 Polybius, 18.11.

49 Much of the report of the campaign and battle which follows is derived from Hammond's magisterial treatment in 'The campaign and battle of Cynoscephalae in 197 BC', in *The Journal of Hellenic Studies* (1988).

50 Livy, 33.6.

Chapter 6

51 This may not have happened. By some reports the bones of the fallen remained unburied half a decade later.
52 Livy, 33.12.
53 Polybius, 8.36.
54 Appian, *The Syrian Wars*, 12.

Chapter 7

55 Livy, 39.24.
56 Regrettably the relevant text of Polybius is fragmentary or missing at this point, or we should have a clearer picture of an incident which was, even at the time, shrouded in palace secrecy and rumour.
57 Livy, 40.58.
58 Livy, 42.12, Appian in his *Macedonian Wars* says much the same: 'Perseus was popular partly due to the hatred felt for the Romans, hatred which Rome's generals had aroused.' fragment from Constantine Porphyrogenitus, *The Embassies*, 17.

Chapter 8

59 Livy, 42.63.
60 Some annalists have blown this into a major battle with thousands dead on each side. Livy reports these accounts, but does not give them much credence. Nor does the subsequent behaviour of the protagonists suggest such a battle took place.
61 For details of Eumenes and other Greek states see Eckstein, A. M., 'Rome, the War with Perseus, and Third Party Mediation', in *Historia: Zeitschrift für Alte Geschichte* (1988).
62 Plutarch, *Life of Aemilius Paulus*.
63 This is possible, because we do not know enough about the exact position of the coastline to know how it influenced the positioning of the armies. Generally speaking, one would expect the Romans to be facing north, and the Macedonians to be looking south, in which case the time of day would not significantly affect how much sun was in each side's eyes.

Chapter 9

64 Polybius, 30.6.
65 This version of events is to be preferred to a confusing and implausible

account in Pausanias, book 7, which suggests that the Achaeans did nothing until bribed, and then Callicrates swung into action. However, at the Achaean approach the Athenians abandoned the city, pillaged what they could once more and withdrew into Attica.

66 This much we get from Cassius Dio in a fragment of his book 21.

67 For a full discussion of this issue see Morgan, M., 'Metellus Macedonicus and the Province Macedonia', in *Historia* (1969).

68 For discussion see *ibid.* but note that it is my belief that Andriscus divided his forces before the entry of Metellus into Macedonia, simply because this makes more military sense. Dio's description, on which Morgan bases his chronology, has Andriscus splitting his army and sending half away when on the verge of a crucial battle, which he then lost.

69 The view of Polybius (38.9.6) which has been built into a detailed argument by Gruen, E., 'The Origins of the Achaean War', in *The Journal of Hellenic Studies*, Vol. 96 (1976).

Chapter 10

70. However, recent archaeological studies have confirmed the statements of some ancient authors who feel that the destruction, though vast, was not as total as once believed.

71. Strabo on Corinth, *Geography*, 8.23.

72. Thus Cicero at the trial of Verres affected to know none of the great works of art that Verres is said to have misappropriated, and ostentatiously had to look each one up when he referred to it.

73. Plutarch, *Moralia*, 737a. The youth quoted from the Odyssey: 'Three, no, four times happier were the Greeks who died then'.

Select Bibliography

Adcock, F. E., *The Greek and Macedonian Art of War:Sather Classical Lectures vol. 30* (Berkeley, 1957).

Anderson, J. K., 'A Topographical and Historical Study of Achaea', in *Annual of the British School at Athens*, 49 (1954), pp 72-92.

Balsdon, J. P. V. D., 'Rome and Macedon, 205-200 B.C.', in *The Journal of Roman Studies*, 44 (1954), pp 30-42.

Astin, A. E. (ed.) et al. *Cambridge Ancient History Vol 8 Rome and the Mediterranean to 133 BC* (Cambridge, 1989).

Dorey, T. A., 'Macedonian Troops at the Battle of Zama', in *The American Journal of Philology*, 78, No. 2 (1957), pp185-187.

Eckstein, A. M., 'Rome, the War with Perseus, and Third Party Mediation', in *Historia: Zeitschrift für Alte Geschichte* (1988).

Eckstein, A. M., *Rome Enters the Greek East: From Anarchy to Hierarchy in the Hellenistic Mediterranean, 230-170 BC* (Chichester, 2008).

Eckstein, A. M., 'Polybius, Demetrius of Pharus, and the Origins of the Second Illyrian War', in *Classical Philology*, 89, No. 1 (1994), pp 46-59.

Eckstein, A. M., 'T. Quinctius Flamininus and the Campaign against Philip in 198 BC', in *Phoenix*, 30 (1976).

Gabbert, J. J., *Antigonus II Gonatas* (London and New York: 1997).

Gaebel, R. E., *Cavalry operations in the ancient Greek world* (Norman, 2002).

Gruen, E. S., *The Hellenistic World and the Coming of Rome* (Berkeley, 1984).
Gruen, E. S., 'The Origins of the Achaean War', in *The Journal of Hellenic Studies*, 96 (1976).

Hammond, N. G. L., 'Antigonea in Epirus', in *The Journal of Roman Studies*, 61 (1971).

Hammond, N. G. L., 'The campaign and battle of Cynoscephalae in 197 BC', in *The Journal of Hellenic Studies* (1988).

Hammond, N. G. L., & Griffith, G. T., *History of Macedonia* (Oxford, 1979).

Liati, A., et al. 'The age of ophiolitic rocks of the Hellenides (Vourinos, Pindos, Crete): first U–Pb ion microprobe (SHRIMP) zircon ages', in *Chemical Geology*, 207, Issues 3-4 (2004).

McDonald, A. H., & Walbank, F. W., 'The Origins of the Second Macedonian War', in *The Journal of Roman Studies* 27 (1937).

Morgan, M., 'Metellus Macedonicus and the Province Macedonia', in *Historia* (1969).

Shuckburgh, E. S. (tr), *Polybius on Roman Imperialism* (South Bend, 1980).

Walbank, F. W., *Philip V of Macedon* (North Haven, 1967).

Warrior, V. M., *The Initiation of the Second Macedonian War: An Explication of Livy Book 31* (Stuttgart, 1996).

Wilkes, J., *The Illyrians*, (Chichester, 1995).

Index